A New Endeavour
Selected Political Essays, Letters, and Addresses

FRANK R. SCOTT

Edited and introduced by Michiel Horn

Articulate, thoughtful, resonant with integrity, these writings of F.R. Scott express the political convictions of one of Canada's most respected intellectuals. The collection spans four decades of outspoken opinion on the political issues that were dear to Scott's heart: the advocacy of socialism, civil rights, Quebec politics, labour rights, social justice, and the political destiny of Canada. Presented in chronological order, the writings include letters to the editor of the *Montreal Gazette*, speeches, magazine articles from *Canadian Forum* and *Saturday Night*, and letters to such political colleagues as David Lewis and J.S. Woodsworth.

Scott played many roles in Canadian intellectual life: as a teacher, lawyer, social activist, and poet, he was one of Canada's most skilful communicators. The clarity of his prose and the depth of conviction behind it created a powerful vehicle for his ideas on the political and social issues of his day.

MICHIEL HORN is professor of history at Glendon College, York University.

FRANK R. SCOTT

A New Endeavour

Selected Political Essays, Letters, and Addresses

Edited and introduced by MICHIEL HORN

UNIVERSITY OF TORONTO PRESS
TORONTO BUFFALO LONDON

© University of Toronto Press 1986
Toronto Buffalo London
Printed in Canada

ISBN 0-8020-5672-5 (cloth)
ISBN 0-8020-6603-8 (paper)

Printed on acid-free paper

Canadian Cataloguing in Publication Data

Scott, F.R. (Francis Reginald), 1899–
  A new endeavour: selected political essays,
  letters, and addresses

  ISBN 0-8020-5672-5 (bound). – ISBN 0-8020-6603-8 (pbk.)
  1. Canada – Politics and government – 20th century.
  2. Canada – Social conditions – 20th century.*
  3. Socialism – Canada – History. I. Horn, Michiel,
  1939– II. Title.
  FC609.S36 1986   971.06   C86-094272-4
  F1034.S36 1986

Contents

Editor's Preface

The public life of Frank R. Scott had three major elements: the law, poetry, and politics. Towards the end of his life Frank decided that he wanted to sum up each of these in a book. His *Essays on the Constitution* (University of Toronto Press 1977) was the first of these volumes; *The Collected Poems of F.R. Scott* (McClelland & Stewart 1981) was the second. *A New Endeavour*, a selection from Frank's political writings and speeches, is the third and last.

This book was intended as a sort of companion piece to *Essays on the Constitution*, a selection from his legal writings, because Frank's lifelong concern for civil liberties involved both law and politics. Not long before the *Essays* appeared, in fact, Frank began to put together a volume of his political writings, interpreting the word 'political' in a broad sense. He was encouraged in this project by Michael Gnarowski of Carleton University, who wanted the volume to appear in the Carleton Library series. Feeling unable to do the editorial work that he considered necessary, Frank asked me to take on the job. A representative of the Carleton Library editorial board had already approached me to write an introduction to the volume, and I was glad to become its editor as well.

Although Frank was open to suggestions for changes in his original selection of documents, he retained control over the table of contents. Working with him was enjoyable as well as instructive. Still, the process of collaboration took more time than either of us had anticipated. Further delays occurred because the Carleton Library was experiencing difficulties in its arrangements with publishing houses. The manuscript was essentially complete by 1981; three years later the Carleton University Press, which had been established in order to publish further volumes of the Carleton Library, finally decided to abandon the project on financial grounds. Fortunately, the University of Toronto Press then decided to publish the book. I am immensely glad that Frank heard this good news just before his death, but I regret that he did not live to see the book in print.

As editor my chief debt is to Frank himself. He continued to work on the project in spite of his deteriorating health: the final draft of his own preface was not finished until the spring of 1983. I am grateful to both Frank and Marian Scott for the hospitality they gave me during the preparation of the manuscript. The late David Lewis gave useful support to the project. Sandra Djwa read my introduction and offered helpful criticism and advice, as did my wife Cornelia Schuh. Michael Gnarowski, and R.I.K. Davidson of the University of Toronto Press, deserve thanks for their efforts on the book's behalf. I am grateful to Lorraine Ourom for her editorial work.

Denyse Smith and Julie Parna Stief typed successive early versions of the editorial material. Claude Tatilon helped with some fine points of translation. The address 'Confederation Is a True Alliance' was translated into English by students of the Translation Programme of Glendon College, under the supervision of Jane Couchman. I acknowledge the financial support of the Glendon Research Grants Committee. Generous contributions to the cost of publishing this book were made by the Boag Foundation, Vancouver, and the Douglas-Coldwell Foundation, Ottawa.

The book is dedicated to the memory of Frank Aykroyd, Thérèse Casgrain, Harry Cassidy, M.J. Coldwell, George Grube, David Lewis, Angus MacInnis, Leonard Marsh, George Mooney, Graham Spry, Frank Underhill, J.S. Woodsworth, and other warriors gone to rest, and of Frank Scott himself.

Michiel Horn
April 1986

Author's Preface

The papers and the essays I have included in this volume cover the period from 1931 to 1971, and speak for themselves. They are placed in the context of the Canada of their time by the introduction and notes of Michiel Horn. I felt a few words should be added to explain some of the influences which changed the starry-eyed Oxford graduate of 1923 into the active participant in Canadian politics.

Oxford added depth and historical background to my faith in the principal values of the Anglican church in which I had been reared and of which I was still a communicant. I went through no major shift in moral or religious outlook. The first book I was told to read for the History Schools was Aristotle's *Politics*; the book that most influenced my thinking was R.H. Tawney's *The Acquisitive Society*, which was only published in my second year, but which a group of students selected one term for intensive analysis. The real education, I realize as I look back, came from immersion for three unbroken years in the whole miracle of European art, especially painting, architecture, and music. Poetry was a private affair, which I maintained without special attention to an outside world.

I knew very little of my country when I settled in Montreal as a teacher at Lower Canada College in October 1923. I had never read a page of Canadian history in the course of taking three degrees in history (one at Bishop's College and two at Oxford), and indeed had never even left the province of Quebec till I stepped into the liner that was to take me away to Europe. I had had the inestimable advantage for a Canadian, however, of growing up in Quebec City, the very nursery of Canada. My father, the rector of St Matthew's Anglican Church, was proud of the fact that his parish contained the Plains of Abraham. Being very high church, ordained in England during the height of the Pusey Anglo-Catholic movement in the 1880s, he was most happy to be in a Roman Catholic milieu. He would take me into the St Jean-Baptiste Church on the way back from St Matthew's to the rectory so that we might 'smell the incense.'

My first eight years in Montreal, from 1923 to 1931, forced me to find my place in Canada and to evolve a theory of Canada's place in the world. Every experience that touched me closely in those years was a Canadian experience, and had to be understood in Canadian terms. If to be a Canadian nationalist is to involve oneself actively in things Canadian then I was a Canadian nationalist. I would have repudiated the term because I am first of all an internationalist.

Being both a teacher and a college student in those years, I was confronted with the problem of changing from Oxford tutorials to McGill's compulsory lectures. I cannot claim that I ever solved it, but my negative views of McGill's system were expressed in several pieces of satirical verse. It was easier to define the aims of education than to detail its means. Alongside of McGill were the two French-Catholic universities of Montreal and Ottawa. The aims of their education were laid down from on high. Montreal announced in its calendar of 1928 that it would take special care to protect its students against the three great dangers of 'materialism, liberalism and modernism,' while the newer University of Ottawa later permitted the opening of the students' mail. All education in Quebec was either under Catholic clerical control or Protestant school boards, except for a very few public and private schools. McGill operated under a Royal Charter dating from 1821. Founded by a wealthy public figure, it was financed entirely by private and corporate donations, and fees. It was under a Board of Governors, first elected, later self-perpetuating, drawn from the dominant corporate and professional leaders of eastern Canada. When I emerged as a democratic socialist in their midst, certain confrontations were inevitable. Of this long story I shall say here simply this, that I never at any time felt my position as teacher and writer was threatened, and while my behaviour was under close scrutiny and doubtless constrained in consequence, I owed the university my freedom from the much more inhibiting restraints imposed by the active practice of law in which I was first engaged. A group of law partners can be even more repressive than a Board of Governors, as I was eventually to learn in the Padlock Act and Roncarelli cases.

Chief among the catalytic events that deeply engaged me as the 1920s moved on were the meeting with A.J.M. Smith and founding of the *McGill Fortnightly Review*, the decision to quit the practice of law for a teaching post at McGill, and the Great Crash of October 1929. Then there were several occurrences that demonstrated to me the corruption of the prevailing business order and its corrupting effects on politics: the Laurier Palace fire in Montreal, the Beauharnois scandal, and the Westmount Water Works deal.

When the first wonder of poetic discovery dimmed in me, I found myself hurled into a new set of economic ideas and a new group of friends with whom to discuss and share them. The Great Depression had arrived. This, too, sharpened my view of what Canada was and what it might be. In incident after incident, starting with my letter to the Montreal *Gazette* in 1931, I met aspects of Canadian life of which I had been totally unaware. This strengthened my interest in civil liberties, providing many examples of the need to enlarge and protect them, and brought to the surface again that fundamental analysis of our economic society which I derived at Oxford from the two study groups I had attended. These ideas had remained relatively quiescent during the 1920s, but now had a new meaning in everything I saw about me in Canada. This projected me into politics in the League for Social Reconstruction and the CCF (later in the NDP). The drafting of the Regina Manifesto in 1933 completed the theoretical definition of what I wanted my 'new endeavour' to strive for. It was no less than the remaking of Canadian society on the basis of the co-operative and democratic socialist principles which in my case derived mainly from the English socialist tradition, but which were now widespread in the world.

The title of this book, *A New Endeavour*, is taken from a line in a poem I wrote in 1938. I was returning from Australia, where I had attended the British Commonwealth Relations Conference at Lapstone Hills, forty miles outside Sydney. I had written the main Canadian paper for this conference in the summer of 1937, with assistance from Escott Reid, then national secretary of the Canadian Institute of International Affairs. In due time it appeared in the form of a book, *Canada Today*.

Through studying the Commonwealth from a labour point of view I saw my way clear to supporting it, provided it accepted its obligations to the higher authority of the United Nations. I also came to think of a future Commonwealth that would consist entirely of socialist countries freely associated: a union of democratic socialist republics. This allowed me to square my Canadian nationalism and respect for the achievements of the Commonwealth with the principle of international association.

I want to conclude with my poem 'Dedication':

From those condemned to labour
For profit of another
We take our new endeavour.

For sect and class and pattern
Through whom the strata harden
We sharpen now the weapon.

Till power is brought to pooling
And outcasts share in ruling
There will not be an ending
Nor any peace for spending.

Frank R. Scott
Montreal, May 1983

MICHIEL HORN

Introduction: Frank Scott's Life in Politics

Frank Scott's life in politics was, like all of his life, multi-faceted and creative. In 1971, discussing the decision he made forty years earlier to become a university professor, he said: 'I jumped at the opportunity of teaching instead of practising law, early in my career, because I was attracted to the wider view of law as a potentially creative instrument for the building of a better society – the same attraction that led me into politics. All I was doing seemed creative. Poetry was but one form of my creative expression and I would not have been satisfied using it alone.'[1] Scott linked the desire for creative expression to the ideal of service to his fellow human beings, especially the weak and needy. Together these impulses helped to form the conditions for a life of great effort and achievement.

McGill University, when the former Rhodes Scholar joined it in 1928, was the most prestigious institution of higher learning in Canada. Scott married the painter Marian Dale the same year. He was intelligent, charming, well-connected: a secure future lay before him. As for his province and his country, although the wounds of the Great War had not yet fully healed, the apparent prosperity of the later 1920s augured well for what was to come. Or so it seemed.

Scott's thirtieth birthday fell on 1 August 1929, a few weeks before the stock-market crash that has come to symbolize the start of the Great Depression of the 1930s. More than any other event in Canadian history, the Depression influenced the attitudes of intellectuals towards their country. The mounting evidence of human misery and social dislocation distressed many educated men and women. As the effects of the economic crisis and the inability of business, charitable institutions, and governments to cope with them became clearer, a conviction grew in the minds of some of the younger intelligentsia that economic and political changes must take place. Various more or less radical ideas of reform gained currency. To a small but growing group of intellectuals some form of socialism seemed to be the way of the future.

Frank Scott was a typical member of this group both in his profession and in his ideas, attitudes, and interests. His father, Archdeacon F.G. Scott, and his mother, Amy Brooks, had cultivated in their seven children a strong sense of Christian service. This religious upbringing gave Frank, the sixth child, a strong concern for human welfare, but did not give him a very coherent view of society or the economy. At Oxford, exposure to the thought of some of the Christian socialists, notably R.H. Tawney, left him with a general distrust of capitalism on moral grounds and reinforced his disdain for mere money-making. At the same time his outlook became more secularized. However, he was not yet a radical critic of society. He recognized some of the world's stupidities and inequities, but felt no great desire to try to correct them. His interests, passions even, were the study of history and constitutional law and the writing of poetry.

Scott later credited a small circle of friends in Montreal with his increasing interest in economics and politics. 'The Group,' as he later called it, was a handful of young men almost all of whom had been at Oxford. Among its members, Scott recalled, were Brooke Claxton, John Farthing, Eugene Forsey, G.R. 'Ronnie' McCall, T.W.L. 'Terry' MacDermot, and Raleigh Parkin. It is not clear whether this group was, or became, the Montreal branch of the Canadian League, a small organization that was in existence as early as 1927 and had a close link to the much larger Association of Canadian Clubs. In this group, and in the Canadian Institute of International Affairs, which he joined in 1929, Scott became more aware of his country and the world. At roughly this time, too, he seems to have become acquainted with J.S. Woodsworth, pacifist, socialist, and Labour MP from Winnipeg North Centre.

By early 1930 Scott was helping to plan a book that would propose remedies for 'the political, economic and social problems of the country.'[2] The book was a project of the Canadian League, whose Montreal members by 1930 also included P.E. Corbett, then dean of the McGill Faculty of Law, Francis Hankin, and Carleton Stanley. The volume took shape during 1930, with Claxton, a corporate lawyer, and MacDermot, a historian at McGill, acting as the organizers. MacDermot was to write the general introduction; other chapters were to be contributed by Corbett, Forsey, and Scott, as well as George Ferguson, a Winnipeg newspaperman, Burton Hurd, an economist at Brandon College, Graham Spry, the indefatigable national secretary of the Association of Canadian Clubs and organizing genius of the Canadian Radio League, and the Toronto historian Frank Underhill.

For reasons that none of the surviving participants were able to recall when I asked them, the book was never published. One possibility is that disagreement developed among the contributors about the degree of change that ought to be proposed. In any case, Scott was among the contributors who were taking an increasingly jaundiced view of Canadian society.

His criticism seems to have begun as an ethical observation: the system was unfair. Not only were a growing number of Canadians denied an opportunity to work, but protests against this state of affairs were met with repression. Both his background as a Christian and his profession as a lawyer contributed to the protest which, on 31 January 1931, he registered in a letter to the Montreal *Gazette*.

The immediate cause was that, the evening before, the Montreal police had broken up a meeting of the Canadian Labour Defence League (CLDL) and arrested the speakers. The meeting had been called to protest against earlier police interference with meetings of the unemployed. The CLDL was communist-led, which in the eyes of the police sanctioned the interference. But not in Scott's. 'Whether or not these meetings are attended by communists or merely by unemployed labourers makes not a particle of difference,' he wrote, 'for communism is no more criminal than liberalism or socialism.'[3] It was for the courts to decide whether seditious words had been uttered, he said; he wished to address the legality and wisdom of interfering with freedom of speech and assembly. On the basis of newspaper reports, he suggested, the behaviour of the police at four recent meetings was probably illegal and certainly provocative. There had been plain violations of the rights of free assembly and free speech. The actions of the police, furthermore, had had the unintended result of drawing attention to the meetings: attendance had grown from 250 at the first to 1,500 at the most recent meeting. In concluding, Scott wondered 'how many converts to communism had been made by this procedure.'

Cliché though the phrase may be, the letter marked a turning-point in Scott's life. Suddenly he had come to public notice. The reaction to his comments was mostly negative. The chief of police and the editor of the *Gazette* took issue with him. At McGill some of the governors were unhappy that he had identified himself as 'associate professor of constitutional and federal law.' Although he had not mentioned McGill, his link with the university was known. The principal, Sir Arthur Currie, told Scott that he was not to use his title if he should write to a newspaper about a controversial matter again, and that such letters in themselves were less than desirable. However, he did not tell Scott *not* to write controversial letters. And criticism from the police and press confirmed Scott in the view that he was right. It pushed him further along a new course of social and political criticism.

Other Canadian academics were on the same path. Two weeks before Scott wrote to the *Gazette*, sixty-eight members of the University of Toronto teaching staff had written an open letter to the four Toronto newspapers in protest against police interference with 'communistic' meetings. Public reaction to the professors had been largely unfavourable, and the university governing board treated the incident as an unfortunate aberration that ought not to be repeated. This failed to intimidate the letter's chief drafter, Frank Underhill. He was the president of a small, informal group of young academics that had been meeting since the previous fall to discuss the shortcomings of Canadian society and what might be done about them. Among the others were the economists Irene Biss, Harry Cassidy, and J.F. Parkinson, and Eric Havelock, a Victoria College classicist.[4]

At this time Scott and Underhill knew each other by name only. Both were involved in the book that Claxton and MacDermot had been trying to pull together. Both contributed to *The Canadian Forum*, the Toronto-based monthly that since 1920 served as an outlet for avant garde intellectuals. Not until August 1931, however, did the two men meet in person, when both attended the annual Institute on Politics at Williams College in Williamstown, Massachusetts. They immediately hit it off together. They enjoyed each other's style, saw Canada's problems in much the same light, and were groping towards similar solutions.

During a Sunday hike to the summit of nearby Mount Greylock, Scott and Underhill reached agreement that Canada needed a sort of Fabian society. The historian believed that a new political party, drawing support from radicalized farmers and urban blue- and white-collar workers, would soon emerge in response to the Depression. He said that a group of intellectuals should help this new party to formulate its ideas. This would give it the ideological core that the Progressive movement of the early 1920s had lacked, Underhill argued, and would prevent the new party from fading away as the Progressives had done. Persuaded by his new friend's analysis and enthusiasm, Scott undertook to do what he could in Montreal in order to get the society started.

The Williamstown meeting was the immediate cause of the formation of the League for Social Reconstruction. First stirrings had already been taking place in both Montreal and Toronto, but now things went much faster. The founding conference of the LSR took place in Toronto in January 1932. A small group in Montreal, consisting of Scott, Forsey, King Gordon, and David Lewis, had done the lion's share of drafting the manifesto for the new organization. Forsey, like Scott a member of the Canadian League, lectured in economics at McGill. Gordon was a professor of Christian ethics at United Theological College, and Lewis was a McGill law student. The document that they drew up described the LSR as 'an association of men and women who are working for the establishment in Canada of a social order in which the basic principle regulating production, distribution and service will be the common good rather than private profit.'[5] Highly critical of the capitalist system, the manifesto stopped short of using the term 'socialism' and, for the present at least, eschewed political partisanship. Scott and others did not wish to limit the LSR's appeal to middle-class Canadians.

During the first months of its life the LSR grew rapidly, aided by invaluable free publicity gained in April when Prime Minister R.B. Bennett attacked it in a House of Commons speech. Having got hold of a copy of the LSR manifesto, Bennett identified its author as none other than Vincent Massey, president of the National

Liberal Federation, and denounced this alleged evidence of the Liberals' 'new parlour socialism.'[6] The press gave considerable attention to Bennett's erroneous charges and J.S. Woodsworth's correction of them. Soon the league had almost twenty branches from Montreal west to Victoria.

The formation of the Co-operative Commonwealth Federation in the summer and fall of 1932 led to demands within the LSR that it affiliate itself with the new 'farmer-labour-socialist' party. Like Woodsworth, who was the league's honorary president and leader of the CCF, Scott opposed these demands. He feared the move would damage the LSR in the eyes of the politically uncommitted and in the eyes of French Canadians. The CCF seemed like 'the long looked-for article,' he wrote to Underhill, 'and therefore I agree the LSR should help it as much as possible. I am doubtful whether any sort of official connection should be established however. At present I rather favour keeping the LSR at its educational job alone.'[7] He was gratified when an attempt to link the LSR and CCF formally failed in early 1933.

Although he opposed affiliation, Scott greeted the CCF with enthusiasm. He welcomed Woodsworth's request that the LSR draft a manifesto and program for the new party. He became one of the party's first members in Quebec and, in July 1933, attended its Regina convention as a representative of the Montreal CCF Council. At Regina he took an important part in the process of amending the draft manifesto prepared by Underhill, Harry Cassidy, and a couple of other Toronto LSR members. Asked to address the convention on the constitutional implications of the new manifesto, he said, in part, that 'not only would the use of French not be curtailed, but that it would actually be extended.'[8] The *Winnipeg Free Press*, whose coverage of the convention was excellent, quoted Scott as saying that 'the CCF is likely to encourage the learning of French. There is no reason why we might not come out with a bi-lingual currency.' Provincial rights in education, moreover, would in no way be changed by the CCF.[9] These indications of his strongly held views on the subjects of minority rights and English-French co-operation were favourably noted in his home province. He returned from Regina appalled by what he had seen of the prairie dustbowl, but with the comfortable feeling that the LSR had made its presence felt and that the future looked bright for a Canadian socialism.

He stopped in Toronto to confer with Cassidy. 'Frank Scott called on me this morning on his way back from the CCF convention ...,' Cassidy reported to a friend: 'He said that the LSR had scored a brilliant success at the convention, since the members of our group who were on hand had succeeded in having their views accepted pretty generally with respect to the programme.'[10] This was no exaggeration: at the convention itself more than one delegate had commented on the contribution made by the LSR participants, Joe Parkinson of Toronto, Forsey and Gordon as well as Scott of Montreal.

Scott's hopes for the CCF's future gained strength from the investigation he and

Cassidy made of wages and working conditions in the men's clothing industry in Ontario and Quebec. They undertook the study at the joint request of the Canadian Garment Manufacturers' Association and the Amalgamated Clothing Workers' Union of America. Completed late in 1933, the Cassidy-Scott report described a demoralized, dog-eat-dog industry. 'Both the manufacturers and the workers have suffered greatly in recent years, the former from cut-throat competition, disorganized marketing and general industrial instability, and the latter from unemployment, under-employment and the revival of the sweatshop in its most obnoxious forms.'[11] One major problem was that a few large-scale buyers exercised an inordinate degree of power over the market. Harry H. Stevens, the federal minister of trade and commerce, seized on this when he received an early copy of the report, and it reinforced the attack which in December 1933 he launched on monopoly and monopsony in Canadian industry. In due time that attack led to the establishment of the Royal Commission on Price Spreads, Stevens's departure from the Cabinet, and his formation of the Reconstruction party to contest the federal general election of 1935. To Scott the investigation suggested that the free market system was in the process of destroying itself.

Scott already believed that capitalism was immoral because it brutalized human beings. The study he carried out with Cassidy seemed to show that capitalism's claim to efficiency in distributing goods and services was very much open to question. Capitalism often did not, could not, deliver the goods. Scott commented on this in a satirical poem, 'Efficiency: 1935.' It was the last of a series of six poems that he published in 1935 under the title 'Social Notes.' These poems make two main points: capitalism is inhumane and immoral in treating human beings as if they were commodities, and is also inefficient.

The efficiency of the capitalist system
Is rightly admired by important people.
Our huge steel mills
Operating at 25% of capacity
Are the last word in organization.
The new grain elevators
Stored with superfluous wheat
Can load a grain-boat in two hours.
Marvelous card-sorting machines
Make it easy to keep track of the unemployed.
There is not one unnecessary worker
In these textile plants
That require a 75% tariff protection.
And when our closed shoe-factories re-open
They will produce more footwear than we can possibly buy.

So don't let us start experimenting with socialism
Which everyone knows means inefficiency and waste.

Socialism, Scott wrote in *Queen's Quarterly*, would in fact prove to be more efficient than modern capitalism was.

This theme also ran through *Social Planning for Canada*, the LSR's first book, published by Thomas Nelson & Sons in the autumn of 1935. Scott had helped to push this volume to completion as part of an editorial team that also included Forsey, Leonard Marsh, a young social scientist at McGill, and Marsh's wife Helen. Aside from his editorial duties, Scott had particular responsibility for the section on the Canadian constitution.

Scott's centralism was manifest in this section, as in an earlier booklet written for the LSR and published by Nelson, *Social Reconstruction and the B.N.A. Act* (1934), in his advice to J.S. Woodsworth and the CCF on constitutional issues, and later in the LSR's brief to the Royal Commission on Dominion-Provincial Relations. As he saw it, only the Dominion government was able to deal with the pressing social and economic problems posed by the Great Depression. Besides, unless the central government seized control of the economy, the big corporations would continue to take advantage of the division of power in the Canadian federal system and bend governments to their ends. The British North America Act had at the outset been strongly centralist, and in spite of a fairly consistent record of judicial interpretation favouring provincial rights, Scott felt confident that it could be used to advance socialist aims. 'There are great opportunities in the existing constitution,' he wrote in *Social Planning for Canada,* 'for Dominion control over economic matters of national importance.'[12] Some amendments would be necessary, however, chiefly in the field of social legislation.

Without uniformity in some degree, laws dealing with wages, hours, insurance benefits, health services, etc., must necessarily fail of their purpose, or at least work under enormous disadvantages and at greatly increased cost. The Dominion has done something to assist uniform standards, but its powers are cramped by the general understanding that social legislation belongs for the most part in the category of the provincial power over property and civil rights .... An amendment is needed to transfer to the Dominion unquestionable power to establish a national labour code, ... and to legislate regarding the subject of social legislation generally.[13]

Certain other amendments, notably in regard to control over companies and insurance and in order to abolish the Senate, were also necessary.

As for the method of amendment, it should be by action of the Dominion Parliament. Scott rejected the notion that provincial assent was required for the changes he proposed. He judged the provincial rights movement to have had harmful consequences not only for the Dominion's control of the economy but also for minority rights. Rights such as those of Roman Catholics in Ontario and Protestants in Quebec to their own publicly supported schools merited the strongest possible guarantees. Scott therefore proposed entrenching the sections of the BNA Act dealing with minority rights. 'Provincial powers over economic matters and social legislation, be it noted, are not in this group. Quebec's right to tolerate sweatshops whose existence holds down living standards in other provinces, is not a minority right.'[14] Civil liberties, too, were to be protected by means of 'an entrenched Bill of Rights clause in the B.N.A. Act.'

Although he was concerned to safeguard the rights of French Canadians within Quebec, and to expand their rights outside that province, Scott found many of the claims of French Canadian nationalism unacceptable. He rejected Quebec's hostility to centralism as irrelevant to the economic needs of French Canadians. Whatever might be said about this attitude from a constitutional point of view, as a political stance it was suicidal. This is not to suggest that the CCF would have enjoyed greater support in Quebec if the party, the LSR or spokesmen like Scott had been less centralist in their views. The CCF had more than one strike against it where Quebec was concerned.[15] But its centralism certainly did not help.

In reading what Scott had to say about French Canadian nationalism during the 1930s one gets the impression that he found it too offensive to assess carefully all the political implications of his criticism. He deplored the intolerance and attacks on civil liberties that often accompanied the expression of nationalist views in Quebec and elsewhere. For example, in October 1936 University of Montreal students threatened to break up a meeting at which representatives of the Spanish republic were scheduled to speak. Opinion in Quebec was generally hostile to the anti-clerical republic and favourable to General Franco's insurgents, seen as 'good Catholics,' and the student threat led the executive committee of the City of Montreal to ban the meeting.

Another example was the Act to Protect the Province against Communistic Propaganda, better known as the Padlock Act, passed in early 1937. Scott interpreted this action by the Duplessis government as a device to use the 'property and civil rights' clause in section 92 of the BNA Act in order to legislate in the area of criminal law, a federal responsibility. The purpose of the Padlock Act also seemed clear. Although it undertook to protect the province against communistic propaganda by padlocking (i.e., sealing) premises used for its dissemination in any form, the act did not define the term 'communism' and could be used against any sort of radicalism of which the attorney general, Duplessis himself, happened to disapprove. Moreover, the act placed a burden of proof of innocence on the victim of padlocking, rather than a burden of proof of guilt on the authorities, before the padlock would be removed.

It was not only the great majority of French Canadians who welcomed the

Padlock Act. To Scott's distress, English-speaking politicians and newspapers in Quebec also indicated their support. Those opposing it were clearly a small minority, mostly of left-wingers. Some of them founded the Canadian Civil Liberties Association and attempted to have the federal government disallow the act, or at least refer it to the Supreme Court of Canada for an opinion on its constitutionality. When the minister of justice, Ernest Lapointe, rejected this attempt, Scott was among those who sought a way of bringing a test case before the Supreme Court. This proved to be a long haul: ultimate success was almost two decades off.

In 1935 Scott succeeded Underhill as national president of the LSR and went on to serve for two years. He continued to see the role of the league as primarily educational. 'Slogans are all very well in the political field,' he told delegates to the 1936 national convention in Toronto, 'but the LSR tries to convince people by the sheer force of its logic and the accuracy of its analysis.'[16] Rarely did anyone express quite so boldly the LSR's faith in political education, or the conviction of its members that they really had solutions to the many difficult problems facing Canadians.

Its purchase of *The Canadian Forum* in the spring of 1936 was very much in the interest of spreading the league's message. Until 1934 the *Forum* had received an annual subsidy from the publishing house of J.M. Dent & Sons. When that ended a group of Liberals led by Steven Cartwright assumed control, but gave up after a year, Cartwright selling the periodical to Graham Spry for one dollar. Spry, who held a number of badly paid and unpaid positions, among them that of LSR national secretary, for a year tried in vain to make the *Forum* pay for itself. Then the LSR came to the rescue, having some money of its own and further encouraged by the promise of $1,000 from a well-to-do member, W.C. 'Bill' McNaught. Without this the *Forum* would surely have disappeared. To Scott the monthly was important not only as a means of publishing political commentary but also as an outlet for his poetry.

In 1937 he shared with Eugene Forsey and Leonard Marsh the task of preparing the LSR's second book. Essentially an abridged and updated version of the earlier volume, *Democracy Needs Socialism* was published by Nelson in 1938. In the same year Scott joined the national executive of the CCF. This was perhaps a natural development. Although Scott continued to oppose a formal affiliation between the LSR and the CCF, he believed that the league should be useful to the party. During his presidency of the LSR, two closed meetings of the LSR executive and the CCF members of Parliament took place, in March and May of 1936. Their purpose was to discuss the direction that the CCF members might take in Parliament and the help that the LSR might be able to give them. By 1938 the increasingly central role taken within the CCF by LSR founding members like Frank Scott and David

Lewis – in 1936 the latter became CCF national secretary on a part-time and in 1938 on a full-time basis – underlined the close link between the two groups.

Scott's first major contribution as a member of the executive was to join Lewis in writing a pamphlet, *CCF et propriété privée*. It was a response to a condemnation of the party made by Cardinal Villeneuve in November 1938. Roman Catholic hostility to the CCF was nothing new. The Dominican Georges-Henri Lévesque in 1933, and Archbishop Gauthier of Montreal in 1934, had condemned the CCF program for its alleged errors and similarity to communism. The latter condemnation had led the CCF to publish a pamphlet written by the bilingual Grace MacInnis, Woodsworth's daughter and wife of a CCF MP from Vancouver, Angus MacInnis. Entitled *La CCF réplique*, the pamphlet tried to controvert Gauthier on every major point. Villeneuve's condemnation was even more serious than Gauthier's, Scott pointed out to Woodsworth. 'Hitherto the only [sic] condemnation had been from a single bishop; now it is from a cardinal representing the entire Catholic Church in Canada or 41% of the population.'[17] A reply directed to French-speaking Quebeckers seemed essential. The pamphlet by Scott and Lewis drew on two papal encyclicals, *Rerum Novarum* (1891) and *Quadragesimo Anno* (1931), in support of the CCF's views and asserted that 'there is a great difference between the CCF and the communism described by his Eminence, Cardinal Villeneuve, a fundamental difference in philosophy, outlook and goals.'[18] Although the party made a valiant effort to distribute the pamphlet in Quebec, it is unlikely that it had much influence.

Scott was increasingly being drawn into partisan politics, but his creative energy continued to find expression in other fields. In 1936, for example, he was co-editor of and a contributor to *New Provinces,* an anthology of modern Canadian poetry. Two years later the Canadian Institute of International Affairs (CIIA) published his book *Canada Today.* It was a survey of current affairs whose major argument was that most Canadians had no wish to participate in the next European war. As things stood, however, Canada had no right of neutrality should Britain go to war, and the powerful pro-British faction would opt for participation in any major war which involved Britain.

With Underhill and Escott Reid, national secretary of the CIIA as well as an LSR member, Scott shared the view that Canada would be wise to take whatever steps were necessary to secure the right to neutrality in case Britain went to war. Then, if war broke out in Europe and Britain did become a belligerent, Canada should opt for neutrality. Scott feared a repetition of the conflict between English and French Canadians, and between social classes, that had afflicted the country in 1917 and 1918. He also feared that war would strengthen the most reactionary elements in Canadian society.

War in Europe was a growing threat during the later 1930s; after Germany's take-over of Bohemia and Moravia in March 1939, and Britain's subsequent guarantee to Poland, it became a virtual certainty. Nevertheless Scott continued to hope that the almost inevitable might yet be staved off, and that Canada might stay outside the conflict.

In the winter of 1938–39 he helped to draft *Canadian Unity in War and Peace,* a twelve-page pamphlet that demanded 'the immediate declaration by Parliament of Canada's right to decide issues of War and Peace.'[19] The demand arose out of fear that Prime Minister Mackenzie King's promise, that 'Parliament would decide' whether Canada would go to war, was hollow: that Parliament constitutionally had no freedom of choice once Britain had become a belligerent. The seventy-five signatories, some of them French but mostly English Canadians, were drawn from law, medicine, education, journalism, business, farming, and the clergy. Scott was the only one among them to be prominently associated with the CCF.

During the summer Scott entered into conversations with some young French Canadian intellectuals, among them François-Albert Angers, Gérard Filion, and André Laurendeau. They were generally hostile to the CCF, its centralism and its socialism. Its opposition to war, however, seemed to provide a basis for co-operation. The small group worked on a statement on Canadian foreign policy, but what they did was 'too little, too late.'[20] A weekend conference held at Scott's house on 2 and 3 September 1939 took place under the shadows cast by Germany's invasion of Poland on 1 September and the British and French declarations of war two days later. Canada's belligerency was now a foregone conclusion. This removed the main objective of the attempted alliance, which was to try to keep Canada out of war, and there were no further meetings.

At both an LSR national executive meeting, held in Montreal on 5 September, and an emergency meeting of the CCF national council in Ottawa on the 6th and 7th, Scott argued that Canada was already technically at war. To oppose her entry would be a waste of time; what mattered was to limit the extent of the country's war effort as much as possible. To some extent he agreed with Woodsworth's passionate argument for a non-interventionist stance. 'The last war settled nothing,' Woodsworth said: Canada had no business in this one.[21] Unlike the party leader, however, Scott was not a thorough-going pacifist, and ultimately he supported Angus MacInnis's compromise proposal. The CCF would oppose the conscription of manpower and the sending of a Canadian expeditionary force to Europe. It would oppose, too, the interference with civil liberties that was already under way, sanctioned by the War Measures Act and the Defence of Canada Regulations. However, it would support full economic assistance to Britain on a non-profit basis, while urging that munitions factories and other war industries be run by the government. Canadians would also be urged to start thinking about the shape of the post-war world.

Woodsworth opposed the policy of limited participation; so, from their very different perspective, did the interventionists, led by the Saskatchewan CCF leader, George Williams. The policy prevailed by a final vote of fifteen to seven at the council meeting, however, and remained in effect until the following summer. It certainly had Scott's support. He believed limited participation would prove attractive in Quebec. But in the federal election of March 1940 the CCF contested only four Quebec constituencies, and captured a mere 0.6 per cent of the province's vote, the same minuscule proportion it had taken in 1935. Elsewhere the party also fared disappointingly, although it gained 8.5 per cent of the popular vote with only 96 candidates – in 1935 it had taken 8.8 per cent with 118 candidates – and won eight seats instead of seven.

In hindsight the policy of limited participation seems unrealistic, not only politically but also militarily. That judgment can be extended to the policy of neutralism or quasi-isolationism that the LSR and CCF adopted in the later 1930s. Scott admitted as much in two articles early in 1942.[22] In the late summer and early autumn of 1939, however, the military forces in western Europe seemed to be evenly balanced. More important, no *military* contribution that Canada was able to make in the short or even medium term was likely to make any difference to that balance. Beyond that, it was legitimate to question, as Scott, Underhill, Reid, and others did, whether either the defence of Canada or the merits of Poland's or Britain's case warranted Canadian intervention on the European continent. More than one official in the Department of External Affairs, including the undersecretary, Dr O.D. Skelton, believed in 1939 that Canada should stay neutral. During the week between the British and Canadian declarations of war Skelton 'argued that the surrenders and hypocrisy of appeasement, from Ethiopia onward, had undermined all the moral purpose for which the war ostensibly was to be fought. Since no moral question was involved, Canada, like Ireland, should keep out.'[23] Loring Christie, who was the second most important official in the department, leaned to a policy of passive belligerency rather similar to the policy proposed by the CCF.

Hindsight, of course, has the advantage of knowing not only the course of military events after 1939 but also the full extent of Nazi *Schrecklichkeit* (horror). In some people's minds these eventually came to justify full Canadian participation in the war from the very outset. During the autumn of 1939, however, neither of these was known as yet. At that time the main argument in favour of belligerency was that Canadians had a duty to join the mother country. As J.L. Granatstein has aptly written: 'Canada went to war because Britain went to war. Not for democracy, not to stop Hitler, not to save Poland. Canada decided to fight ... only because Prime Minister Neville Chamberlain felt himself unable to escape the commitments Great Britain had made to Poland six months earlier.'[24] But public opinion was not united on the issue, and so long as the 'Phony War' of 1939–40 lasted the conflict in Europe probably seemed remote and even unreal to many. In any case, although in the election of March 1940 the policy of limited participation may have cost the CCF two of its experienced MPs, A.A. Heaps and Grant MacNeil, it did not fatally damage the party.

In the spring and early summer of 1940 the military situation changed dramatically. In April Germany invaded Denmark and Norway and in May attacked the Low Countries and France. The German armed forces quickly demonstrated far greater strength than most people had imagined them to possess. The fall of France in June was deeply disturbing to Canadians. With France out of the war, was Britain safe? Scott had been critical of British foreign policy in the 1930s, but he had real affection for the country. Under the new national government led by Winston Churchill it stood as a last western defence against the Nazi tide. Like the CCF generally, Scott came to support a whole-hearted Canadian war effort.

He continued to be critical of the many infringements of civil liberties that took place under the authority of the War Measures Act and the Defence of Canada Regulations. The official persecution of Communists, Jehovah's Witnesses, and others who were deemed to be hindering the war effort gave the Civil Liberties Association more work than it could handle. Intolerance of unpopular minorities reached a peak in 1942 when more than 20,000 Japanese Canadians were forcibly deported from the West Coast. Scott deplored outrages of this kind. Yet he did not lose sight of the CCF's major domestic goal, the making of a Canada that took greater responsibility for the welfare of its citizens. He recognized that, from the CCF's point of view, the war had some unexpected beneficial effects. During the Depression years he had argued that the federal government's emergency power should be used to deal with serious economic distress. That argument had been effectively rejected by the Privy Council decisions of 1937, which found much of the Bennett 'New Deal' legislation of 1935 *ultra vires*. The war, however, enabled the Dominion to do all sorts of things that were not possible in peacetime. Writing a valedictory for the LSR early in 1942, Scott noted that a number of its proposals, especially on economic planning, had since the outbreak of war been instituted by a government intent on running the war effort efficiently. 'The only thing wrong with the LSR idea, it seems, was that we did not adopt it.'[25]

If Scott took pleasure from his assessment that some of the LSR's policies were being adopted by Ottawa, he took more from evidence that the CCF was gaining public support. The war, in fact, took the party – as it did Canada – out of the stagnation of the later 1930s. 'Although few in the party saw the war as an opportunity to advance, it would not be far short of the truth to argue that the immediate result of the war was that it helped save the CCF.'[26] The party needed new causes; the conduct of the war, profiteering, labour relations, and government interference with civil liberties provided plenty. And then there was the shape that post-war Canada would take. Canadians were reluctant to return to the conditions of the Depression. The CCF's image was that of a party of reform. As the war grew older the party picked up steam.

From October 1941, when the CCF captured a plurality of the votes in British Columbia and became the Opposition, until June 1944, when it triumphed in Saskatchewan, it scored a number of successes. They included several federal by-election victories, as well as the 1943 provincial election in Ontario which saw the CCF go from no seats to thirty-four. These were heady days for CCFers, and Scott shared in the mounting enthusiasm. If there was a fly in the ointment it was the continuing weakness in Quebec. David Lewis ran a bad fourth in a by-election in Montreal-Cartier in August 1943, even though he had grown up in the area. Moreover, although one year later the CCF did better in the provincial election than it ever had before in Quebec, it still took only 2.6 per cent of the total vote and elected just one candidate.

Scott had a strong personal reason to be pleased about the CCF's advance: in 1942 he was elected national chairman of the CCF. Lewis was chiefly responsible for persuading Scott to take on these duties, which were often onerous. Furthermore, they made his relations with the administrative officers of McGill a bit more difficult.

Ever since Scott's letter to the *Gazette* in 1931 those relations had not been altogether easy. There was at McGill reluctance to instruct professors not to get involved in left-wing politics, but also some concern about that involvement. This was chiefly because of the critical questions it aroused outside McGill. As early as 1932 there had been an inquiry from General J.H. McBrien, commissioner of the RCMP, as to the opinions and connections of Forsey, Gordon, and Scott. Principal Sir Arthur Currie co-operated with the inquiry, and his executive assistant, Colonel Wilfrid Bovey, replied to General McBrien at length. The three men were not communists, he said: 'they desired change in the existing economic arrangements ... by parliamentary action, not by revolutionary action.'[27] That might be good enough for the RCMP, but it did not satisfy everyone. As McGill's official historian indicates, the activities of Scott and some of his associates were a source of occasional discussion between high administrative officers and the man who had been McGill's chancellor since 1920, Edward (later Sir Edward) Beatty.[28] Although Beatty did not question the right of left-wing professors to express their opinions, he regretted that these tended to associate the name of McGill with socialism and with 'unsound' ideas generally. Concerned about the university's financial welfare, he was almost bound to take a dim view of anything that to him reflected unfavourably on it.

Beatty probably agreed, for example, when the Montreal *Gazette* in 1938 questioned Scott's right to serve on the CCF national council: 'Ought a professor of civil law at McGill University, or a professor of any other faculty in any university, identify himself directly and actively with a political organization? Surely there is a line to be drawn somewhere, and surely the time has come to draw it?'[29] Neither he nor the new principal, Lewis Douglas, seems to have contemplated taking steps to force Scott to reconsider. As a senior and tenured member of faculty, and one who was respected and well-connected, Scott was close to being inviolable. But Douglas, who was very much Beatty's choice for principal, did manage to create the conditions for the dismissal of two of Scott's close associates, Forsey and Leonard Marsh, in 1941. As junior members of faculty they did not enjoy the tenure that protected Scott. They were not given the real reason for the non-renewal of their contracts, however, which was that their voluminous writings helped to give the social sciences at McGill too radical a reputation. Because people were uncertain about the circumstances of their release it was not the *cause célèbre* that it should have been.

When in 1942 Scott was asked to serve as CCF national chairman, he became aware of some sentiment among the governors that this was inappropriate and should be prevented if possible. In August 1942, Cyril James, who had succeeded Douglas as principal, asked Dean C.S. LeMesurier of the Faculty of Law whether Scott's new duties would not be too heavy for a full-time professor. LeMesurier must have 'a frank talk' with Scott in order to 'find out the exact demands of his political duties upon his time in order that we might be able to arrive at a satisfactory solution of the problem.'[30] In any case, Scott was not to use the stenographic and telephonic facilities of the Law Faculty for his political work.

Scott recalled in talking to me that he was able to reach an understanding with his dean, and that his CCF duties did not interfere with his work as teacher or scholar. However, his political work did for years keep him from becoming dean. In early 1947 he wrote to Principal James noting that, as he had not made dean because of his chairmanship of the CCF, he would look for some supplementary paid work, such as writing articles and acting as legal counsel in the Roncarelli case.[31] He had mixed feelings about being repeatedly passed over for the deanship. 'Actually the situation suited me admirably,' he later wrote: 'No one in his right senses wants to be Dean, but he certainly wants even less to belong to a university which discriminates against its staff for political reasons.'[32] McGill, let it be said, was not the only offending Canadian university in that respect.

As chairman of the CCF Scott was apparently effective. David Lewis wrote in his memoirs:

Although I was the one who was mainly responsible for persuading Scott to undertake the heavy responsibilities of the position, I did not realize at the time how valuable a chairman he would prove to be. We had all learned to admire his quickness of mind in the National Council and Executive debates and in discussions with the CCF caucus. We also knew that his wide knowledge, intellectual curiosity, and flexibility would help in the search for appropriate policies and for consensus within the party. What surprised many was to find that the man who was an academic, poet, philosopher, theorist, and satirist could also be a practical and often tough executive.[33]

Scott was 'never petty'; he did not look at issues from a self-interested point of view because he had no personal political ambition. He invariably took a comprehensive view of an issue. But he could also be irritating: his attention would wander, especially when the matter under discussion seemed to him to be trivial. 'Too often his tall, cutting aloofness and intellectual impatience caused annoyance and hurt to people who deserved better.'[34] It was perhaps in reference to such behaviour that a member of the Quebec CCF wrote of Scott in 1945: 'Unfortunately, it seems to me that he has the customary contempt of the academic mind for the rank and file.'[35] Probably it was unavoidable that the academics who became active in the CCF should feel that they knew better than the less well-educated what policies were most suitable. It was also unavoidable that this attitude should occasionally be resented.

Scott's stature within the CCF, already great, gained further from his co-authorship, with Lewis, of *Make This YOUR Canada* (1943). The book was low-priced and set forth in non-technical language the CCF's version of Canada's past, present, and future. It also appeared in a French edition, and enjoyed an excellent sale, aided by the mounting interest in the CCF in the war years. The book was very much a collaboration, except for the last chapter, which was mainly Scott's. 'I have always thought that the last chapter ... was an eloquent and valid statement of the democratic socialist's political thesis,' Lewis later commented.[36] But Scott resisted the only serious attempt that seems to have been made to induce him to run for office. Lewis told him in 1948 that he might be offered the federal nomination for the CCF in Sudbury. Scott turned this down, saying he thought he could be more useful to the party in Quebec than anywhere else. 'I have often said to you that the CCF has scarcely begun to realise the importance of Quebec in the total picture. The more we grow in strength elsewhere the more this problem emerges as of crucial significance in our long-range plans.'[37] Whether Scott would have made it into Parliament must remain a matter for speculation.

Scott was active on hehalf of the CCF, but he was never in danger of becoming a single-minded propagandist for the party. He continued to write poetry, and in 1945 published his first collection, *Overture*. His academic accomplishments as an expert on constitutional law secured him a Guggenheim Fellowship in 1940–41, one of the first to be awarded to a Canadian scholar. This enabled him to take a sabbatical at Harvard University. One of the fruits of that year was a long booklet, *Canada and the United States*, published in 1941 under the auspices of the World Peace Foundation. In it Scott took an internationalist view of the relations between the two countries. Although he recognized the affinities between Canada and her neighbour, he rejected the notion that Canada's early annexation to the United States was at all likely. 'A small power may move in the orbit of a larger power without thereby losing its identity. Any union in the future is less likely to come through annexation than through joint merging in some supra-national organization.'[38] What sort of organization might this be? He suggested that in the post-war world Canadians should support a reconstructed and improved League of Nations.

His calmness in contemplating the eventual demise of an independent Canada indicates that Scott was no diehard nationalist. Centralism has in Canada often been associated with English Canadian nationalism. But Scott's centralism was no more than a means to the end of introducing the social ownership of large enterprises, a planned economy, and vastly improved social welfare services. Any sort of ethnically based and exclusive nationalism certainly troubled him, as his writings on Quebec made clear. He rejected the claims of French Quebec nationalism, while at the same time showing concern for the place of French Canadians in Canada. This concern showed itself most clearly during the war in his assessment of the opinions of French-speaking Quebeckers with respect to conscription for overseas military service.

Late in 1941 Prime Minister Mackenzie King decided to ask the Canadian people whether they would release his government from its pledge not to introduce conscription for overseas service. His reason for doing so was partly military – the Army General Staff wanted to expand the forces overseas – and partly political. The government was under Conservative attack because of its failure to introduce conscription for overseas service – under the National Resources Mobilization Act of 1940 there was already conscription for home defence – and King wished to defuse criticism that he saw as dangerous to his government and to the cause of national unity. But many Quebeckers thought it was dishonest that all Canadians were to be polled in a plebiscite. The pledge had been made to Quebec, they argued, both before the war and during the Quebec provincial election in the fall of 1939. Why ask all Canadians to vote on it?

Scott believed that the CCF ought to oppose the introduction of conscription for overseas service. Accordingly, when the government's plan for a plebiscite became known he urged that the CCF call for a 'no' vote. But most of the National Council took a different line. The needs of the party in English Canada dictated a 'yes' vote. The justification was that this would show support for conscription of all of the country's resources, including private wealth. Scott acceded to the majority opinion, but he was unhappy about it. And when on 27 April 1942 the eight predominantly English-speaking provinces voted 'yes' while Quebec overwhelmingly voted 'no' he felt compelled to try to explain what this meant. Writing in *The Canadian Forum* he explained that French Quebec's negative attitude to conscription for overseas service would recede only when it became clear that the old British imperialism was receding, and that Canada was fighting the war in her own right and for her own reasons. 'All that Quebec means by the 'no' vote is that she does not want her children to die for any country other than their own.'[39] The article excited favourable comment in Quebec, and the CCF decided to issue it as a pamphlet. In talking to me, Scott recalled that the eminent Toronto economist Harold Adams Innis wrote to congratulate him on it. On the whole, however, the *Forum* article was 'not popular' in English Canada.

The article added to Scott's notoriety in conservative circles, as did his election to the chairmanship of the CCF later in 1942 and his co-authorship of *Make This YOUR Canada* in 1943. He was astonished, however, when in 1944 he found himself cast in the role of anti-capitalist villain. The growing popularity of the CCF prompted a vigorous campaign intended to discredit the party and its leaders. A key element in this campaign was a book by a Toronto advertising man, Burdrick A. Trestrail. It carried the title *Stand Up and Be Counted (or Sit Still and Get Soaked)*; a widely circulated comic book based on it had the even more alarming title *Social Suicide*. 'The socialist "Baby,"' Trestrail wrote, was 'the brainchild of a few college boys ... the professional social students' of the League for Social Reconstruction. He singled out two of them, Frank Scott and David Lewis. Scott was described as a law professor without any 'practical business experience' who nevertheless 'has all the answers.' David Lewis was 'a Jewish immigrant boy,' also without any 'practical experience in dealing with the problems for which he professes to have all the solutions.'

These two boys, with a few cronies, are the 'professional social students' who make the balls for Coldwell, Jolliffe, Winch and the others to fire.

If the C.C.F. Party is returned to power, it is my bet that THESE ARE THE BOYS WHO WILL RUN THE GOVERNMENT! These are the boys who will decide what is to be grown by the farmer; what is to be produced by industry; who is to distribute it; who is to get it; how much is to be paid for it; who can stay in business and who can't. They have spent over twelve years of their lives working and planning for 'Der Tag'. If you think they don't intend to succeed you're going to get a rude awakening.[40]

Trestrail went so far as to compare the 'professional social students' of the LSR to puppeteers who had the CCF leaders on strings, to a Pied Piper who was leading the component groups of the CCF astray, and to Hitler in their capacity for deception! On the whole Scott was inclined to laugh off Trestrail's charges: they seemed too ludicrous to be believed. Harder to laugh off was evidence that many Canadian corporations were taking part in the anti-CCF campaign. This campaign was partly responsible for the CCF's disappointing electoral performance in 1945. On 4 June the party lost twenty-six seats in a provincial election in Ontario and with them the Opposition status it had gained in 1943. On 11 June it won only twenty-eight seats in the federal election, all but one of them in the West. Although this was a marked increase over the eight seats won in 1940, it was well below what party supporters had hoped for and expected. It was particularly distressing that the party failed to get a single seat in either Ontario or Quebec.

The CCF's debacle in 1945 did not have a single cause. The anti-socialist campaign played a role, but probably less in changing voters' minds about the CCF than in reminding them why they had not voted for it earlier. What Canadians wanted was an assurance that the post-war world would not resemble that of the 'dirty thirties'; they also wanted protection against too much change. John English has written of Ontario, the province in which the CCF's collapse was most dramatic, that its 'people wanted a more active state if this meant social security, but not if it meant nationalization.'[41] This worked against the CCF. So did the fact that by 1945 the Liberals and even the Conservatives, now called the Progressive Conservatives, presented themselves as parties of reform. Organizational weaknesses in the CCF also played a part: in few sections of the country was the party in fighting trim.

The failure in Quebec, at least, came as no great surprise. Among French Canadians the CCF's message was still regarded with great suspicion. Episcopal hostility lingered in spite of the party's attempts to dispel it. Late in 1943 Scott accompanied the national CCF leader, M.J. Coldwell, to a luncheon with Archbishop Charbonneau of Montreal. It was held at the house of Murray Ballentyne, the editor of the Montreal edition of the *Catholic Register*, who took a sympathetic view of the CCF. The conversation was encouraging, Scott recalled a third of a century later. Referring to *Make This YOUR Canada*, the prelate said: 'I would not change a word.'[42] A subsequent meeting of the Canadian episcopate, held in October 1943, issued a declaration that was apparently intended to clear the CCF of any condemnation attached to it during the 1930s. The declaration did not mention the CCF by name, however, and was interpreted in more than one way. Some held that Roman Catholics were now free to vote for the CCF; others, especially in Quebec, denied this.[43] What benefits, if any, the CCF gained is not clear. The party did better in 1945 than it had in the elections of 1935 and 1940. Its total vote, however, was no more than a negligible 2.4 per cent of all ballots cast in the province, and of its twenty-nine candidates – this was a record – not one got even close to being elected.

The CCF's lone representative in the Quebec provincial legislature, David Côté, did not last long. He got into debt and asked the national office – the provincial CCF was impecunious–for a full-time salary in addition to his parliamentary salary. 'This was entirely outside our tradition and beyond our treasury', David Lewis wrote in his memoirs: '... I could not do otherwise than reject his demand. Some months later we learned that the Liberals had made Côté an offer he could not refuse. The CCF toe in the Quebec door had been amputated.'[44] In the 1948 provincial election the CCF did not even run a candidate in Rouyn-Noranda, the scene of Côté's victory four years earlier.

That election underlined the continuing weakness of the CCF in Quebec, despite the efforts of people like Scott to make a wider appeal to Quebeckers. In the 1930s the Quebec CCF was limited very largely to English-speaking Montrealers, but by the mid-1940s French Canadian involvement had grown. An increasing number of French Canadians had found their way into the provincial council. The most important of these was Thérèse Casgrain, who had played the leading role in the suffragist movement that had succeeded in finally getting Quebec women the vote in 1940. She and her husband, a judge and former Liberal MP, knew the Scotts socially, and in 1946 Scott took pleasure in signing her membership card. Two years later he informed Lewis: 'Thérèse Casgrain said she would accept a Vice-Chairmanship if elected.'[45] François Laroche, asked whether he would stand aside for her, agreed readily, and later in 1948 Thérèse Casgrain succeeded Laroche as the French Canadian vice-chairman of the national CCF. At two separate times, too, the national party managed to maintain a paid organizer in the province, Jacques Casgrain in 1943–44 and Roger Prévost in 1946–48. Nothing seemed to help, however. After its improved showing in the provincial election of 1944, when the CCF contested twenty-four seats, won one, and got 2.6 per cent of the popular vote, it fielded only seven candidates in 1948. Together they got fewer than one in a hundred votes. In the 1949 federal election the party nominated twenty candidates in Quebec, thirteen of them in the Montreal area, and received a mere 1.1 per cent of the ballots cast. The biggest vote-getter in Quebec that year was Scott's fellow poet A.M. Klein. He contested Cartier, the constituency that had rejected his friend David Lewis six years before, and got 14.2 per cent.

The 1948 and 1949 elections were a low point for the CCF in Quebec. In the elections of the 1950s – there were provincial elections in 1952 and 1956 and federal elections in 1953, 1957, and 1958 – it did somewhat better, though never again matching the results of 1944 and 1945. The CCF continued to be unattractive to French Canadians, though in 1955 the Quebec party abandoned the untranslatable name of Co-operative Commonwealth Federation and rebaptized itself the Parti social démocratique du Québec. Its essentially English Canadian roots and its known centralism counted heavily against it even when clerical objections to its socialism and alleged materialism dwindled. Moreover, leading CCFers from other parts of Canada continued on occasion to show themselves insensitive to the concerns of Quebeckers. One striking example was Angus MacInnis's defence of the British Columbia school system against Quebec MPs, who supported a local demand for a French language school in Maillardville, in the lower mainland. This was one of several incidents in 1955 which almost led Scott, among several other Quebec leaders, to resign from the national council.

The CCF's centralism was actually diluted in the early 1940s, a consequence of the growing expectation that the party might well triumph in several provinces before it could seriously expect to form a government in Ottawa. The CCF could not abandon every element of its centralist faith, however. What it and more particularly Scott tried to do was to make centralism and state intervention more acceptable to French-speaking Quebeckers. He was the party's chief spokesman in Quebec, and there were few groups he would not address and issues he would not tackle. His audiences probably listened to him with scepticism. Even intellectuals, with whom Scott's rapport as a speaker was greatest, generally rejected his message. The CCF in Quebec continued to be a forlorn hope.

It was far from being a great success in Canada as a whole. Disappointing as the party's showing in the federal and Ontario elections of 1945 had been, there were other disappointments to come. The only really bright spot was Saskatchewan, where the CCF, led until 1961 by T.C. 'Tommy' Douglas, remained in office for twenty years. Scott acted as constitutional adviser to this government. In British Columbia, however, once the most promising province from the CCF's point of view, a Liberal-Conservative coalition kept the party from power for almost a decade. When in 1952 the coalition faltered Social Credit took its place. In Ontario the CCF regained the status of Opposition in 1948, but only for one term. In 1951 the party was reduced to a mere two seats, and it managed to regain only a small amount of ground during the remainder of the decade.

The federal election of 1949 reduced the CCF's representation in Parliament from thirty-two to thirteen – the party had won four by-elections between 1945 and 1949 – while its share of the popular vote fell from 15.6 to 13.4 per cent. The recapture of York South, which the party had won in a 1942 by-election only to lose it in 1945, fell far short of the hoped-for breakthrough in Ontario. The party showed strength in Saskatchewan (though less than in 1945), British Columbia, and urban Manitoba, and scarcely anywhere else. It was a stunning disappointment. And although the CCF in the federal election of 1953 regained some of the seats it had lost four years before, going from thirteen to twenty-three, its share of the popular vote declined further, dropping to 11.3 per cent.

By this time Scott had ceased to be national chairman. In 1950 he addressed the CCF national convention in that capacity for the last time. He reaffirmed his belief in the essential rightness of the party's cause, and in the basic soundness of its analysis of the Canadian situation. The CCF's socialism still spoke to the problems facing Canada, even though increasing prosperity had altered perceptions of these problems. At the same time, he said, the party should not be doctrinaire with respects to the details of its socialism. 'Socialism is most concerned with the human spirit, with its freedom, its growth, its emancipation, and with ownership only in so far as some of its forms are obstacles to this freedom just as other forms seem essential to it.'[46] Changes in detail might be desirable. An opinion that he had occasion to express more than once during the 1950s was that the CCF's program had to be adapted to changing circumstances.

One of these was the altered international situation. Since the last national convention, held in Winnipeg in August 1948, the North Atlantic Treaty Organization (NATO) had come into being and war had broken out in Korea. The development of the Cold War between the United States and the Soviet Union was bound to affect Canada and the CCF. Initially there was reluctance in party circles to see Canada align herself too closely with the United States. But the weight of CCF opinion, like that of Canadians generally, became increasingly anti-Soviet and pro-American, particularly after the Communist party take-over in Czechoslovakia in May 1948. Indeed, it can be argued that majority CCF opinion shifted along with public opinion, and shifted independently of the merits of the case.[47] Dissidents learned to keep from making their disagreement with the party's cold war stance too open or faced expulsion. In 1949, for example, two Manitoba MLA's were expelled for their outspoken opposition to the American-sponsored Marshall Plan for European economic recovery and to Canadian membership in NATO.

For many CCFers opposition to Soviet Russia was made easier by their long-standing hostility to the Communist Party of Canada, known in the late 1940s as the Labor Progressive party. It is not altogether easy, indeed, to determine whether the CCF's support for American policy was prompted primarily by fear of the Soviet Union or by dislike of the Communists. Both motivations found expression in Scott's address to the 1950 national convention. 'The Communist Party has no right to the word socialist', he said, because it lacked 'respect for the individual human being.' Stalinism 'represented the recapture of Russia by a powerful form of oriental despotism,' whereas socialism continued to be committed to 'the great traditions of democracy, traditions which are still very much alive in the country where capitalism is most powerful, namely the United States.' Socialists would defend their freedom against communist aggression, 'and they will not let the strangeness of some of their capitalist bedfellows deflect them from this fundamental purpose.' He rejected a policy of neutrality for Canada as 'utterly unrealistic' as well as 'a denial of socialist responsibility.' He disagreed with the view, common among liberals and conservatives by this time, that the issue was between freedom and totalitarianism rather than between socialism and capitalism: 'Freedom is endangered by certain capitalist practices and tendencies as well as by totalitarian movements, and the evils of capitalism help to create those movements.'[48] But it is hard to escape the conclusion that Scott saw in Soviet communism a greater danger to Canada *and* to socialism than he saw in capitalism. His somewhat facile analysis was reflected in National Council motions at the 1950 convention expressing support for NATO and the United Nations expeditionary force in Korea. The motions passed, though not without opposition.

One admiring listener to Scott at the 1950 convention was David Lewis, who had himself recently left his position as the party's national secretary. In his memoirs he called Scott's address:

an illuminating contemporary statement about democratic socialism. It was so well received by the majority of convention delegates that the national office published the speech as a pamphlet for wider distribution. To me the address was another example of Scott's intellectual contribution to the CCF which caused me to value highly the opportunity of working closely with him for many years ... Scott's searching intelligence and lucid exposition brought political discussion to a high level. This meant much to me; it responded to my own inclination always to seek the theoretical basis for socialist policy and action.[49]

Although Scott had helped to draft the Regina Manifesto, he did not think it was engraved in stone. The process of rewriting the manifesto began in 1950, as the convention passed a motion instructing the 'National Council to prepare a statement of the application of democratic socialist principles to Canada and the world today.'[50] But if, in Walter Young's words, Scott in 1950 'laid the foundation for the rethinking of the Regina Manifesto,'[51] the process took several years to complete.

Other leading figures in the national party, among them Lewis, who in 1950 joined Thérèse Casgrain as one of the party's vice-chairmen and in 1954 became its national chairman, as well as the leader, M.J. Coldwell, and the veteran MP from Vancouver East, Angus MacInnis, believed that a new statement of principles was necessary. They believed that the prosperity of the post-war years had made some of the stronger language of the Regina Manifesto obsolete, particularly its ringing concluding sentence: 'No C.C.F. Government will rest content until it has eradicated capitalism and put into operation the full programme of socialized planning which will lead to the establishment in Canada of the Co-operative Commonwealth.'[52] A mixed economy had become an acceptable choice. The policies followed in post-war Britain and Sweden seemed examples of what might win the support of a majority of Canadians. Certainly the party's warnings that the post-war prosperity was going to be followed by another depression seemed to be alienating people. Scott was not alone in thinking that the CCF's appeal could be broadened if the party approached the electorate in a less apparently gloomy and intransigent guise.

There were those, however, who believed that the Regina Manifesto spoke to the needs of the 1950s as it had to those of the 1930s. These 'left wingers' opposed the call for a re-examination of party principles in 1950, and continued to do so. A characteristic response was that of Ernest Winch, a veteran member of the British Columbia Legislature: 'So long as the Regina Manifesto stands, we are safe.'[53] The split between those who wanted what they thought of as an updated program, and those who believed the old one to be still suitable, for some years all but immobilized the party. Eventually the growing evidence of weakness, measured in falling membership and worsening finances, pushed the CCF along the path of change. A meeting of the National Council reached consensus early in 1956 that the party seemed to be frightening people with its commitment to socialization, and that a new program should be prepared for consideration at the next National Convention meeting. Scott, who was still on the National Council, strenuously argued the need to restate the CCF's objectives so as to elicit greater electoral support. 'Too much social theory, too little social psychology,' was how he described the CCF's prevailing approach.[54]

In August 1956, the National Convention adopted its new program, the Winnipeg Declaration. It 'lacked the fire of the Regina Manifesto,' Walter Young commented, 'and was accepted only after long, and at times bitter, debate. The members resented the change in policy despite their earlier acceptance of the need for change.'[55] The party's left wing saw in the document a weakening, if not the abandonment, of the CCF's commitment to socialism. Its defenders, Scott among them, held that the Winnipeg Declaration was a clarification of the Regina Manifesto rather than a major departure from it. The declaration's language was clearly less threatening. Contrast, for example, its last sentences with the final sentence of the Regina document quoted earlier: 'The CCF will not rest content until every person in this land and in all other lands is able to enjoy equality and freedom, a sense of human dignity, and an opportunity to live a rich and meaningful life as a citizen of a free and peaceful world. This is the Co-operative Commonwealth which the CCF invites the people of Canada to build with imagination and pride.'[56] More soothing language, however, was hardly the key to CCF success. Scott was surely right when he told the National Council meeting in January that 'the best programme was no substitute for organization.'[57] And in few places was CCF organization good.

The Winnipeg Declaration failed to bring the national party additional support, though it did not lose it any votes. New policy statements scarcely had the power to affect the fate of the 'minor party' that the CCF had become or, perhaps more accurately, had never really ceased to be.[58] The federal election of 1957 brought some evanescent pleasure. The CCF won twenty-five seats, one of them C.D. Howe's stronghold in Port Arthur. Its share of the popular vote fell once more, however, and in the 'Diefenbaker landslide' of March 1958 the party fell to eight seats and a mere 9.5 per cent of the popular vote, the lowest share since 1940. Veterans like Coldwell and Winnipeg North Centre's Stanley Knowles went down to personal defeat.

Even before the election it had been clear to Scott, among others, that the party's base must be broadened. Indeed, for many years David Lewis had been trying to forge ties with organized labour. The disaster of 1958 made a new coalition of forces essential.

The election also made that coalition more likely. Shocked by the results, which weakened gravely the party most favourable to organized labour, the convention of the Canadian Labour Congress (CLC) in April 1958 acted on a recommendation from the executive council and called for a new political movement. The CCF's National Council was eager to meet this initiative. It appointed a small group, of which Scott was a member, to meet with representatives of the CLC. The first meeting of the 'CLC-CCF Political Committee' took place in June 1958; in July the CCF national convention endorsed the council decision.

During the next two years Scott worked hard to help make the 'New Party' a reality. The CLC-CCF committee was rechristened the National Committee for the New Party (NCNP), and spun off New Party clubs. There was resistance, as some CCF stalwarts feared that the old party's socialism was being diluted, and that labour elements would dominate the new party unduly without being able to deliver the anticipated electoral strength. Nevertheless the 1960 CCF national convention unanimously endorsed the establishment of the New Party. There were early indications of success. In October 1960 a New Party candidate won a federal by-election victory in Peterborough, Ontario. More encouraging still from Scott's point of view was that 'early in 1961, the Quebec Federation of Labour endorsed the New Party by a margin of 507 to 5. To a movement perennially shut out of Quebec, the news sounded incredible.'[59]

Over 2,000 delegates from the CCF, the labour unions, and New Party clubs met in Ottawa from 31 July to 4 August 1961, to establish the New Democratic Party (NDP). Scott was one of the few delegates who had also attended the Regina Convention in 1933. The NDP's program was couched in language considerably less radical than the Regina Manifesto's. It also accommodated Quebec views to an extent that would have been scarcely thinkable a generation earlier. The draft program promised equal recognition and respect for French and English and a new, co-operative federalism. When French-speaking delegates from Quebec insisted that Canada was a compact of two nations and should be recognized as such in the program, the convention went along: 'The New Democratic Party strongly affirms its belief in a federal system which alone insures the united development of the two nations which originally associated to form the Canadian partnership, as well as that of other ethnic groups which later made Canada their home. Canada's constitution particularly guarantees the national identity of French Canadians and the development of their culture.'[60] Like his long-time friend Eugene Forsey, Scott recognized that this was questionable history. Unlike Forsey, he was inclined to acquiesce in it for political reasons. In any event, the delegates at the Ottawa convention overwhelmingly accepted it.

The NDP was the culmination of a process whereby those in the CCF who wanted a Canadian version of the British Labour party had their way. In Walter Young's view, 'the formation of the New Democratic Party was, in this sense, the fulfilment of the aims of Lewis and Scott and Coldwell.'[61] Certainly Scott had always taken a favourable view of the needs and interests of the Canadian working class and of organized labour. Unfortunately for the calculations that he and others had made, organized labour in much of Canada, and particularly in Quebec, was relatively ineffective in delivering the vote. In the federal election of 1962 the NDP, led by former Saskatchewan premier Tommy Douglas, polled 13.5 per cent of the total Canadian vote and took nineteen seats. Its share of the ballots cast in Quebec was only 4.4 per cent, however. In the 1965 federal election no less than 12 per cent of Quebec voters chose the NDP, but none of its sixty candidates was elected. And in 1968 the influence of Pierre Trudeau was much in evidence: although the NDP had candidates in all but one of Quebec's seventy-four constituencies, its share of the popular vote dropped to 7.5 per cent. The provincial party's performance was no more encouraging. In Robert Cliche the Quebec party in 1965 found a superb leader, but it was weakened by constant dispute about the nature of the relationship between Quebec and Canada.

As for the national NDP, the party's share of the country-wide vote was 17.9 per cent in 1965 and 17 per cent in 1968. Two decades later it was still trying to expand its electoral support beyond the 18–20 per cent level nationally, and to make a breakthrough in Quebec.

The formation of the NDP ended Scott's active involvement in party politics. He continued to support the party, but after 1961 his main attention was engaged elsewhere. Of course, Scott's ample energies allowed him throughout his life to range over several fields. His interest in international affairs, for example, was as keen as ever. In 1952 he worked for the United Nations Technical Assistance program while on leave from McGill. After being briefed in New York, where his old friend King Gordon worked for the United Nations, Scott went to Burma. There the socialism that in Canada had made him the object of mild suspicion was counted to his credit. 'The millstone around my neck became the halo around my head,' he sometimes quipped.[62] Unhappily he had to be invalided home early because he contracted amoebic dysentery. His experiences in Burma confirmed the belief, however, which he had held since the 1930s, that a socialist commonwealth of nations should be the goal of all socialists.

In the 1950s two more collections of his poetry appeared, *Events and Signals* (1954) and *The Eye of the Needle* (1957). The latter contained some of Scott's most trenchant social and political commentary of the 1930s and 1940s. 'Ode to a Politician' and 'W.L.M.K.' – 'How shall we speak of Canada, / Mackenzie King dead? / The Mother's boy in the lonely room / With his dog, his medium and his ruins?' – viewed critically the two leaders who dominated the main federal parties during that time: R.B. Bennett and William Lyon Mackenzie King. Other poems lampooned life under capitalism and the incapacity of well-to-do men to understand the problems of the poor. One example was 'Practical Men':

'No health insurance for Canada'
  says the Chamber of Commerce
sitting in the Chateau Frontenac
  everyone insured personally
against sickness, accident, fire, theft,
  and housemaids falling off step-ladders.

'It might lead to state medicine'
  warn these prophets
who have been educated in state schools
  and, if lucky
have graduated from state universities.

'Social medicine is not the whole answer to public health,' Scott told the medical students of the University of Montreal in 1949, 'but in my opinion it will represent a great step toward a healthier and happier society.'[63]

In the 1950s and early 1960s, too, Scott successfully pleaded before the Supreme Court of Canada three landmark cases involving civil liberties. After lengthy litigation, in *Switzman* v. *Elbling* the Supreme Court finally, in 1957, declared Duplessis's twenty-year old Padlock Act to be unconstitutional. In 1959 the Supreme Court's decision in *Roncarelli* v. *Duplessis* rendered belated justice to Frank Roncarelli, a Montreal restaurateur who had aroused Duplessis's ire by standing bail for Jehovah's Witnesses. In late 1946 Duplessis had ordered the cancellation of Roncarelli's liquor permit. Thirteen years later the Supreme Court awarded Roncarelli damages of more than $33,000 and assessed Duplessis interest and court costs. By this time the persecution of Jehovah's Witnesses had already begun to wane in Quebec; 'in a real sense,' a historian of the sect writes, the Roncarelli decision was therefore 'anti-climatic.'[64] However, in 1947 it had required courage to take the case. Very few lawyers in Quebec were willing to cross Duplessis, who was attorney general as well as premier.

In 1962 the Supreme Court, in *The Queen* v. *Brodie,* cleared D.H. Lawrence's novel *Lady Chatterley's Lover* of charges of obscenity. (Scott's earlier experiences with this case at a lower level had led him to write an amusing satirical poem, 'A Lass in Wonderland.') But Scott regretted that he lost the last case he pleaded before the Supreme Court of Canada, *Oil, Chemical and Atomic Workers' International Union* v. *Imperial Oil Ltd.* (1963). Associated with him was Thomas Berger, later to become leader of the Opposition in British Columbia and eventually, for a time, a judge of the British Columbia Court of Appeal. They failed by one vote to persuade the Supreme Court to set aside a British Columbia statute barring trade unions from contributing to political parties. (At the time of writing this issue has become the focus of a case under the new Charter of Rights in which an Ontario community college teacher is challenging a union's right to use part of membership dues for political contributions.) The legislation was repealed after the NDP under David Barrett took office in 1972. But the court's decision means the precedent stands. To Scott the statute seemed to be an appropriate comment on lawmaking in a capitalist society: there was no equivalent prohibition against contributions by private corporations.

Scott's sympathy for the labour movement, which prompted his taking the case of the Oil, Chemical and Atomic Workers' Union, was evident in other ways. He had supported the Asbestos Strike in Quebec in 1949. The following year a small group of which he was director, Recherches sociales, got some money from an anonymous donor that was to be used for social education. Scott wrote in 1956:

Our chief aim has been to give financial support to a few daring and imaginative Canadians who are involved in worthwhile intellectual or social pursuits, but who are not in a position to receive one of the too few Canadian government grants available. In particular, we have tried to promote or encourage attempts to make the two great cultural groups of Canada better known to each ... To date, however, *Recherches sociales* has devoted most of its time and money to this series of studies on the asbestos strike of 1949, which we are now publishing.[65]

The book in which these lines appeared was *La Grève de l'amiante (The Asbestos Strike)*. The volume's editor was a young lawyer, Pierre Elliott Trudeau, co-editor of the political and literary periodical *Cité Libre* and a valued ally in the political battle against Duplessis. Trudeau also shared Scott's love of the outdoors, and in the summer of 1956 the two men went down the Mackenzie River together. The publication of the book, whose contributors included Gérard Dion, Fernand Dumont, Gérard Pelletier, and Maurice Sauvé as well as Trudeau himself, ranked with the Asbestos Strike itself as a key event in the background to Quebec's *révolution tranquille*.

It was largely as the result of his acquaintance with Scott that Trudeau moved for a few years in Quebec CCF circles, and in the early 1960s supported the NDP. Both men served from 1958 to 1961 on the editorial committee of a publishing project that eventually saw the light as *Social Purpose for Canada*, and both contributed essays to it. Among the other editors were George Grube, of the Classics Department of Trinity College, University of Toronto, Eugene Forsey, and David Lewis, all of them active in the CCF. The book's editor, Michael Oliver of the McGill political science department, linked its publication to that of *Social Planning for Canada* in 1935:

Among its authors was Professor F.R. Scott who has been intimately connected with this book, both as a most active member of its editorial committee and as a contributor. The sense of continuity from the thirties to the present must have been strongest in him, but it was shared by all of us to some degree. We could not have escaped the influence of the democratic socialists who wrote *Social Planning for Canada* if we had wanted to, and in spite of striking differences sometimes between the remedies (and to a lesser extent the diagnoses) proposed in the two books, their common purpose is unmistakable.[66]

It would be wrong to assume that there was a direct connection between *Social Purpose for Canada* and the New Party, Oliver added: 'Rather, both are products of a revival in social and political concern which will, I think, mark the 1960's as it did the 1930's.' He hoped that the ideas in the book would influence not just the New Party but all the political parties. But its frequent references to socialists and socialism, in the articles by Scott and Trudeau among others, seemed to guarantee that the book would be taken most seriously on the political left.

In 1961, the year that *Social Purpose for Canada* appeared, Scott finally became dean of law, holding the position for a three-year term. Upon leaving the deanship he was appointed to the Macdonald Professorship of Law, one of the most prestigious endowed chairs in the university. He occupied it until his retirement from teaching in 1968, an event he captured in a poignant poem, 'On Saying Good-Bye to My Room in Chancellor Day Hall.' The Law Faculty later made available to him a small office, however, and in 1975 he was named Professor Emeritus.

Scott's lifelong concern to improve the relations between French and English Canadians never found clearer expression than in the 1960s. His interest in the work of French Canadian poets and desire to make them better known in English Canada led in 1962 to the publication of *St. Denys Garneau and Anne Hébert: Translations*. In these two writers Scott found support for his own humanist views. The following year he edited, with Michael Oliver, the book *Quebec States Her Case*. Published in 1964, this volume of documents in translation was an attempt to acquaint English Canadians with the entire range of opinion in French-speaking Quebec on the future of the province and of Canada. The interest in English Canada in the 'quiet revolution' and the varieties of separatism in Quebec meant that the book found wide use in schools and universities.

Scott's conviction that the best and perhaps only way to keep French-speaking Quebeckers in Canada was to give them a larger place within it found recognition in 1963 in his appointment to the Royal Commission on Bilingualism and Biculturalism. It was the creation of the Liberal government led by Lester B. Pearson, an old acquaintance of Scott's. That government was concerned to increase the stake that French Canadians had in the country as the best way of combatting Quebec separatism. (Pearson and one of his Quebec ministers, Maurice Lamontagne, were able to draw Scott's friends Gérard Pelletier and Pierre

Trudeau into the House of Commons as Liberals in 1965. Three years later, of course, Trudeau became prime minister of Canada.) Until the end of the 1960s the royal commission claimed much of his time. Nevertheless he was able to bring out three more collections of poetry: *Signature* in 1964, his *Selected Poems* in 1966, and a book of 'found poems,' *Trouvailles,* in 1967. In that year of Canada's centennial Scott was named a Companion of the Order of Canada, the country's highest non-military honour. He was one of the first group of Canadians to be invested into the new order, another of Mike Pearson's innovations. But in 1969 he declined a seat in the Senate as an inappropriate honour for one who had argued for that body's dissolution.

One organization in which Scott remained active throughout the 1950s and 1960s was the Canadian Civil Liberties Association. Indeed, my first memory of him is of the day he addressed a meeting of the association at the Colonnade on Bloor Street in Toronto sometime in 1965 or 1966. One of his remarks has stuck in my mind. He noted that the RCMP had their origins in the government's desire to exercise surveillance over the Indians in the Canadian West, but since then that surveillance had been extended over all Canadians: 'We are all Indians today!' In view of his long-standing commitment to the rights of individuals as well as unpopular groups, it is therefore surprising that a controversy surrounding civil liberties exposed him to more criticism than he had experienced since the 1940s, but this time from his friends rather than his enemies.

The occasion was Ottawa's invocation of the War Measures Act in October 1970. This startling action was a response to the terrorist activities of the Front de libération du Québec (FLQ) and what the federal government deemed to be a threat of civil disorder. Whether or not this was necessary is a question that will probably be debated for years to come. A highly regarded survey of recent Canadian history published in 1981 notes: 'In retrospect it is difficult to understand what else, legally and politically, could have been done. The government was bound to uphold the law and its application. It would have been ultimately foolish to concede much of the terrorist program, and it may have been unwise to concede any. Politically, it is the government's duty to try to manage conditions, including public opinion, so that danger to the fabric of the Canadian state is avoided or repaired. That it also seems to have done.'[67] At the time, however, some people to whom Scott was very close attacked the use of the War Measures Act as extreme and unwarranted. His long-time friend and political comrade David Lewis, soon to be federal leader of the NDP, was also in this camp. Indeed, sixteen members of the party's parliamentary caucus, led by Tommy Douglas, opposed the federal government's action.

Scott nevertheless gave qualified support to the use of the act. When the government of Quebec, supported by that of Montreal, asked for emergency aid, he wrote in a syndicated newspaper article: 'How could a federal prime minister have possibly refused to respond?'[68] Without denying that as emergency legislation the War Measures Act was extreme, or that its first regulations were unnecessarily severe, Scott believed that Ottawa would have been remiss had it not responded. He reiterated his assessment in an article some months later, comparing the situation in October 1970 to other 'examples of an outbreak of civil disorder' in the province that had left marks on his memory.[69] He noted the conscription riots in Quebec City in 1918 and the threatened student interference with a meeting of three representatives of the Spanish Republic in 1936. The demonstration of strong student support for the FLQ in 1970 reminded Scott of the 1936 episode. Although in the earlier instance the students had taken an anti-radical stand and in the more recent case a radical one, the incidents seemed to have in common a hostility to the give and take of debate in a democratic society.

Scott took comfort from the awareness that a large majority of Canadians supported the use of the act: 87 per cent, with little variation between English and French Canadians, approved its use. However, he distinguished sharply between the invocation and the way it was carried out. 'It was not necessary, in my opinion and that of the Civil Liberties Union of which I am a member, to have had such drastic Regulations accompanying the Act ... There must have been hundreds of unnecessary arrests.'[70] Scott, indeed, was among those who had moved quickly to help provide legal representation to the 436 persons who were arrested and detained under the War Measures during the crisis. This was not enough for some of his critics, however, who thought that he was renouncing forty years of service in the cause of civil liberties. For his part, Scott believed that in 1970 these liberties were endangered by supporters of the FLQ and needed to be protected, along with civil society as a whole, by some form of emergency legislation. In more than one conversation with me he charged his critics with naïveté or inadequate understanding of the troubled state of affairs in the province, and particularly in Montreal, that fateful October.

The FLQ was only the most extreme and intolerant manifestation of a nationalism that Scott found worrying. In the 1930s he had deplored the racist, obscurantist, and reactionary nature of much of Quebec nationalism. If the nationalism of the 1970s was less objectionable on those counts, Scott none the less found much to dislike in it. In so far as it tended to separatism it threatened the country that he loved, and although Scott was not a conventional nationalist he was a loyal Canadian. In so far as it tended to linguistic chauvinism it threatened the position of the English-speaking minority of which he was part and which he refused to see as somehow alien to Quebec. 'I predict there will be more English in Quebec,' he told a student audience in Toronto in 1967: 'There are already, in Quebec, some seven hundred thousand people whose mother tongue is English. In addition, there are new immigrants whose mother tongue might have been Italian or Polish or what have you, but who now use English as their working language. I do not think we shall be far out in suggesting there are nearly a million people in Quebec who use English normally as the language in which they live their lives.

That will not change, no matter what constitutional decisions are made.'[71] It was, as he well knew, the tendency of immigrants to integrate themselves into English-speaking Quebec that particularly bothered French-speaking Quebec nationalists. In the school district of St Léonard, a Montreal suburb, the issue became a heated one in 1967, leading the local school board to rule in 1968 that the children of all Roman Catholic parents must attend French-language schools. This decision was highly unpopular with many Italian Canadians, and forced the Union Nationale government of Jean-Jacques Bertrand to take a stand. In 1969 it tabled Bill 63, which made French the prevailing language of instruction, but offered parents the choice of whether their children should be educated in English or in French. In spite of strong pressure from French-language organizations brought together in the Front du Québec français, the Bertrand government refused to abandon the voluntary principle.

Concerned about the menacing tone of much of the criticism of Bill 63, Scott became active in the defence of minority rights in the province, the Protestant educational rights referred to in section 93 of the BNA Act and the English-language rights referred to in section 133. These were challenged by Bill 22, introduced by the Liberal government of Robert Bourassa and adopted by the National Assembly in 1974, and later by Bill 101, introduced by the Parti Québécois government of René Lévesque and passed in 1977. The first of these, the Official Language Act, 'declared French alone to be the official language of Quebec, thus upsetting the coequal status that English had always enjoyed in Quebec.'[72] It also restricted to some extent the access of the children of non-English-speaking parents to English-language schools. The *péquiste* legislation, the Charte de la langue française as Bill 101 was called, went much further in asserting the French nature of the province, concentrating on the role of French as *the* working language. It also limited access to English-language schools much more severely than Bill 22 had done.

Scott was one of four Queen's Counsel who had written a report in 1969 for the Protestant School Board of Greater Montreal setting out the nature of the rights protected by section 93. In July 1974, with six other McGill law professors, he criticized some of the discriminatory provisions of Bill 22. He saw it as an attack on the concept of equality between the two principal cultures in the province, as well as on the long-established rights and freedoms of English-speaking Quebeckers. He objected to the excessive use of regulations, which in their nature had not been subject to debate, to implement the bill. He found it unacceptable, moreover, that the government should claim the right to limit the development of the English-speaking minority by denying access to its schools to any particular group of children. This led him to act as counsel in the preparation of cases challenging Bill 22 and later Bill 101. The latter, he believed, was blatantly unconstitutional because it made French the only language in which legislation

was presented to and adopted by the National Assembly as well as the language of
the judicial system. By 1978, however, his deteriorating health forced him to
withdraw from further litigation.

Years before he had expressed the view that Manitoba's action in 1890 making
English the sole official language of the province was unconstitutional. He was
naturally delighted, though not surprised, in late 1979 when the Supreme Court of
Canada ruled in the same sense against the denial of official linguistic equality by
both Manitoba and Quebec. In 1984 the Supreme Court ruled further that Bill
101's attempt to regulate the language of instruction contravened the Canadian
Charter of Rights and Freedoms that had become law in 1982. Scott's interest in an
entrenched Bill of Rights went back to the 1930s, and he had welcomed the
successful campaign by the Trudeau government in 1981–82 to entrench the
charter in the constitution. By 1984, however, he was too ill to care much about
judicial decisions, even those that confirmed his own views.

By the 1970s Scott had found himself a subject of increasing interest to scholars.
At the same time he began to reflect more on his own past, and to pull together the
fruits of decades of activity. Encouraged by Sandra Djwa of Simon Fraser
University, who became his biographer, Scott put his reminiscences on tape. They
dealt with his private life, as well as a public life in which teaching, law, poetry,
and politics all loomed large. These did not encompass all of Scott's achievements, but they went a long way towards doing so, and they engaged his energies
until very late in his life.

In 1977 the University of Toronto Press published his *Essays on the
Constitution: Aspects of Canadian Law and Politics,* which won the Governor-
General's Award for non-fiction. It is true, however, as Douglas Sanders observed
at a Simon Fraser University conference in 1981 devoted to Scott's contributions
to Canada, 'that his centralist constitutional views are quite out of line with those
of contemporary lawyers and politicians. Even the New Democratic Party is
decentralist by Scott's standards.'[73]

Four years later McClelland & Stewart published his *Collected Poems*; it won
the Governor-General's Award for Poetry. Scott's accomplishments as a teacher
of law found recognition in an address by one of his former students, Gerald Le
Dain, at the 1981 conference. Le Dain remembered Scott as an excellent teacher,
and one who was clearly engagé: 'Perhaps the outstanding characteristic of Frank
Scott as teacher was his point of view or philosophic frame of reference. There was
no pretense of neutrality in his teaching and writing. He had strong convictions on
what should be the broad goals of government policy, and these provided the
framework within which he considered the implications of the distribution and
exercise of legal power. A consistent thread of social policy and purpose runs
through his constitutional thought. The key ideas are economic planning, social

justice, and the protection of human rights.'[74] This clearly refers to Scott's political convictions, whose central core is that the state ought to create the conditions for a better life for individuals.

Was this the unifying principle of Scott's political activity? Or was it rather a persistent concern for the underdog? Professor Djwa has noted Scott's disposition to see himself as a 'white knight' who succours the oppressed. Certainly there is in Scott's career a good deal of the *chevalier sans peur et sans reproche*, riding into battle against the foes of freedom and for a decent life for the ordinary Canadian.

Some of Scott's political career is bound to seem quixotic. Yet the foes he fought were real enough, even though they included people who hardly saw in themselves the features that Scott recognized. Corporation presidents and the conservative politicians usually allied with them are as apt as the rest of us to believe that they are acting justly and for the common good. Scott believed they were often wrong even though they might be sincere. He did not oppose them *as individuals*, however, but because of the power they exercised, power that was insufficiently restrained, even irresponsible, and because the system they represented frustrated basic human needs.

For most of his adult life Scott thought of himself as a socialist. He was not a theorist of socialism, nor did he see himself as one, although he did help to enunciate the ideas of the LSR and CCF. His most important contributions to those ideas, perhaps, rested in his simultaneous advocacy of a strong central government and the protection of minority rights. Yet he did not lose sight of the dangers of concentrating too much power in the hands of even well-meaning men and women. *Democracy Needs Socialism* was the title of one book he helped to write. He believed that this was true, but he also believed that socialism needed democracy. If he was a collectivist in his economic views, he was a liberal in his political outlook, a strong supporter of what he conceived to be Canada's legal and constitutional traditions, a believer in personal freedom. To be sure, he did not think that freedom should be without restraint: Scott criticized the individualism and selfishness that he associated with capitalism. The needs of co-operative social life demanded that there be limits on individual freedom. But a society should impose these limits upon itself, and should respect the customs of minorities.

Scott believed that the needs of a co-operative society should take precedence over those of a market economy. He believed, too, that individual freedom and economic planning could be reconciled with each other within a political democracy, and that ultimately that democracy would cross national boundaries. 'The world is my country / The human race is my race,' he wrote in his short poem 'Creed.' It was this humanist vision which unified Scott's political thought, and which underlies the documents selected for this book.

NOTES

1 F.R. Scott, 'The Teacher as Writer,' *McGill Journal of Education*, VI, Spring 1971, 65
2 Public Archives of Canada (PAC), Brooke Claxton Papers, vol. 16, Claxton to Burton Hurd, 21 February 1930, copy
3 Montreal *Gazette*, 3 February 1931. Reproduced in this reader.
4 Michiel Horn, '"Free Speech within the Law": The Letter of the Sixty-Eight Toronto Professors, 1931,' *Ontario History*, LXXII, March 1980
5 League for Social Reconstruction, *Manifesto*, reproduced in Michiel Horn, *The League for Social Reconstruction: Intellectual Origins of the Democratic Left in Canada 1930–1942* (Toronto 1980), 219
6 Canada, House of Commons, *Debates*, 26 April 1932, 2405
7 PAC, F.H. Underhill Papers, F.R. Scott Correspondence, Scott to Underhill, 7 September 1932
8 'C.C.F. Program Can Be Realized by Constitutional Means,' *The U.F.A.*, XII, 1 August 1933, 5
9 *Winnipeg Free Press*, 21 July 1933
10 Queen's University Archives, G.M.A. Grube Papers, H.M. Cassidy to K.W. Taylor, 26 July 1933, copy
11 F.R. Scott and H.M Cassidy, *Labour Conditions in the Men's Clothing Industry* (Toronto 1935), vi
12 League for Social Reconstruction, Research Committee, *Social Planning for Canada* (Toronto 1935), 503
13 *Ibid.*, 505, 506
14 *Ibid.*, 508
15 See Andrée Lévesque, *Virage à gauche interdit* (Montreal 1984).
16 PAC, F.R. Scott Papers, 'Report of the National Convention of the League for Social Reconstruction, February 22–23, 1936'
17 Scott Papers, Scott to Woodsworth, 30 November 1938 (copy). Reproduced in this reader.
18 Scott Papers, *C.C.F. et propriété privée* (Montreal, n.d.), 2. Author's translation.
19 Underhill Papers, *Canadian Unity in War and Peace: An Issue of Responsible Government* (n.p., n.d.), 1
20 Joseph Levitt, 'The CCF and French Canadian "Radical" Nationalism: A Comparison in Policy 1933–1942'(unpublished MA thesis, University of Toronto 1963), 151
21 Scott Papers, 'National Council Meetings, Sept. 6, 1939.' These are Scott's own minutes of the meetings.
22 F.R. Scott, 'Canada's Role in World Affairs,' *Food for Thought*, II, January 1942; 'Canadian Nationalism and the War,' *The Canadian Forum*, XXI, March 1942

23 Bruce Hutchison, *The Incredible Canadian* (Toronto 1952), 250

24 J.L. Granatstein, *Canada's War: The Politics of the Mackenzie King Government 1939–1945* (Toronto 1975), 19

25 F.R. Scott, 'Ten Years of the League for Social Reconstruction,' *Saturday Night*, LVII. 24 January 1942, 8. Reproduced in this volume.

26 Walter Young, *The Anatomy of a Party: The National CCF 1932–61* (Toronto 1969), 97

27 McGill University Archives, Principal's Office Files, Wilfrid Bovey to J.H. McBrien, 17 December 1932, copy

28 Stanley Brice Frost, *McGill University: For the Advancement of Learning*, vol. II, *1895–1971* (Kingston and Montreal 1894), 187–209

29 'One of Our Teachers,' Montreal *Gazette*, 15 August 1938

30 Scott Papers, vol. 24, F. Cyril James to C.S. LeMesurier, 14 August 1942, original

31 Scott Papers, vol. 24, Scott to James, 14 February 1947, copy. The Roncarelli case concerned the damages suffered by Frank Roncarelli, a restaurant owner and Jehovah's Witness, who lost his liquor licence because he raised bail for his co-religionists, who at that time suffered persecution in Quebec. See below.

32 Frank Scott to Michiel Horn, 11 September 1968

33 David Lewis, *The Good Fight: Political Memoirs 1909–1958* (Toronto 1981), 220

34 Lewis, 'F.R. Scott's Contribution to the CCF,' in *On F.R. Scott: Essays on His Contributions to Law, Literature, and Politics*, ed. Sandra Djwa and R. St J. Macdonald (Kingston and Montreal 1983), 82

35 PAC, CCF Records, vol. 35, Frank Watson to David Lewis, 18 January 1945

36 Lewis, 'F.R. Scott's Contribution to the CCF' 82. The chapter is reproduced in this reader.

37 CCF Records, vol. 104, Scott to Lewis, 25 July 1948, in reply to Lewis to Scott, 22 July 1948, copy

38 F.R. Scott, *Canada and the United States* (Boston 1941), 74

39 F.R. Scott, 'What Did "No" Mean?' *The Canadian Forum*, XXII, June 1942, 73. Reproduced in this reader.

40 B.A. Trestrail, *Stand Up and Be Counted* (Toronto 1944), 29. M.J. Coldwell led the national CCF, E.B. Jolliffe the Ontario party, and Harold Winch the CCF in British Columbia.

41 John English, 'Canada's Road to 1945', *Journal of Canadian Studies*, XVI, Fall-Winter 1981, 107

42 Conversation with Frank Scott, July 1979

43 On this, and the subject of Roman Catholicism and the CCF in general, see Gregory Baum, *Catholics and Canadian Socialism: Political Thought in the Thirties and Forties* (Toronto 1980), esp. 119–32.

44 Lewis, *The Good Fight*, 211

45 CCF Records, vol. 104, Scott to Lewis, 25 July 1948

46 Scott Papers, 'The Fundamentals of Socialism: Opening Address of the National

Chairman,' Co-operative Commonwealth Federation, Eleventh National Convention, Vancouver, 26 July 1950. Reproduced in this reader.

47 See: J.T. Morley, *Secular Socialists: The CCF/NDP in Ontario, A Biography* (Kingston and Montreal 1984), 156–7; Nelson Wiseman, *Social Democracy in Manitoba: A History of the CCF/NDP* (Winnipeg 1983), 55–62.

48 Scott, 'The Fundamentals of Socialism'

49 Lewis, *The Good Fight*, 380

50 CCF Records, vol. 18, Report of the National Convention, 1950

51 Young, *Anatomy of a Party*, 126

52 'Programme,' *C.C.F. Research Review*, I, August 1933, reproduced in Michiel Horn, 'Frank Underhill's Early Drafts of the Regina Manifesto 1933,' *Canadian Historical Review*, LIV, December 1973, 409–18

53 *CCF News*, 31 August 1950, quoted in Leo Zakuta, *A Protest Movement Becalmed* (Toronto 1964), 92

54 Quoted in Lewis, *The Good Fight*, 440

55 Young, *Anatomy of a Party*, 128

56 'Winnipeg Declaration of Principles,' reproduced in D. Owen Carrigan, comp., *Canadian Party Platforms 1867–1968* (Toronto 1968), 215

57 Quoted in Young, *Anatomy of a Party*, 128

58 Leo Zakuta has claimed that from 1942 to 1949 the CCF was a 'major party'; Kenneth McNaught disagrees. On the whole I find the latter view more persuasive. See the review by McNaught of *A Protest Movement Becalmed* in the *Canadian Historical Review*, XLVI, March 1965.

59 Desmond Morton, NDP: *The Dream of Power* (Toronto 1974), 22

60 *The Federal Program of the New Democratic Party*, adopted by its Founding Convention, Ottawa 1961, reproduced in Carrigan, *Canadian Party Platforms*, 279

61 Young, *Anatomy of a Party*, 134

62 As in a conversation with Michiel Horn, July 1979

63 Scott Papers, 'Social Medicine,' address delivered in French to the medical students, University of Montreal, 19 January 1949. Reproduced in this reader.

64 M. James Penton, *Jehovah's Witnesses in Canada: Champions of Freedom of Speech and Worship* (Toronto 1976), 222

65 F.R. Scott, 'Foreword,' *The Asbestos Strike*, ed. Pierre Elliott Trudeau, trans. James Boake (Toronto 1974; Montreal 1956), ix

66 Michael Oliver, 'Preface,' *Social Purpose for Canada* (Toronto 1961), vi–vii. Scott's essay in the book, 'Social Planning and Canadian Federalism,' is reproduced in this reader.

67 Robert Bothwell, Ian Drummond, and John English, *Canada since 1945: Power, Politics, and Provincialism* (Toronto 1981), 394

68 F.R. Scott, 'Global Attack on Our Institutions,' *The Gazette*, 24 October 1970. Reproduced in this reader.

1 Introduction

69 Frank Scott, 'The War Measures Act in Retrospect,' *CAUT/ACPU*, II/4 May 1971, 1. Reproduced in this reader.
70 *Ibid.*, 2
71 F.R. Scott, 'Quebec's Future in Canada,' *Quebec: Year Eight* (Toronto 1968), 71
72 Kenneth McRoberts and Dale Posgate, *Quebec: Social Change and Political Crisis*, rev. ed. (Toronto 1980), 172
73 Douglas Sanders, 'Law and Social Change: The Experience of F.R. Scott,' in *On F.R. Scott*, ed. Djwa and Macdonald, 130
74 Gerald Le Dain, 'F.R. Scott and Legal Education,' in *On F.R. Scott*: 103–4

A NEW ENDEAVOUR

I

Letter to the Editor, *The Gazette*, 1931

By 1931 Canada had a growing army of unemployed people, public provision for whom was quite inadequate or even non-existent. The three levels of government quarrelled about their spheres of responsibility while doing as little as possible. It was not long before meetings of the unemployed began to worry the authorities. The Communist Party of Canada played a prominent role in trying to organize the discontented, and its leaders were frequent speakers at gatherings of the unemployed. In cities like Toronto and Montreal the police routinely attended such meetings and often broke them up. In Montreal they eventually began to arrest speakers and charge them with sedition. Late in January 1931 Frank Scott criticized police tactics in a letter to the Montreal Gazette. *He followed this with an article in the* Canadian Bar Review, *'The Montreal Sedition Cases,' which demonstrated the unreliability of the evidence given by mostly French-speaking police constables as to speeches delivered in English.*

Scott signed himself as 'Associate Professor of Constitutional and Federal Law.' As this had made it easy to identify him as a teacher at McGill, and as both the chief of police and the editor of the Gazette *soon criticized his views, Scott received a request from the Principal's Office not to use his title in writing to newspapers about controversial matters.*
From *The Gazette* (Montreal), 3 February 1931

The recent activities of the Montreal police in breaking up by force meetings of the unemployed in this city should not, I feel, be allowed to pass without comment ...

It is necessary first to clear the issue from the confusion likely to be introduced by the word 'communism.' Whether or not these meetings are attended by communists or merely by unemployed labourers makes not a particle of difference, for communism is no more criminal than liberalism or socialism. If the police were to break up a meeting of CPR shareholders gathered to discuss a petition to parliament it would be equally objectionable.

I have no wish either to express any opinion as to whether or not the speakers may have uttered seditious words. Sedition has never been defined by our criminal law with any exactness, and the term could no doubt be easily stretched to include some of the phrases attributed to these speakers. This is a matter for the courts to decide after a full hearing of the evidence.

What I wish to question is first the legality of enforcing the law by these methods, and secondly the wisdom of interfering at all.

If the reports in your news columns are accurate the action of the police has been clearly high-handed, and apparently illegal. To send hundreds of police to arrest two men (as was done at the Prince Arthur Hall meeting on January 23rd) is high-handed. To order a crowd assembled in a hall to disperse when all that has been done is to listen to what may be seditious words is high-handed and probably illegal. To begin tearing down bunting and destroying pictures, even of Lenin, is clearly illegal, and obviously likely to cause a riot.

At not a single one of the four meetings recently broken up has the crowd itself been accused of disorder until *after* the police have arrested speakers and started to disperse the audience. At the Rosemount meeting the police were gathered in such numbers that the people dared not assemble. That is, the methods of the police amounted to a pre-judging of the case before any evidence of crime existed. The rights – and they are rights – to freedom of assembly and freedom of speech have thus been plainly violated.

As to the wisdom of interfering at all in any meeting which is held indoors and is not disorderly, opinions of course will differ. The British method in such cases is to let the radicals blow off steam to their hearts' content. The method of our police is to make a stirring incident out of every meeting. What is the result? At the first meeting broken up some two hundred and fifty people were in attendance. At the last, over fifteen hundred attended. It would be interesting to know how many converts to communism have been made by this procedure.

II

Communists, Senators, and All That

Section 98 of the Criminal Code dated from 1919, when the Union Government, led by Sir Robert Borden, disturbed by the Winnipeg General Strike and infected by the worldwide 'Red Scare' of that year, adopted draconian measures for dealing with revolutionaries. The section made possible very severe penalties for criminal sedition and seditious conspiracy. During the 1920s the section went unused, but attempts by the Liberal government of William Lyon Mackenzie King to repeal the section failed because of opposition from the Senate. In the early 1930s the section proved useful to provincial governments, most of them Conservative, that sought to deal with radical troublemakers. The attorney general of Ontario used it in August 1931 when he ordered the arrest of Tim Buck, the secretary of the Communist Party of Canada (CPC), and a number of other Communist leaders. Eight of them subsequently came to trial and were convicted of being members of an 'unlawful association.' The CPC was thus held to be illegal. Not until 1936 was section 98 repealed.

Scott wrote about the trial in Queen's Quarterly *('The Trial of the Toronto Communists,' reprinted in his* Essays on the Constitution *[University of Toronto Press]). In the article that follows he discusses section 98 and contrasts the treatment of the Communists with that of two Liberal senators implicated in the Beauharnois scandal. A report of a House of Commons committee in July 1931 strongly condemned Senators Andrew Haydon and W.L. McDougald for accepting money from the promoters of the Beauharnois power project on the St Lawrence River. Although one of them, Senator McDougald, eventually resigned his seat after a second investigation again condemned their actions, neither man ever went to trial. As Scott noted acidly, the eight Communists were not so fortunate.*

From *The Canadian Forum*, vol. 12, January 1932, pp. 127–9. Reprinted by permission of *The Canadian Forum*

No one can deny that under Mr. R.B. Bennett Canada has become a leader in the movement of world ideas. Where others have vacillated, we have acted. Hard hit though we were by the depression, and despite the thousands of unemployed starving in our streets, we had the courage and unselfishness to announce that we would not sell our soul – or our machinery – for Soviet gold; that we would not support by interchange of trade a country which maintained a low standard of living and which forced workers to work instead of forcing them to be idle. Recently a Toronto court has held that under Canadian law Communists can be sent to prison for any period up to twenty years, just for being Communists. In banning Russian goods we stood, and still stand, proudly alone. In outlawing the Communist party we are not alone, but the company in which we move is select. Japan, Jugo-Slavia, and Bulgaria have proscribed Communism; Italy permits no right of association to any non-fascist body, whether Communist or Conservative; under the Polish dictatorship no one is allowed to think at all. With Japanese, Jugo-Slavs, Italians, Bulgarians, and Poles, Canada marches toward a higher social order. Only in decadent and backward countries like Great Britain, the United States, France, Germany, Belgium, Spain, Norway, Sweden, Denmark, Holland, and the other British

Dominions can the horrid plots of the Marxian idolators be carried out in the broad light of day.

Canadians must be pleased to discover that they are protected by such a reliable system of laws, and that they have fine, clean-cut stool-pigeons of the type of Sergeant Leopold to see that our British tradition of fair play is not undermined by skulking foreigners.[1] It is true that certain senators affiliated with Beauharnois are still senators, and that they have not had to undergo any civil or criminal action whatsoever. But these men merely abused positions of high public and social trust to transfer to their own pockets millions belonging by moral right to unsuspecting investors. Whereas the Communists have probably got hold of the wrong ideas about how to make the world a better place to live in. Obviously the two cases are totally different.

A friend of mine – I think he had been an investor in the old Canada Power and Paper Company[2] –suggested that Sergeant Leopold should now be disguised as a cunning fellow and ordered to worm his way into the secret conclaves of the Canadian financiers. But I pointed out promptly that you couldn't do that sort of thing. You mustn't start weakening the faith of Canadians in their financial institutions. If you once give them the idea that the money they keep losing oughtn't to have been lost, they may start asking questions or something. And how can the system possibly work if people start asking questions?

It is shocking to realize that we very nearly had no law at all under which the Communist party could be declared an unlawful association. The totally inadequate criminal law which we inherited from England had nothing in it nearly so efficient as the present section 98 of the Canadian Criminal Code, in virtue of which the Toronto Communists were chiefly sentenced. There was only a vague rule about seditious conspiracies, which had hardly ever been enforced, which no one understood, and for which the maximum penalty was a paltry two years. It wasn't until 1919, after the world – and Winnipeg – had been made safe for democracy, that the new section was added. It was apparently invented by the State of New York, and it suited so well the famous American methods of repressing crime that we thought we had better copy it. But later it very nearly got taken off the statute book. Prosperity seemed to weaken the moral fibre of the public. On no less than five occasions the Canadian House of Commons passed a bill to amend the Criminal Code by repealing section 98. Five separate times – in the sessions of 1926, 1926–7, 1928, 1929, and 1930. If it had not been for our Senate of picked men, who manfully threw out the bill every time it came before them, we should have been in a pretty fix now. In the session of 1929 the bill failed to pass the Senate by only three votes. If two members had been a little sleepier that day, Canadian institutions might be tottering. No wonder we insist that every senator shall own at least four thousand dollars worth of property.

It must not be thought that the Beauharnois senators were amongst those who wanted to maintain section 98. On the contrary, the records show that in 1928 Messrs. Haydon and McDougald voted for the repealing bill.[3] Apparently they were in favour of a fairly lenient Criminal Code.

The idea of deporting Communists and other radicals is another good example of the present government's methods in handling a grave social problem. There is nothing like getting rid of a disease by sending away to foreign countries all persons who have it, so that other people may become infected instead of ourselves. Then we can keep clear of future contagion by asking all immigrants as they enter Canada whether they intend to undermine Mr. Bennett and other Canadian institutions. If they say they do, we can turn them away. This is really rooting out the cause of the trouble, isn't it?

Our parlour Bolsheviks had better understand what they are in for if the present law is to be enforced to the full. Canada doesn't need to put up with their nasty new ideas if she doesn't want to. Section 98 creates so many new crimes and establishes so many presumptions of criminality that lots of people who are not actually Communists are liable to prosecution. It is a good red-blooded article, with 115 lines of definitions, offences, and penalties, all so obscurely worded that no one can be sure just how much liberty of speech and association survives – except that it is pretty small. The following examples of its provisions will show what the authorities could do if they really got on the warpath. After defining an unlawful association as one whose purpose is to bring about any governmental, industrial, or economic change within Canada by use of force, or which teaches or defends the use of force to accomplish such change, or for any other purpose, the article goes on to say amongst other things:

(1) Any person who sells, speaks, writes or publishes *anything* as the representative or professed representative of such association;
(2) Any person who wears or displays *anywhere*, any badge, banner, motto, button, etc., indicating or intending to indicate that he is a member of or in *anywise associated with* such association;
(3) Anyone who solicits subscriptions or contributions for it or contributes *anything* to it or to anyone for it as dues or otherwise; shall be guilty of an offence punishable by twenty years.

How about that for getting after friends and sympathizers of Communists? The italics are added to show the whole-hearted way in which Parliament tackled the job in 1919: lots of all-embracing *anywheres, anywises* and *anythings*. Then comes a still better clause:

(4) In any prosecution under this section, if it be proved that the person charged has, –
    (a) attended meetings of an unlawful association; or

(b) spoken publicly in advocacy of an unlawful association; or

(c) distributed literature of an unlawful association by circulation through the Post Office mails of Canada, or otherwise;

It shall be presumed, in the absence of proof to the contrary, that he is a member of such unlawful association.

Just examine that for a moment, all you red college professors. None of your old-fashioned ideas that a man is presumed innocent until he is proved guilty. All the police need to do here is to show that you once attended a Communist meeting, perhaps through curiosity, or spoke publicly in advocacy of the party, or distributed literature (presumably any kind of literature) of the party, and at once the Canadian legal machinery gets to work and says you are a criminal liable to twenty years. You won't escape gaol unless you can prove that you are not a member of the party. And think what it will be like trying to make this proof! Obviously no member of the party will dare to testify that you are a non-member, because by coming forward he would at once give notice to the police that he is a criminal. You will simply have to give your own word – and why should a college professor's red word destroy a legal presumption?

This is by no means all. The owner of any building who knowingly permits therein any meeting of an unlawful association *or any subsidiary association or branch or committee thereof*, or any assemblage of persons who teach, or defend the use, without authority of the law, of force, violence, etc. shall be liable both to a five thousand dollar fine and to imprisonment for five years. This will stop all nonsense in the way of radical meetings of any sort, Communist or otherwise. For how is the owner of a hall to know whether or not a society is a 'subsidiary' of an unlawful association? He won't take the risk of a five thousand dollar fine and five years in gaol. What about the Friends of the Soviet Union, for instance, a society which actually teaches that we should love and not hate the Russians. Isn't this a subsidiary association, and isn't its teaching tantamount to defense of the use of force without authority of the law? And the Workers' Unity League?[4] And the Canadian Labour Defense League, which collects money to defend Communists in the Law Courts – isn't this a 'branch' of the Communist party, or at any rate does it not solicit money 'as dues or otherwise' for the party so as to make every member of it liable to twenty years? What about you misguided people who have subscribed to the defense of Tim Buck – aren't you pretty close to twenty years in gaol yourselves?

The section warms up as it proceeds, and new crimes come thick and fast. Here are three more specimens: (1) every person who prints, circulates, sells, or offers for sale, etc., any book, pamphlet, etc. (there are 13 synonyms), in which is taught, advised, or defended the use of force, or threats of injury to person or property, etc. as a means of accomplishing any governmental, industrial, or economic change;

(2) every person who *in any manner* teaches, advises, advocates, or defends such use of force, etc.; and (3) every person who imports or attempts to import such literature, shall be liable to twenty years' imprisonment. This really gets down to business, and should rid our radicals forever of the obsolete idea that under the Canadian constitution the personal liberties of the subjects give the subject personal liberty. Has any Canadian bookseller ever sold a copy of the Communist Manifesto? Twenty years for him. Has any Canadian professor ever taught a class of students in political science that there are occasions when revolution is morally justifiable? Clap him in gaol with the Communists: defending the use of force in any manner is a crime even if it is done in the privacy of the classroom or home. Has any Canadian citizen ever brought into Canada any book in which the use of force to effect political or industrial change is defended under any conditions whatsoever? Let him shiver in his shoes; Sergeant Leopold, disguised as a friend, may be after him, and a long spell in the penitentiary awaits him.

Just to round out the law it is declared to be the duty of every person in the entire civil service of the Dominion to seize all literature of the prohibited kind, whether found in the mails or in any vehicle or vessel, and to transmit it at once to the Commissioners of the Royal Canadian Mounted Police. It was a happy idea of Parliament to think of this ingenious way of creating a censorship service. Without additional cost to the Canadian taxpayer, at once some 40,000 people were given the job of confiscating dangerous books. And by having a police commissioner as final judge the law is sure to be administered in a manner conducive to the purity of Canadian thought.

Enough of section 98 has been explained to show the citizens of Canada the sort of law which governs them. The best thing for every good Canadian to do, if he wants to keep out of gaol, is to cling to the stock of reliable and well-tried ideas which have made Canada exactly what she is today. If he is built so queerly that he finds he cannot agree with Mr. Bennett, try as he will, let him then be radical with Mr. King. But that is as far as he can expect to be allowed to go. Canada is a country which has inherited British traditions of law, of justice and of government. It is a land of golden opportunity, where everyone who can do a good day's work will get along fine. We have admitted a lot of foreigners to build our railways and dig up our minerals, but they ought to be grateful to us for letting them live here, and not go about organizing to alter the present system in any way. If they do not like the way we treat them, then let them pack up their belongings and travel back to Europe, via CPR. We won't stand for their talk about the downtrodden masses and the class war. There aren't any classes in Canada; it is a democratic country. And as for Soviet Russia, let it be understood once and for all that a state which is run for the workers, where the land and natural resources and means of production are owned by the people and not by financiers, where there are no sharp contrasts of riches and poverty, and where the motive of personal profit has been replaced by that of public service is a state utterly foreign to Canadian traditions and practice. We won't have it, that's all.

EDITOR'S NOTES

1 Sergeant John Leopold, alias J.W. Esselwein, was an undercover RCMP agent who for seven years belonged to the Communist party and who in 1931 was the Crown's chief witness in the case against Tim Buck and the other Communists.
2 Formed in 1929, the Canada Power and Paper Company was a conglomerate controlled by the Montreal financier Sir Herbert Holt. Its expansion had been financed by borrowing and issuing additional stock. Worth $10 per share before the stock market crash of October 1929, the stock had fallen to one dollar a share by 1931. At that time the affairs of the company were wound up, and the shareholders got one share of the new Consolidated Paper Corporation in exchange for ten of the old Canada Power and Paper Company. Heavily burdened by debt, the Consolidated Paper Corporation did not pay a dividend to its common share holders until after the second World War.
3 Senators Andrew Haydon and W.L. McDougald were at the centre of the Beauharnois scandal.
4 Active from 1929 to 1936, the Communist-sponsored Workers' Unity League sought to organize semi-skilled and unskilled industrial workers in whom the older craft unions were not interested.

III

The Future of the Legal Profession

This article appeared in a short-lived student magazine at McGill University. Called The Alarm Clock, *it was avowedly socialist. The first issue appeared in January 1933 and was promptly banned from sale on campus by Principal Sir Arthur Currie after protests reached him from the Montreal business community and from members of the Board of Governors, notably J.W. McConnell. It continued to be sold in neighbouring stores, however, and in due time a second issue appeared which carried Scott's article. This seems also to have been the last issue.*

Scott owed his proposal concerning no-fault automobile insurance to a report by a committee of American jurists, set up in New York in 1928. The idea is still being discussed today. The report of the Ontario Task Force on Insurance in 1986 calls for some form of no-fault insurance. A headline in the Globe *and*

11 The Future of the Legal Profession

Mail's *'Report on Business' of 8 May 1986 reads: 'Call for no-fault insurance worries Ontario lawyers.'*
From *The Alarm Clock,* December 1933, pp. 5, 10

Lawyers as a class command small respect in contemporary society. What little admiration they arouse is largely due to their capacity to make money. To say that a man has a lawyer's mind is not a compliment: it means that he is quick rather than wise, clever rather than sincere. Nor is the ordinary citizen much impressed by the working of our judicial machinery. He looks upon the modern trial as simply a contest in wits between two opposing counsel, with justice generally on the side of the strongest battalions, and in which the only thing certain is that litigants, whether they win or lose, will have to pay through the nose for their experience. Expense, delay, and, at most, an even chance of justice being done – such is the popular view of the law.

There is much to be said for this criticism. Professions are notoriously conservative, but the legal profession has probably guarded itself from reform more carefully and more successfully than any other, not even excepting the teaching profession. A recent writer on law reform, Mr. Claude Mullins, declares that 'the fact has to be faced that the record of the (English) legal profession shows no enthusiasm at any time for law reform, but rather a steady opposition to the fundamental changes that experience has proved necessary and wise.' This seems true of every country. In consequence the technique of administering justice has changed less in the past two centuries than have the methods of applying medicine or engineering, for example. The scientific method has invaded these spheres, but not that of the law to any extent. Doctors have reduced mortality rates, controlled infectious diseases, increased the chances of life; engineers have made it possible to fly and to speak around the world. The lawyers have diminished neither the cost nor the delays of litigation to any appreciable extent; nor have they improved the quality of justice obtainable in the courts.

Changes, then, are due and overdue. For those who care to look below the surface, the direction of reform is already evident. In a more civilised society the lawyer will be in part eliminated, in part reformed through different training.

The elimination of the lawyer will come in two ways, through the development of the idea of insurance, and through an increase of state administration. Insurance has already cut down to some extent the field of litigation. Workmen's Compensation is a case in point. Formerly a workman injured at his place of employment had to collect damages by the cumbersome process of a legal trial. The big corporations made a point of fighting important cases through to the Privy Council, so that it might take anywhere from three to six years to get a final judgement. Usually the lawyers took 25 to 50% of the compensation actually paid. Today progressive countries handle all cases of workers' injuries by means of a fund created by a tax on industry, out of which compensation is paid regardless of the question of fault. The expenses of a trial are thus saved from being added to the inevitable medical expenses. The lawyer has one less pie to dip his finger into, and society is the richer.

Recently a proposal has been made by a responsible committee of American jurists to treat all automobile cases in the same way. The idea is much too radical and sensible to be adopted by contemporary legislatures, but it will come in time. Automobile accidents are on the increase. The disputes they create clutter the courts. In them it is notoriously difficult to apportion fault; two witnesses never see the accident in the same way. Instead of doubling or trebling the cost of the physical damage by an attempt to find out who caused it, the proposal is to provide by compulsory insurance for the payment of compensation, and to forget about the legal fault. Only the lawyer will suffer. There is no reason why most accident causes could not be similarly dealt with.

Social legislation and the equalisation of wealth, as both develop, will still further reduce the work of the courts, particularly in the realm of criminal law. Theft, burglary, vagrancy and other crimes related to property, which today produce 75% of the criminals in Canada, will diminish as society organises its economic life so that each individual is given the chance to earn a decent livelihood. The elimination of slums will greatly reduce the number of prisons. In a fully scientific age crime will be considered a form of disease, to be handled by psychologists and psychiatrists rather than lawyers and judges. Some form of trial will no doubt always be necessary to decide who has committed the crime, and this will involve legal defense for the accused; but the actual number of offences will be far less.

Accident insurance and social legislation indicate one sort of change that is coming; the increase of state administration suggests another. It takes two to make a lawsuit. As society takes over the operation of services and industries now privately owned, the number of individual corporations, and hence of potential litigants, will enormously diminish. There can be no suits between banks, if Canada adopts a unified banking system; no suits between railroads, if all are under the CNR; no suits between insurance companies, if all insurance is handled by the state. Private enterprise stimulates, public enterprise eliminates, the lawyer. In the economic warfare which our competitive capitalist system creates the lawyers are trained warriors ready to do battle for their financial overlords. They are (with obvious exceptions for the truly professional practitioners) the knights of this economic feudalism, without even the advantage of the 'truce of God' over the weekends. All big corporations maintain a staff of lawyers, either in the company or permanently retained in law firms, ready at a moment's notice to advise on how to ruin a competitor through a merger or an injunction, or how to fleece the public through a holding company, a stock flotation or a combine. In an economic society of socially operated monopolies all this now lawful racketeering would disappear. Only non-commercial suits between citizens, and between citizens and the State, would remain. Administrative tribunals and trades unions committees would take care of most disputes between the individual and public officials.

So much for the partial elimination of the lawyers. Those that are still needed must be reformed through better training. The obvious criticism of our present law-schools is that the legal education they give is too exclusively technical. The young lawyer is taught the law as it is; he is taught to hold his own in the professional struggle for existence; but he is not taught enough, if anything, about the science of law and the sociological approach to law. He is not taught to see law as 'social engineering,' to borrow the phrase of Pound;[1] he does not think of it as a public service, as a social function, like medicine or education, which it is his duty and privilege to modernise and improve. The ideas of progress, of reform, of experiment, are alien to the profession.

The education of the lawyer in criminal law is especially one-sided; of modern penology and the scientific treatment of crime he is taught nothing. Criminal law to him is simply a question of legal definitions of crimes, and training in procedure. And yet it is from this class that our judges must be selected – men who have power to impose punishment on all the various classes of criminal that come before them. At the present moment the sentencing of the criminal in Canada is in the hands of persons who, from the standpoint of modern science, can only be called amateurs. Yet no Bar Association is showing the least concern over the matter.

To secure a more progressive attitude on the part of the legal profession, however, more will be required than a change in the law school curriculum. The operation of the practice of law on the basis of individual profit-seeking will have to change. The best professional traditions of the lawyers are corrupted today by the opportunities of making money which await the unscrupulous practitioners. The Morgan directors did not evade the American income tax laws without legal aid, nor did Samuel Insull erect his vast corporation superstructure without fat fees to counsel.[2] The lawyer who undertakes this form of work today will feather his own nest very smoothly. The difficulty is to devise a system in which the public service idea would predominate, and money-making would be secondary. Free legal aid clinics paid by the State would help. The State might also shoulder the expense of defending the accused as well as prosecuting him, if he is willing to use a Public Defender. The question of other fees would probably have to be controlled by strict rules within the profession itself, permitting only a variation within defined limits appropriate to different categories of work. It might then be possible to ascertain beforehand how much a law suit would cost. Lawyers admitted to the Bar would be guaranteed a minimum income, and not allowed to rise above a certain maximum. All members would be paid out of pooled resources, as is done within most law firms today.

When all this is considered, the future appears safe for the lawyer. He will be needed somewhere in any social order that can be imagined. He has survived even the Russian revolution, the most thoroughgoing the world has ever seen. Probably he might be dispensed with in a society of pure communism. If the state ever 'withers away,' the law, and the lawyer, might wither away too. Law could then melt into social habit, and we should all behave socially by instinct, like bees or ants. There were no lawyers in Mr. Huxley's Brave New World.[3]

EDITOR'S NOTES

1 Roscoe Pound, the distinguished American jurist, was the author of *Introduction to the Philosophy of Law* and other works.
2 J.P. Morgan and Company was a major American banking and investment firm. Samuel Insull, American public utilities magnate, put together a corporate empire with assets of more than $2.5 billion before failing spectacularly in 1932.
3 Aldous Huxley's novel Brave *New World*, published in 1932, presented a satirical view of a utopia resulting from the idea of progress. Since Scott was bound to be hostile to this utopia, his comment was really a way of saying that he expected lawyers to exist in any society that he could imagine.

IV

The Unholy Trinity of Quebec Politics

This article originally appeared under the title 'The Fascist Province' and was signed with a pseudonym, J.K. Keith. Scott occasionally decided not to use his own name if he thought that an article he was publishing might strain his relations with the McGill Board of Governors unduly, or might cause difficulties for the university in its relations with the provincial government.

Upon reading the article again in the 1970s Scott decided that the title was in error. There was a good deal of authoritarianism in Quebec in the 1930s, as well as sympathy for fascism in its Italian form, but to call Quebec fascist seemed too extreme. The new title is one that he chose himself.

Although Scott could not in early 1934 discern an effective challenge to the provincial Liberals, precisely such a challenge arose in 1934–35 in the form of the Action libérale nationale, *led by Paul Gouin. It formed an alliance with the provincial Conservatives, led by Maurice Duplessis, just before the election of November 1935. The* Union nationale Duplessis-Gouin *(UN) dealt a major blow to the Liberals in that election, and the following year*

the UN, now led by Duplessis alone, replaced the Liberals in office after a further election.
From *The Canadian Forum*, vol. 14, April 1934, pp. 251–2. Reprinted by permission of *The Canadian Forum*

The Liberal government in Quebec is liberal in the sense that the National Socialist government in Germany is socialist – that is to say, in the non-sense. Its programme, as disclosed by action taken while in office (it does not bother to offer a paper programme), may be described as pure laissez-faire illuminated by touches of fascism.

Mr. Taschereau stands for private ownership in industry and public utilities, especially electric power, and is himself closely tied up with the power trust.[1] He has refused to bring the province under the Dominion Old Age Pensions scheme, although advised to do so by his own Social Insurance Commission in 1932.[2] The shamefully inadequate labour legislation which is on the Quebec statute books is not even properly enforced, as recent evidence before the Stevens Committee made startlingly clear,[3] and ... the Montreal *Gazette*, purest spokesman for high finance, can find no stronger denunciation for the Department of Labour at Quebec than that its activities are 'creating uncertainty where formerly there was a sense of perfect security.' A new law is about to be passed making collective wage agreements, when adopted by an employer, compulsory on all similar firms in that district; the international unions see in the measure a threat to the right to strike and the beginning of the corporative state.[4] No attempt is being made to lessen the gross inequalities of wealth by a fairer system of taxation.

The suppression of freedom of speech is ruthless and persistent. The latest move in this direction, the David Bill,[5] which would make it an offence to distribute circulars calling a public meeting unless the chief of police approved, is merely symptomatic of the general attitude. The iron heel is showing itself with a vengeance.[6] So far to the right is Mr. Taschereau that there is no room for the provincial Conservatives except on his left and theirs are the only voices calling – but how faintly! – for a more humane and liberal policy. The party roles are completely reversed.

Four and a half years of depression, in fact, have done little else than reveal how harmonious are the relations between the three persons in the provincial trinity: the Liberal Party machine, the Roman Church, and St. James Street.[7] Scarcely a rift has appeared to disturb the equilibrium of the theo-pluto-bureaucracy. The editorials of the Montreal *Gazette* would make ideal pastoral letters from the parish priests to read from pulpits; the episcopal denunciations of Socialism and Communism must turn the *Gazette* leader-writers pale with envy; Mr. Taschereau could not denounce the CCF as divinely as Archbishop Gauthier has done it.[8] The totalitarian state could hardly be more united.

It must be admitted that all these three powers have handled the difficulties of these latter years with considerable skill. Mr. Taschereau rides more firmly in the saddle than ever. The Conservative opposition, with a heaven-sent opportunity, is too supine, too bound by political tradition, to lead a vigorous attack. Being Conservative, it cannot be radical, and only a radical party could break the governing machine. The once-threatening Fédération des clubs ouvriers is petering out, blind and unled. To complete the Liberal stranglehold it only remains to deprive Montreal of its self-government and put it under a Quebec-appointed Commission, in order to prevent Mr. Houde or some other unorthodox fellow from obtaining control of the city.[9] On the excuse of economy and good government, with full backing from banks and manufacturers, this change is apparently about to be accomplished. Nothing short of a revolution can prevent Mr. Taschereau's return to power at the provincial elections of 1935. This is the brand of Liberalism Mr. King will have to cope with if he becomes Prime Minister.

On the side of religion, a similar strength prevails. The leaders of the Church have interpreted the depression as a sort of punishment from God upon greedy individuals. It follows that the individual who wants to help matters must contribute more of penance and of pence; he must return to God before he can hope to return to work. It is difficult to know how far this doctrine is believed, but it is certainly preached, and radical movements are denounced far more strongly than the capitalist injustices which produce them. The increased burden of municipal taxes is causing some people to cast critical eyes upon the enormous tax-free properties of the Church, but no hands have as yet been laid upon this source of revenue, except in Ste Hyacinthe, where in consequence a balanced municipal budget was produced in 1933. With the great investments of the Church not only in lands but in utilities and industrial stocks and bonds, it is not difficult to see why the ecclesiastical authorities attack organizations like the CCF which, they fear, would imperil their economic privileges.

No anti-clerical movement shows any signs of appearing. The only champion of that dangerous cause, Albert St Martin, has at last been effectively silenced.[10] Hailed into court time and time again for sedition, blasphemy, and numberless other charges usually employed to suppress opinion, he was assaulted and nearly killed last autumn by a band of French hooligans who broke up a meeting of his Université ouvrière and then attacked him with sticks, cracking open his head. It was his 67th birthday; the police were present in large numbers, but no arrests were made. All is now quiet on the religious front. Mr. Gobeil's devastating charge at Ottawa that the University of Montreal actually had atheists on its staff caused a slight upset recently,[11] but the statement was so vociferously denied, and it was so uncontrovertibly established that no one was allowed to teach any subject at the University unless he had been previously approved by a board of clerics, that there is obviously no danger of error from that quarter.

And St. James Street? Its position has in many ways been consolidated. The Montreal Light, Heat and Power Company has absorbed some twenty municipal distribution systems since the depression started. Beauharnois power, after the 'cleansing' of the 1930 investigation, has passed quietly into the pockets of the Holt interests.[12] Not one of Quebec's major financial scandals has yet been exposed: Canada Power and Paper, McDougall and Cowans, Price Brothers, etc., have come and gone, leaving ruin for the small investor but no punishment for those responsible ... One lone Galahad – Harpell – assaulted the financial fortress, but he won only silent sympathy to compensate for his gaol sentence.[13] Even the United Church is feeling pressure from its wealthy laymen for its mildly Christian utterances in favour of social justice.[14] If St. James Street is ever to be called to give an account of its stewardship, the call will have to come from outside the Province of Quebec. Not a person here who knows the facts dare open his mouth.

The outlook for progress in the province, then, is dark at the moment. There are currents moving, bodies of criticism forming, but they have not reached the surface. One or two that have are clearly under expert guidance from above. Les Jeunes Canada,[15] for instance, have espoused a programme of social reconstruction which goes as far as public ownership of power and a certain measure of social insurance; yet significantly enough, some of its members threatened to break up the meeting at which Mr. Woodsworth spoke on March 3rd, shortly after Archbishop Gauthier's denunciation of the CCF. They are potential, if not actual fascists.

If discontent grows too prominent among the French masses we may expect a concerted move to deflect it into fascist channels, and to provide the people with scapegoats lest they come to see where the real evil lies. The increasing anti-semitism of the French Canadian (where are minority rights now?) is evidence of this, and a natural enough tendency to associate trusts with the English race lies ready for exploitation. If there were any French socialist leaders they could use this lever first, and could show how public ownership is the easiest method by which the French Canadian may regain control of the natural resources which English and American capitalists have stolen from him. But there are no such leaders yet, and the masses are being taught that all will be well if only English capitalists are replaced or controlled by French ones, and all chain and department stores replaced by small, independent retail merchants, and all unemployed persons set to work on the abandoned farms. So completely is the French Canadian deprived of literature not approved by the authorities that very little of the fundamental criticisms of capitalism available for English Canadians have reached him. His mind is so indoctrinated that one would probably have to go to the Ontario Orangemen to find its equal.[16]

There are two possible ways in which an intelligent reform movement might start. One is that a leader may spring from the people. All one can say of this is that he is not in sight. The other possibility is that the CCF might take root, and might provide a rallying point for the progressive forces. The Church's attitude by no means makes this impossible – in fact, it probably assists through publicity. It must not be forgotten that there is no absolute ban on the CCF. The Church as a whole has not spoken, but only one bishop, and he has merely issued a strong warning. The Church made a similar attempt to destroy the youthful Laurier, and failed.[17] The last meeting held by Mr. Woodsworth in Montreal, at which over 1,300 French Canadians were present, was enthusiastic. If French leadership can be found, the miracle might be worked. The political field is wide open for radicals: both the other parties are thoroughly discredited at the moment. One thing is certain. If Quebec should ever adopt socialism, even of the CCF brand, Canada will be an exciting place to live in. We Anglo-Saxons are dull fellows beside the French when it comes to politics.

EDITOR'S NOTES

1 Louis-Alexandre Taschereau was Liberal premier of Quebec from 1920 to 1936. While he was premier he served on the boards of directors of many corporations, arguing that 'the head of a government should meet businessmen around a directors' table, learn about business, and give the province the benefit of it.' *Canadian Annual Review*, 1928–9, quoted in Herbert F. Quinn, *The Union Nationale: A Study in Quebec Nationalism* (Toronto 1963), 67

2 This scheme, introduced by the Mackenzie King government in 1927, committed Ottawa to paying half the cost of any provincial old age pension scheme that would give pensioners $20 per month, subject to a means test and a residence requirement.

3 In February 1934 Prime Minister R.B. Bennett had introduced a motion establishing a select House of Commons committee to investigate the causes of the large spread between the prices received by producers and those paid by consumers. The chief instigator of such a committee was Bennett's minister of trade and commerce, Harry H. Stevens, who also chaired its proceedings.

4 Corporatism was an economic-political doctrine associated closely with Benito Mussolini's fascist Italy. Representation in government would be by corporations representing the major economic functions.

5 This bill was named after Athanase David, the provincial secretary.

6 The reference is to a speech by R.B. Bennett in November 1932 in which he said: 'We know that throughout Canada ... propaganda is being put forward by organizations from foreign lands that seek to destroy our institutions, and we ask every man and woman to put the iron heel of ruthlesssness against a thing of that kind.' *Mail and Empire*, Toronto, 10 November 1932, quoted by J.S. Woodsworth in the *Debates* of the House of Commons, 1 February 1933

7 St James Street was symbolic of the Montreal business community.

8 Msgr Georges Gauthier, archbishop-coadjutor of Montreal, in February 1934 warned against socialism and the CCF in a pastoral letter.

9 Camillien Houde, who had been mayor of Montreal and served as leader of the Quebec Conservative party from 1929 to 1932, recaptured the mayoralty of his city in 1935.

10 Albert St Martin was a Montreal court stenographer who singlehandedly ran and staffed a 'people's university' in his spare time until he was closed down by vigilante action.

11 Samuel Gobeil was Conservative member of Parliament for Compton.

12 Sir Herbert Holt, who died in 1941 at the age of eighty-five, was during the last forty years of his life the leading Canadian financier and businessman. He was president of 27 major corporations, among them the Royal Bank of Canada, and director of some 300 more. He founded and controlled the enormously profitable Montreal Light, Heat and Power Company, the epitome of the hated 'electricity trust.'

13 The owner of a small printing press in Ste Anne-de-Bellevue, Harpell had written a pamphlet accusing the directors of the Sun Life Assurance Company of improper financial behaviour. He was sued for libel, convicted, and imprisoned.

14 In 1933 the Montreal-Ottawa and Toronto Conferences of the United Church of Canada both passed resolutions calling for the introduction of a Christian social order. The Toronto conference also, by a narrow majority, condemned capitalism as unchristian.

15 This was a movement of right-wing students, chiefly at the University of Montreal. In one of its early actions the group organized a counter-demonstration when the Jews of Montreal in 1933 demonstrated in protest against the anti-semitism of Germany, where Adolf Hitler had led the National Socialists to power earlier in the year.

16 The Orange Order was militantly Protestant and loyal to the monarchy and the British Empire. In the 1930s it still played an important role in the politics of Ontario.

17 In the late nineteenth century the church favoured the Conservative party (*les bleus*) and was hostile to the Liberals (*les rouges*). In the federal election of 1896 the bishops opposed Wilfrid Laurier because of his decision not to seek legislative remedy for the Roman Catholics in Manitoba, who had been deprived of public support for their schools. Laurier nevertheless easily carried his own province.

V

The Efficiency of Socialism

The collapse of business firm after business firm, the growth of unemployment,
and the misery and even starvation of the unemployed affected Scott powerfully.
His work with the University of Toronto economist Harry M. Cassidy on labour
conditions in the clothing industry confirmed his growing belief that capitalism
was not only immoral but also inefficient. In 1935 this belief found expression in
a series of poems that he called 'Social Notes.' At the same time Scott wanted to
show that socialism was a more efficient way of organizing the economy. He
hoped this article in Queen's Quarterly *would prove the point.*
From *Queen's Quarterly*, vol. 42, no. 2 (Summer 1935), pp. 215–25. Reprinted
by permission of *Queen's Quarterly*

A popular objection to socialism is that public ownership and state operation of
industry will inevitably produce inefficiency and graft. This belief is carefully
fostered by capitalists, who thereby achieve the double purpose of injuring
socialism and at the same time creating the impression that their own undertakings
are honest and well run. In Canada their task is assisted by the example of the
Canadian National Railway. This particular experiment in state capitalism,
undertaken in order to recoup some of the losses of rugged individualism out of the
pockets of taxpayers, is always held up as the typical example of socialism. 'Look
at the CNR,' says the unthinking citizen (who of course never has looked at the CNR
to see why or how it was nationalized), 'Socialism will simply multiply failures of
that sort. Give me the efficiency of capitalism any day, even with its injustices, rather
than the incompetence and corruption which public ownership will involve.'

The obvious retort to this sort of person is to explain what the 'efficiency' of
capitalism really is, so that he may properly understand his alternative. He must be
reminded that capitalism pays farmers money to destroy cotton and corn, while
underclothed and undernourished workers eke out an existence in sweat-shop or on
relief. He should remember that capitalism has burnt millions of bags of coffee in
Brazil. He should consider the intelligence of a system that first of all produces
mass starvation because of over-production of wealth, and then sets out to end the
starvation by destroying the wealth. All our schemes of control are simply scarcity
planning, aimed to reduce production to meet the lower levels of consumption –
aimed, in other words, to reduce our standard of living, and to starve us into
prosperity. He should compute the 'efficiency' of the permanent army of
unemployed that capitalism always has within it. He should estimate the cost of

competitive advertising, of the overlapping of services like gasoline distribution, and the delivery of bread and milk; the losses due to the reckless exploitation of natural resources like the Turner Valley gas field, or pulp and paper in Quebec, and the hundred other ways in which wealth is wasted even when the individual undertaking is run efficintly. He should ponder over the fact that ever since its beginnings capitalism has been, in the sphere of economics, a series of booms between ever deepening depressions, and in international politics a series of unstable balances of power and armament races between increasingly murderous wars. That is the boasted 'efficiency' which he is afraid to lose.

Socialism, through national planning, and the conscious co-ordination of economic activity, offers a hope of equating consuming power and production, of spreading the available work amongst those capable of working, and thus of abolishing for ever the problems of unemployment and overproduction. As this goal is progressively achieved (no socialist pretends that it will be attained at once), prosperity will be established on an increasingly permanent and equitable basis. The necessary consequence will be that the occasions for war will be far fewer; not only will economic stability produce political calm, but the control which the peoples of the world will have over their national economies will make possible, ultimately, the planned development of the world's resources and the consequent elimination of those uncontrolled economic rivalries, the struggle for markets and the competition of powerful interests, which now set nation against nation exactly as they set corporation against corporation. Socialism, in other words, will operate to remove those colossal wastages, of war, competition and depression, which are part of the normal functioning of capitalism, and make the high efficiency of the capitalist corporation so pathetically useless. Socialism could stand a considerable amount of inefficiency within the organs of its planned society before the total amount of waste began to approach that which our present system, for all its individual skill, continually forces upon us.

But there is a more direct answer to the critic who says that government ownership means inefficiency and graft. If that were true, why did every government in the last war become more and more socialist as the crisis deepened? Were they aiming at inefficiency? If private enterprise is the most efficient system of production why abandon it when the enemy is at the gate? Great Britain, for instance, rationed the national food supply, took over the railways, controlled shipping, bought and distributed whole ranges of commodites, fixed prices, and generally supplanted private business. The same development occurred to a greater or less degree in the other belligerent countries. Once efficiency became a matter of life and death for the state, capitalism had to be replaced by a type of socialism. Only in times of peace can the wastes of capitalism be tolerated. At the end of the war the countries reverted to capitalism, not because their socialist experiments had been proved a failure but because the capitalists wanted to regain their 'liberty' to make profits without restriction from the state.

In other words, we already have ample experience in capitalist countries, quite apart from the evidence of the Soviet Union, to show that national planning increases efficiency, instead of reducing it. And socialism is merely planning based on social ownership and carried on for public benefit instead of private profit. Where the war socialism failed was just in so far as it left private interests active (as in the armament business), or paid them overmuch for their rights of ownership.

The same conclusion follows from a study of individual socialist experiments in Canada and other countries. It is not true to say that they prove government ownership to be inefficient. No one would suggest that our roads and bridges should be handed over to private companies, that our canals should cease to be government property, that liquor should again be distributed by private individuals, and electricity in Ontario placed under the control of a privately-owned monopoly. It is clear from experience in both private and public management of these undertakings that public operation better serves the public interest. Individual experiments may have failed, but the number of public enterprises which the people of Canada have found beneficial greatly exceeds those which they have regretted. This is true despite our reliance on patronage and our indifference to corruption in public matters, both of which are costly and in large part remediable. Moreover, isolated experiments in public ownership, carried on in the hostile environment of capitalism, constantly subject to misrepresentation in newspapers and deprived by lower salary rates of the best technical skill available for private business, inevitably work under a great handicap. Conditions in a fully socialized community would be vastly more favourable for efficient operation.

There is in fact only one serious obstacle that the advocate of public ownership in Canada meets, and that is the example of the CNR. This is rapidly ceasing to be an obstacle, as the history of the national railway becomes better known. The CNR is one of the typical wrecks of capitalism which a Conservative government bought at a ridiculously high price in order to shift to the Canadian public the losses that should have been borne by the investors. It is one of the best examples, not of the inefficiency of public ownership, but of the waste of private enterprise, which built a hodge-podge of competing railways in Canada without any unified plan or control and then ran them all, except the CPR, into bankruptcy. Having brought them to the verge of ruin, the owners of these private lines then turned to the government as an alternative to the bankruptcy courts. So the 'credit of the country' was saved by an unwise public investment.

It was inevitable that the railways composing the CNR should be unable to pay interest on their bonds out of earnings. They were not economically sound, or they would never have been handed over. All that the experience of the CNR shows is that public ownership will prove costly if it is merely used to save the investments of careless capitalists. But it can be predicted with absolute certainty that no socialist government in this country would make this mistake. A socialist party in office will not play the fairy god-mother to stock and bond holders. Wherever governments have socialized a profitable business, like liquor, they have made plenty of money. If the governments were now to take over the distribution of gasoline, for example, enormous profits could be made even without getting rid of the present wastage of four filling stations on the same corner.

The CNR, however, does not really need the excuses that have been made for it, valid though they are. A more positive defence for government operation can be found in the actual achievement of the lines. Out of the hundred and thirty-nine private corporations that went to the making of the railway a single system has been created that functions with an efficiency comparable with that of the CPR. And this has been accomplished in spite of the evil of patronage in the appointment of directors – an evil, be it noted, which the Drayton-Acworth Report in 1917 expressly provided against in its recommendations to the Dominion Parliament,[1] although members at that time failed to adopt them.

Much of the argument against public ownership is based on the old idea of direct government operation – the idea that government management of economic undertakings should be carried on by a government department, like the Post Office. This is a technique of state action which derives from a time when almost all the functions of government were political. It is a technique appropriate to, say, the conduct of foreign affairs, but not to the distribution of electricity. The modern technique of state management through the publicly owned corporation is a development out of capitalist experience, and enables the state to carry on economic activity with almost the identical checks and safeguards that operate to make an individual capitalist business efficient. The public corporation is not directly under state control; it has an independent existence of its own; it can be run on a strictly cost-accounting basis and be made to show profit and losses in an annual balance sheet just as do privately owned firms to-day. In this way if there is waste anywhere it can be soon tracked down and dealt with. So far there have been few experiments with this type of public ownership; most of our government 'commissions' in Canada are still very largely under political direction, and proper accounting is lamentably scarce. Under socialism the newer method of management would become normal for almost all economic activity not undertaken by co-operative institutions – and these have a record of achievement behind them, in this and other countries, that needs no defence.

The view that government ownership necessarily leads to inefficiency does not bear examination. The allied objection that the public services are always corrupt is equally fallacious. Admittedly there is much dishonesty surrounding the administration of government in Canada. No one would deny it, any more than he would deny that there is also a large number of civil servants who perform their duties honestly and well. The socialist, however, is under no obligation to prove that governments are always honest and that the socialist state will never know corruption. All he need show is that it is reasonable to expect enough honesty to make national planning workable. He must show that a wide extension of social ownership is not likely to increase graft to such a point that the savings due to planning are lost in the pilfering of officials.

Capitalism has shown itself to be infected with a greater degree of graft than has ever been disclosed in government undertakings. This point is important, not because it enables the socialist to use the *tu quoque* argument on the capitalist, but because it shows that we do not escape dishonesty by clinging to rugged individualism. Where can be found a list of public officials comparable in their ethic to those whom a few Senate 'probes' revealed in the United States? In Canada our democracy has not proved strong enough to insist that its financial mis-leaders be called to account, but the Ottawa enquiry into price-spreads and mass buying has given us inklings of what exists,[2] and not a person in the country doubts that if the affairs of some of our financial 'rackets' had been aired there might have been a list of Canadian names to match the American record. The corruption of capitalism is *systematic*, that is, part of its normal working, whereas that of government bodies is individual and spasmodic. It is normal for capitalist corporations to water stock so that profits are turned into dividends instead of higher wages, lower cost for articles, or improved service to the public. It is normal to erect combines so that the public are cheated out of a fair price for commodities. It is normal for the big executives in private businesses to vote themselves large salaries and bonuses while their workers remain poorly paid or are being turned into the street. And capitalism is directly corrupted by bribery which takes the form of commissions on contracts and sales, the hiding of profits, and so on. Capitalism continually confronts honest business men with the choice between bankruptcy or the chiselling of wages and other evil practices necessitated by the force of competition. It is a form of economic warfare. Employers are frequently faced with a choice between scrapping their morality or scrapping their business, and all the honesty and decency of individual capitalists, who, it is willingly conceded, are in the great majority in numbers, are powerless before the inherent immorality of the system. It matters not a whit whether these normal practices are technically illegal or not; from the point of view of the morality on which the socialist works, they are wrong, and he sees clearly that they can only be eradicated by changing the economic system which produces them. Indeed, the very fact that some of these practices are not illegal is the best proof that the ethic of capitalism is inadequate.

The system of private enterprise thus produces anti-social behaviour on a large scale. If we turn now to examine the principal kinds of corruption in government services to-day, we find a significant thing – they are nearly all connected with the making of profits by the private owners of the means of production, distribution and exchange. Take the three biggest political scandals exposed in Canada in the past forty years – the public works contracts in 1891–3, the customs scandal of 1926, and the Beauharnois affair of 1931.[3] The first was bribery by private corporations who wanted to obtain contracts from the government; the second was bribery of customs officials by private traders – chiefly liquor interests – who wanted to import goods more cheaply; the third was bribery of party members by promoters of a privately-owned power production scheme. In the same way the recent probe into the Ontario Hydro, if it disclosed corruption at all, showed that it occurred precisely where the public system came into relations with private corporations. Obviously under socialism, whatever forms corruption might take, it could not take these forms. There would not be any powerful private corporations to make profit out of graft. The incentive to corruption will have gone. Government contracts will be filled by government construction departments or in socially owned factories the profits of which do not go to individuals but to the community as a whole. Customs laws will be replaced by import and export quotas for the various public distributing bodies. The development of waterpower and other natural resources will be undertaken in accordance with the national plan by public utility commissions. Who would want to bribe whom for what? It would be as sensible to expect the chief inspector of hotels for the CPR to bribe the superintendent for CPR trains, or the Deputy Minister of Railways and Canals to bribe the officials in the Department of Trade and Commerce. Corruption in politics to-day is mostly due to private ownership of the economic processes. Socialism, by eliminating competition and the private appropriation of profits, strikes at the root motive of corruption, and is indeed the only method of effecting a cure.

Beside the major forms of political graft which are due to private ownership and which socialism will necessarily eradicate, the petty pilfering of officials, which of course will occur under socialism for some time, is a very minor affair. It will certainly be a no more serious problem for socialist governments than it is to-day for individual corporations, who have always to take the risk that the cashier may abscond or the treasurer may embezzle funds. The criminal law, careful accounting, and normal social pressure keep this evil within manageable bounds. There is not the slightest reason why it should increase under socialist operation; indeed it should vastly diminish once the state guarantees security for all. It is insecurity of employment which drives many men to desperate remedies.

A more serious danger is political patronage – the distribution of office as a reward to friends, and generally the filling of positions on grounds other than those of merit and public interest. We in Canada have suffered and still suffer greatly from this evil. In so far as socialism increases the number of positions to be filled by the state, which it will do, it will increase the opportunities for patronage. But this danger on examination turns out to be not nearly so insurmountable as it appears at first sight. The public corporation lends itself to promotion for merit from below just as does the private corporation, which, it should be remembered, it itself always liable to nepotism from directors. The development of the panel system of appointments, selection by the Civil Service Commission in appropriate cases, increased supervision by trades unions and workers' organizations, will all help to check the evil. In the socialist state, also, there will be no place for the best brains to go outside public service of some sort, and the best brains will come to the top positions under any system. Once official positions become the real centres of social power, comparable to the great executive posts now found chiefly in private enterprise, the ablest citizens will find them. Certainly patronage did not stand in the way of socialist construction in Russia; she made no bones about hiring capitalist experts at high salaries in order to hasten industrial development until she could train a personnel of her own. We can be as intelligent.

One other danger that confronts the socialist state is the danger of political pressure on public authorities to make them embark on costly public works in order to placate sectional interests. This is a real danger, but one which is present in any system, capitalist or socialist. If ever humanity is to substitute control for blind endeavour in economic matters it is a risk that must be taken. There is no reason to suppose that the mistakes of socialism, with its careful planning and the wide publicity which will be given to all public enterprises, will be anything like as large or as costly as under a system in which economic development takes place wherever a short-sighted capitalist thinks he sees a profit for himself, regardless of whether or not it is at someone else's expense.

In short, socialism instead of being a likely cause of economic inefficiency and political corruption, holds the promise of being the cure for these evils.

EDITOR'S NOTES

1 Sir Henry Drayton, chairman of the Board of Railway Commissioners, and W.M. Acworth, a British railway economist, gave their names to the Royal Commission on Railways though neither was its chairman. He was A.H. Smith, Vice-president of the New York Central Railroad, who dissented from the finding of his two fellow-commissioners that the Canadian Northern, Grand Trunk, and Grand Trunk Pacific railway systems should be placed under trusteeship and operated within a government-owned system.

2 The Royal Commission on Price Spreads, also known as the Stevens Commission after its first chairman and best-known member, H.H. Stevens, from 1930 to 1934 R.B. Bennett's minister of trade and commerce. See note 3 in 'The Unholy Trinity of Quebec Politics.'

3 The first was the scandal involving Thomas McGreevy, Conservative MP for Quebec West, and Sir Hector Langevin, the minister of public works in the cabinets of Sir John A. Macdonald and Sir John Thompson. The second and third were sources of serious embarrassment to the federal Liberals when William Lyon Mackenzie King was leader.

VI

French Canadian Nationalism

This article appeared in two issues of The Canadian Forum. *At the time the* Forum *was in danger of going under, and it was only because the LSR, of which Scott was at that time the national president, decided in May 1936 to buy the monthly from its owner, Graham Spry, that it survived.*

Scott used the pseudonym 'Quebecer' in publishing the article. Raised in the Church of England, his father an Anglican clergyman, Scott was conscious of the likelihood that he might be regarded, and by French Canadians dismissed, as 'just another anti-Catholic.' Actually his father had very high church views, and Scott had been brought up to think of himself as an Anglo-Catholic. He therefore had considerable sympathy for Roman Catholicism. However, he could not be blind to the great and often reactionary influence that the Roman Catholic hierarchy had on Quebec politics in the 1930s.

From *The Canadian Forum*, vol. 15, March 1936, pp. 12–13; vol. 16, May 1936, pp. 12–14. Reprinted by permission of *The Canadian Forum*

There is a movement on foot amongst the French-Canadians that Canadians would do well to study. Unnoticed by the English press, unsuspected by the public at large, it is steadily gaining strength in Quebec. It has its own clubs, its youth organizations, its newspapers. What is of vastly more importance, it has the backing of the Catholic Church.

This is the movement for the creation of an independent French and Catholic republic on the banks of the St. Lawrence.

It is well known that the Abbé Groulx has been preaching this idea for many years.[1] The world war gave it popularity amongst a people conscripted to fight others people's battles on foreign soil, but during the years of 'prosperity' little more was heard of it. With the depression, however, it has again sprung into prominence, and this time it is a force to be reckoned with. For Paul Gouin, the leader of the Action Libérale Nationale party,[2] which now holds 42 seats in the provincial legislature, has himself publicly voiced the hope of French-Canadian independence. Basing himself on the remarks of Cardinal Villeneuve made in 1922,[3] he recently spoke of the 'supernatural vocation' of the French race in America, where, in the midst of this North American Babylon, it was destined to become the 'modern Israel.' The hope, he admitted, could not be immediately realized, but it was something towards which his fellow countrymen would never cease to strive.

To understand the full character of the movement, one must read some paper like *L'Indépendance*. This is the official organ of the 'Jeunesses Patriotes,' a youth organization most active in promoting the new nationalism. From the most recently published number, dated February 1936, and specially dedicated to the Abbé Groulx, the following ideas are taken ...

In the first place, the call for independence from the Dominion is made in ringing tones. 'The French-Canadian people will not exist as a nation until it has freed itself from the foreign yoke. This is a right we claim, we demand, and we shall acquire.' Confederation is an absurd attempt to bind together provinces divided by race, culture, geography and religion. There is a natural right to secession. A new name is suggested for the state-to-be: Laurentia. 'O Laurentie, terre de nos aieux.'

It is to be a Catholic state. Just what that means in the political field is not very clear, but some idea of how theocratic it will be may be gained from the fact that the present control of the Church in Quebec is apparently considered inadequate. It is notorious that one reason why Mr. Taschereau is so near defeat at the moment is because the Church has turned against him.[4] He has not conceded the clergy the full freedom they demand. At present the priesthood merely controls all education, the press, the French trades unions, and social behaviour generally. In the new republic it will not be so hampered.

It is to be a corporative state. 'The parliamentary regime can lead us only to ruin, because it requires the existence of parties which dissipate our national energies.' The corporative state is said to be the 'juridical affirmation of the real man' as opposed to Marxist materialism. Democracy is to be scrapped, and in its place will come 'the centralization of power, wherever it may be necessary, in the person of the man who will impose himself and who will symbolize the spiritual unity of the factory, the municipality, the district or the nation.' A long speech from the Belgian Fascist, M. Hoornaert, is quoted with the advice that the reader should substitute 'French Canada' for 'Belgium' whenever that word appears; the gist of the speech is that 'authority' must be restored and democratic parties destroyed.

It is to be a country of the petty bourgeoisie. Those two great scapegoats of fascist ideology, the trusts and the chain stores, will be liquidated. French Canadians are said to be naturally adapted to small proprietorship; they will apparently revert to some mediaeval form of social structure, based on peasants, craftsmen and small traders, governed by a hierarchy of professional men with the priesthood at the top. Very like the province of Quebec today if English and American capital were removed from it. Industrialization, father of liberalism, marxism and all things evil, will be utterly cast out.

It will be a thoroughly masculine state, as is appropriate to Catholicism. This particular copy of *L'Indépendance* does not devote any space to the suppression of women's rights, but the idea is gaining in the province despite the valiant fight of those who are striving for the women's franchise. Mayor Houde of Montreal from time to time urged that all the jobs now occupied by women in the city be vacated to make room for men.[5] Recently M. Pellisson, representing the Junior Liberal Association of St. Roch, complained to M. Taschereau that there were no less than 800 women employed in the Parliament Buildings at Quebec. The char-women were not included in this figure; no good fascist, of course, could expect men to do dirty work of that sort.

... It will be an anti-semitic state. While M. Gouin is pointing out the civilizing mission of his 'Israel in Babylon,' his cohorts will be proving the point by organizing local pogroms. A writer in *L'Indépendance*, commenting on the evil state of present day society, concludes: 'C'est un malaise universel qui n'a qu'une source: le libéralisme juif.'

This ideal state cannot, of course, be achieved just yet. Meanwhile the 'Jeunesses Patriotes' intend to get what they can. All centralization of power at Ottawa is to be fought. Provincial rights are to be extended rather than curtailed, because the more power Quebec can obtain the more easy it will be to make the transition to independence. Good French Canadians are asked to take a solemn oath never to use the English language in their own province. All attempts to induce Canada to oppose Italy through the League of Nations must be prevented, since this will merely extend the nefarious influence of the British Empire. If France supports the League's efforts to help Abyssinia, it is only because France is governed by Free Masons.[6] The word loyalty is quite inaccurate to describe the relations between the French Canadians and the British Crown; the true relationship is one of political expediency. Loyalty was shown in 1776, in 1812 and in 1867 only because it was a necessary condition of French survival, and assisted in the realization of the ideal of independence.

Such are the principal ideas that move the French Canadian nationalists today. They have passed the stage of being secret aspirations and parlor revolutions. More and more they are permeating the new political party which, under the leadership of M. Gouin, may shortly be expected to achieve power in Quebec.[7] It would be wrong to suppose that they are shared by all French Canadians; it would be wrong to suppose that they will necessarily prevail. Whether they do or they do not prevail, however, will depend to a large degree upon the way they are received by the rest of Canada. If they are simply met with Imperialist ballyhoo, Orange cries, Protestant bigotry and Anglo-Saxon conceit, they will prevail. If they are met with sympathy, understanding and reasonable concessions, [French Canadians] may be satisfied with something less than the break-up of the Dominion. Ideas of this sort do not spring from mere cussedness, but from a frustrated desire for self-expression.

The roots of the present movement lie deep in the Canadian past. The seeds were sown at the Battle of the Plains of Abraham in 1759 – that preliminary skirmish in the centuries-long racial conflict which is slowly being decided against the British in eastern Canada. Since then the French Canadians have maintained themselves, their religion, habits and traditions, against every influence making for their assimilation by the alien culture which surrounds them. Attacks upon them have been of two kinds: overt attempts by the English to suppress their language, their schools and their political liberties, and the cultural corrosion that comes from daily contact with Anglo-Saxon America. The former has been the easier to meet, though the struggle has been long and is not yet over. Lord Durham's belief in the possible extinction of the French Canadian race,[8] belief which the Union of 1841 was intended to realize, is no longer tenable outside of Orange lodges, though its abandonment is an admission of failure rather than a gesture of generosity. Against the cultural influences, however, French Canada finds it more difficult to fight, but the struggle never ceases to stem the disintegrating effects of the press, the radio, the movies, and of English industrialization.

It is well for the English to understand this struggle, and particularly to realize that the British institutions for which the French Canadian is expected to be so grateful by no means appear to him to be models of fairness and freedom. He knows that in 1760 his civil law was taken from him, to be restored by the Quebec Act of 1774 through fear of revolt in the Americas; he knows of his struggle for political freedom up to 1837, when he was driven to violence to force concessions; he knows that the Act of Union of 1841 took away the official use of his language ...; he knows that Manitoba entered Confederation promising equal rights to the French language, and later took them away;[9] he knows that the special protection for his schools in the Manitoba constitution was virtually destroyed by the Privy Council decision in 1892, although the Canadian courts had decided in his favour;[10] he knows that Ontario made a drive against the use of his language in schools by the enactment of Regulation 17 in 1912, and only dropped the attempt in 1927 after a bitter fight; he knows that freedom for his own school system has never been accorded in the Maritimes, in Saskatchewan or Alberta, in a way satisfactory to him. Above all he knows that the British connection has meant and will probably mean again that he will be expected to leave the peaceful shores of the St. Lawrence and travel to some distant country in which he is not interested, to fight people with whom he has no quarrel, for the sake of an Empire in which he does not believe.

There is another side to the picture of course, and every French Canadian knows that also. But the picture here painted is black enough and true enough for the purposes of a nationalist movement. Nor is this all. As the French Canadian looks around his own province today, what does he see? He sees his people ground down under a foreign economic imperialism. English or American capital has a stranglehold over the natural resources of the province, and exploits that wealth, not for the common good, but for the sake of profits to distribute amongst their largely non-French shareholders. He reads the lists of directors of the great corporations whose head offices are in Montreal, and finds hardly a French Canadian amongst them. He is a servant amongst foreign owners; a serf in a new feudalism. He sees his unemployed in Montreal living in misery, too poor to pay for the light and gas which are laid on to their crowded homes, having to cook with coal-oil bought at a price pegged by the oil interests, burning candles for light, and being sent to gaol in batches by the Montreal Light, Heat & Power Company because some of them have enough initiative to jump the meters by tapping the wires and mains. Is it a wonder he becomes aggressive? But for the Church's control he would have rebelled.

Thus it is that two streams of indignation meet today to swell the flood of nationalist sentiment. So long as the purely cultural struggle was uppermost, the movement remained the persistent but moderate influence which it has been since Confederation. Even the Nationalist Party of Mr. Bourassa in 1900 had no secessionist plank in its platform,[11] and was completely democratic in aim; the Abbé Groulx and his associates in Action Française were talking of independence in the early 1920s but had no wide following. During the Great Prosperity there was no active nationalist movement. Now, however, the economic crisis has stirred deeper mass feelings than could ever appeal to race or religion, and certain nationalist leaders have been quick to seize their opportunity.

It is in relation to the economic situation that this new nationalism needs the most careful analysis. The first pinch of the depression did not make the French Canadian more nationalist; it tended to make him socialist. He did not rush to join the Communists or even the CCF; his press is far too controlled to enable him to know anything truthful about these movements, and the Church has damned them both. But he did turn instinctively against big business and the trusts generally; there were even murmurings against the wealth of the Church. Criticism of the whole social system, by a genuine proletariat, sprang spontaneously from capitalist decline. Obviously the classes in control had to do something to canalize this revolutionary sentiment, or else intelligent radicals might capture it. The present talk of independence is in part a deliberately planned attempt to steer social discontent away from socialist thinking. The propaganda of the new journals like *L'Unité, La Nation, L'Indépendance*, chief organs of the movement, is quite clear on the need for complete autonomy, to fight communism and socialism, which they indiscriminately confuse. Are not the western provinces full of Bolshies, and would it not be safer to cut loose from them at once? Thus the new French republic is to be a haven of bourgeois society.

Further parts of the nationalist programme spring directly from the economic realities. To hold the new proletariat, the nationalist leaders must attack the trusts and chain stores as vehemently as do the genuine radicals. Hence the movement today, in contrast to its earlier stages, is filled with the spurious radicalism which is the main weapon of fascist demagogy. The hungry masses are being told that the trusts are dangerous because they are controlled by English, Americans or Jews; that once an independent corporative state is established it will deal with them effectively, either by putting them in French hands or by destroying them; and that the way out lies in back-to-the-land movements and in a revival of small industry. Whereas the truth of course is that the trusts exploit English, American and Jewish consumers as cheerfully as they exploit everybody else; that to substitute French boards of directors for the present ones would make just exactly no difference at all to the economic system; that a return to a peasant society is a return to the poverty and servility of the eighteenth century; and that the only way out without losing all the efficiency and wealth of large scale production is the creation of a planned, co-operative society based on social ownership of natural resources and monopolies. What these nationalists fail to see also is that one principal reason why French Canadians have seldom advanced to positions of general importance in the economic life of Quebec is not due to the fact that they are constitutionally incapable of adapting themselves to modern industry, nor is it due simply to English unwillingness to give them jobs; it is due in great part to the fact that their schools and colleges, every one of which is in the grip of the Church, are giving them an education that is totally inadequate to the needs of today. It may train them to become good Catholics, but it certainly does not train them to become good scientists or businessmen. This is scarcely to be wondered at, when you may read in the Calendar of the University of Ottawa that all letters sent or received by the students may be opened and read by the Rector, and in the Calendar of the Université de Montréal that the authorities will take special care to prevent the students falling into the three awful errors of 'liberalism, materialism and modernism.'

Because of its reactionary economic philosophy, however, it follows that the present independence movement will not get very far. For sooner or later the Church is going to understand that it has need of the big corporations and trusts. Much of the wealth of the Church today consists of investments in stocks and bonds. Those investments would be largely destroyed by an attempt to create an economic unit out of a single province. Independence would therefore cost the Church a great deal in terms of dollars and cents. It was only a few years ago that Mr. Taschereau countered the attack upon the Quebec Power Company, then accused of charging too much for lighting the city of Quebec, by pointing out that amongst its largest shareholders were various ecclesiastical authorities. The Church, indeed, is caught in a dilemma; it must play with the anti-trust sentiment in order to control the nationalist movement and head off communism, but it must also prevent any sudden dislocation of the economic system for fear of losing its investment. Many individual parishes and religious orders are in serious difficulty as it is. This dilemma is exactly the sort of situation which produces fascism, for fascism talks socialism before it achieves power, and practices monopoly capitalism afterwards. Quebec will only establish her separate state, as the choice of the lesser evil, if the rest of Canada carries its economic radicalism to extremes so that the Church faces confiscation of its wealth.

In addition to this financial factor which hampers the secessionist policy, there is also the racial dispersion factor. At one time Quebec and French Canada were synonymous terms. Today French Canadians are scattered throughout the Maritimes, Ontario and the prairie provinces. Quebec can only achieve her independence at the cost of some 650,000 of her children. That is also a price which at the moment seems too great to pay.

What then of the future? What solution is there to this nationalist problem?

In the first place, English Canadians must accept the bi-racial character of this country, with all its implications. If the future of Canada is to be a country where union for national purposes is based on cultural diversity and racial equality, then the English must make further contributions to this ideal than they have yet done. Complete bilingualism in national matters must be accepted; a gradual extension of bilingual rights must be willingly conceded in those parts outside Quebec where French minorities develop; the English schools must teach French more effectively, as a native language; greater freedom for separate schools will have to be permitted in English provinces. Above all the attitude of the English must harmonize with this national policy; bigotry, smug superiority, must somehow be educated out of them.

In the second place Canadian capitalism, which is controlled by the English and not by the French, must be replaced by social ownership. Strong racial feelings today are in large part due to the failure of the economic system to function. The privately owned trusts and monopolies, besides underpaying workers, exploiting consumers and piling up wealth in the hands of the few, are also doing their best to smash Confederation. They set race against race, class against class, West against East. And they will go on doing this until they are socialized. Socialization will give back to the French Canadian the ownership of his natural resources, for through his provincial government and its various controlling commissions he will be in a position to be master of his economic destiny. He will be able to integrate his provincial planning with the national economic policy, to the mutual advantage of the province and of the Dominion. But any French socialist party which comes forward must recognize that compensation will have to be paid for all expropriated property unless it is willing to add anti-clericalism to its programme. A policy of confiscation would mean war to the death with the Church; a policy of constitutional socialism, drawing its strength from the masses, co-operating with movements like the CCF outside Quebec, would find a wide support without necessarily becoming committed to a complete overturn of the social structure. After all, Quebec has already got rid of one antiquated social system, when she bought out the rights of the Seigneurs and destroyed the relics of feudalism by law in 1854.

On their part the French Canadians will have to do a great deal more careful thinking about the economic structure of Canada than they appear to have done. If they really want to try to put back the economic clock, to abolish large industry and to turn all cities into small towns, then there is no solution to the nationalist problem, either before or after the independence of Quebec. This ideal is of course particularly favoured by the present Church authorities, who would undoubtedly have a more obedient and subservient population in such a society. But a feudal Catholicism is not the only nor the best Catholicism. There are plenty of Catholics today who see the possibility of a social order in which large scale industry is socially operated for the benefit of the people, in which the family and home life are sustained by steady and decent wages, and where the efficiency of modern power production is preserved. Such a society is indeed compatible with, if not proclaimed in, the Encyclical *Quadragesimo Anno*.[12] The trouble is that the Quebec branch of the Catholic Church has become inbred and unprogressive. Its reactionary outlook exceeds the bounds of what the faith requires. Henri Bourassa is reported to have made the remark that 'There are two Churches, the Church of Rome and the Church of Quebec, and I belong to the Church of Rome.' When enough French Canadians belong to the Church of Rome the nationalist problem can easily be solved within the framework of Confederation by a joint French and English movement for the building of a co-operative society based on economic planning for the public good, and proud of the richness of its two great cultures.

EDITOR'S NOTES

1 Abbé Lionel Groulx was the most prominent Quebec historian before the 1960s and one of the leading French Canadian nationalist spokesmen of this century. Professor of history at the University of Montreal from 1915 to 1949, during the 1930s he was active in l'Action Nationale, which blamed the Depression in large part on American, English Canadian, and Jewish industrialists and financiers.

2 Paul Gouin, the son of a former Liberal premier of Quebec, Sir Lomer Gouin, was at this time the co-leader of a coalition called the Union Nationale Duplessis Gouin. This alliance of Gouin's reformist Action Libérale Nationale (ALN) and the provincial Conservative party led by Maurice Duplessis gained forty-two seats in the 1935

provincial election, with the ALN taking most of them. In June 1936, shortly before a new election, Gouin broke with Duplessis, but most of Gouin's former associates failed to follow him out of the coalition. Duplessis quickly gained full control of the Union Nationale, and after the election became premier, a position that he held from 1936 to 1939 and from 1944 until his death in 1959.

3 Jean-Marie-Rodrigue Villeneuve became in 1932 archbishop of Quebec and in 1933 the fourth Canadian cardinal. During the 1920s he had been active in the nationalist circle led by Abbé Groulx.

4 Not long after Scott wrote this, Liberal Premier L.-A. Taschereau, in office since 1920, resigned in favour of Adélard Godbout, who soon therafter lost a provincial election to the Union Nationale.

5 Camillien Houde, leader of the Quebec Conservative party before Maurice Duplessis, was mayor of Montreal for most of the years from 1928 to 1954. An admirer of the ideology of Mussolini's Italy, he was interned for four years during the Second World War after calling for defiance of registration for military service under the National Resources Mobilization Act of June 1940.

6 In the fall and early winter of 1935, the League of Nations faced in the Italian invasion of Abyssinia a major test of the doctrine of collective security. Under Article 10 of the League of Nations Covenant, member nations were to come to the aid of a nation undergoing aggression from another nation. The league failed this test, a tragic development to which the Canadian government led by William Lyon Mackenzie King made a regrettable contribution. Quebec opinion, opposed to intervention in foreign affairs that might lead to war and generally favourable to Italy, played a significant role in the shaping of the policy of the King administration.

7 This prediction was right so far as the victory of the party was concerned, but quite wrong about its leader. See above, note 2.

8 The belief is clearly stated in Lord Durham's *Report on the Affairs of British North America*. See Gerald M. Craig, ed., *Lord Durham's Report* (Toronto 1963), 145–60.

9 The official use of French in Canada was restored in 1848. A decision by the Supreme Court of Canada in 1979 restored the official use of French in Manitoba.

10 The reference is to *Barrett's Case*, dealing with an application by Dr Barrett, a Roman Catholic ratepayer, to quash a by-law of the City of Winnipeg fixing a rate of taxation for public school purposes, passed under the authority of the Manitoba Schools Act of 1890, which had removed public support from Roman Catholic and other separate schools.

11 Henri Bourassa, journalist and politician, was elected to the House of Commons as a Liberal, but broke with Sir Wilfrid Laurier in 1899 over the government's handling of Canadian assistance to the British in the South African war. Bourassa became the exponent of a pan-Canadian nationalism which would give equal place to French and English throughout Canada.

12 Promulgated by Pope Pius XI in 1931, this encyclical was an important and powerful statement on social questions. It favoured a 'middle way' between capitalism and socialism.

VII

Letter to David Lewis, 11 July 1937

Scott first met David Lewis when the latter was a freshman student in law at McGill. Obviously intelligent, and already a committed and well-informed socialist, Lewis took part in the drafting of the LSR manifesto and in January, 1932, attended the Toronto meeting at which the LSR took formal shape. He went to Oxford in 1932 on a Rhodes Scholarship, but when he returned in 1935, having taken a degree in law, he quickly became active in the LSR and CCF. He was appointed national secretary of the CCF, part-time in 1936, full-time two years later, and served in that capacity until 1950. From this time on Scott and Lewis worked ever more closely together, culminating in an eight-year period, from 1942 to 1950, when Scott chaired the national CCF.

The Lachute meeting to which Scott repeatedly refers in this letter to Lewis was a gathering of the provincial CCF council in Quebec.

Our Lachute meeting did not come to any very definite conclusions. We were rather feeling our way toward what we felt was the right political line for the CCF at the present time. My impression of the argument is as follows. The CCF started as a loose federation of ill-united groups. Gradually it began to solidify its ranks and to weld the groups into a single party. This was partly due to a natural desire for unity, partly to the effect of the Regina manifesto which gave a unified political philosophy to the movement, and partly to the efforts of the Communists to destroy the movement from within by capturing affiliated labour groups. The net result is that today we are more closely organised and more unified in purpose than we have ever been. But we have been so intent on putting our own house in order that we have failed to bring in the steady stream of converts which we must have if the movement is to grow.

Today there is a real stirring going on amongst the people. The Liberals have failed horribly to make progress, the CIO has enlivened the labour movement,[1] the Communists have turned into Liberals, the French-Canadians are on the move though they do not know where they are going. All this has loosened people's loyalties and made the political situation fluid. The CCF has a heaven-sent opportunity to canalise this fluidity in the general direction of social democracy. How is this to be done? *There is no single answer to this question which is good for all Canada.* I think we came to that conclusion. The way CCF'ers in Quebec talk to the Quebec nationalists must be different from the way CCF'ers in Alberta talk to disappointed Social Credulites.[2] In Quebec the immediate need is to stop corporatism and fascism; the only hope that this may be done lies in the chance that a genuine French liberal party may grow; therefore we in Montreal are anxious to help liberalism, not to attack it. We shall not disband as a party, but we shall co-operate in all sorts of ways with the nascent liberal group.

It also seems likely that out of the turmoil will arise other small labour parties and progressive groups which will ask us for co-operation. While our group at Lachute agreed that another request for affiliation from the Communists would have to be turned down, if it came, nevertheless we felt that the CCF must avoid giving the impression that it is too pure to associate with anyone else. We must appear publicly as being co-operative in character rather than as being doctrinaire. Because though the Liberals have failed liberalism was never more the zeitgeist than it is today. Therefore I welcome the spirit of the Ontario convention resolution on affiliation with other groups.[3] The CCF can now afford to broaden its base again, because it is strong enough knit to keep its objectives clear. It can discard from strength. And when we begin co-operating with others we must not be surprised nor disturbed to find the Communists popping up again as members of the other bodies.

But again we must remember the different situations in the various parts of the country. In BC a single, unified and non-co-operative party may be quite justified, simply because the CCF there is already a broad movement and there are no other obvious groups with which to seek co-operation. In Quebec the popular front idea, or something like it, is at the moment a reasonable tactic. But personally, and I think most of those at Lachute would agree, I would not include the Communist party amongst those groups with which the CCF should have any public co-operation. They are still not a Canadian party; their tactic of co-operation may change overnight on instructions;[4] they have by no means yet lived down their evil reputation in the public mind; the situation in the Soviet Union may go from bad to worse,[5] and some of that stink will cling to the local party; and anyway they are more of a nuisance than an influence in the country. The CCF has suffered from the enthusiasm of the young convert; it has extolled too much the severe religious virtues of self-denial, fasting and martyrdom. The Communist has been the Indian fakir of the left wing; he has been brave enough to lie down on a board of nails, and to endure untold suffering for his faith. This has dazzled and attracted many CCF'ers. To them its complete futility was not as apparent as the courage of the individual, and though they did not join the Communists they kept thinking more of the political left than of the political right. Yet it still remains true that the CCF is too far left for most Canadians even now, and in the political arena we must find our friends amongst the near right.

Lastly, do not think that I have lost sight of the concept of the CCF as being itself a popular front. It is that to some degree now; our principal aim at all times must be to make it more so. The very best weapon of social change is a single united party, as in Sweden; the French or Spanish method[6] is third rate by comparison. To get more people into the CCF, however, it may be necessary in some parts of Canada to stop saying 'We are the united front: join us,' and to say 'On this immediate issue, which we share in common, we will join forces with you.' Many of those who come to co-operate will remain to affiliate.

Well, this is partly the Lachute discussion and partly just me. Whatever it is, however, it should not go into your secretary's report except as though it were entirely your own. I would be glad to know how far you agree with it.

As regards my allowing my name to stand for the National Council should I be nominated. I have no objections except that I cannot be an active member. And I shall be taking no more active part in the day to day work of the party in Montreal next year than I have in the past. I shall remain the objectionable 'intellectual.' I don't know that as such I ought to be on the Council ...

EDITOR'S NOTES

1 The Committee for Industrial Organization (CIO) was founded within the American Federation of Labor (AFL) in 1935 but expelled in 1938, when it was renamed the Congress of Industrial Organizations. The CIO was active in trying to organize semi-skilled and unskilled industrial workers that had been very largely ignored by the craft unions which dominated the AFL ,and, associated with it, the Trades and Labour Congress in Canada. The CIO spread into Canada in 1936 in the form of affiliated unions like the United Auto Workers, which in 1937 went on a highly publicized and dramatic strike at the General Motors plant in Oshawa.

2 CCFers like Scott found it hard to hide their contempt for Social Credit and its 'funny money' ideas. Social Credit had formed the provincial government in Alberta in 1935, and seventeen Social Crediters, fifteen in Alberta and two in Saskatchewan, gained seats in the federal election of October 1935.

3 The Ontario CCF Council in October 1936 voted to support a policy actually dictated by the national council in the summer: the CCF would maintain complete political independence, but would 'co-operate and participate in immediate struggles.' This permitted co-operation with the Communist Party of Canada (CPC) in such matters as support for the Spanish government in the civil war which had broken out in the summer of 1936. Many Ontario CCFers were not happy about this policy, however, fearing it would compromise the party in the eyes of the public. Earlier in the year the

provincial CCF council had voted against the united front with the CPC in any form.
4 Scott's comment reflected his awareness that the conversion of the CPC to the policy of a 'united front against fascism' had been dictated by the Communist International in a major policy shift in 1934–35.
5 The reference is to the show trials and attendant terror in the Soviet Union at the time.
6 That is, the united or popular front of anti-fascist parties.

VIII

Letter to J.S. Woodsworth, 30 November 1938

The attitude of the Roman Catholic Church to the CCF in the 1930s was generally hostile. Nowhere was this more true than in Quebec. In 1934 Msgr Georges Gauthier, archbishop of Montreal, issued a mise en garde *to the faithful against the new party. Four years later Cardinal Villeneuve, speaking with much greater authority, condemned the CCF. The outcome of the letter which Scott sent to J.S. Woodsworth, leader of the national CCF, was a pamphlet,* C.C.F. et propriété privée, *which the national office of the CCF distributed in Quebec in the hope of countering the attack. Scott later doubted that this had any significant effect on Quebec opinion.*

As you doubtless realise, Cardinal Villeneuve's recent condemnation of the CCF (Montreal *Gazette*, Nov. 30th) is a matter of major importance. Hitherto the only condemnation has been from a single bishop; now it is from a Cardinal representing the entire Catholic church in Canada or 41% of the population.

I saw your answer in this morning's *Gazette*, but useful as it is it cannot quite meet so serious and all embracing a statement as the Cardinal's without going more to the heart of the matter. In particular the argument that we differ from Communists because the latter have opposed us at elections ought not to be used again; it is quite apparent that we have also been supported by Communists in many elections, and Liberals oppose Conservatives in elections though they both support the same kind of social system. The Cardinal's condemnation rests on moral and philosophical grounds; and if he is not met on those grounds he is not met at all. His implication that we differ from the Communists only in method ought I think to be specifically met.

Actually the CCF differs completely from the Cardinal's concept of Communism. If Communism is as he describes it – atheistic, totalitarian, repressive, destructive of all private property – then we differ from it fundamentally. It is not for us to say whether he is misrepresenting Russia; the Communists can undertake their own defence on this point. While it is true that anyone who tries to find out for himself will understand the mis-representation of the CCF in the Cardinal's statement, nevertheless, the fact remains that most people will not find out for themselves. They will only find out if we come back hard. I feel that something further ought to be done to clarify the whole position of the CCF in regard to private property, religious toleration and respect for spiritual values in society; the present seems an appropriate moment to do it. If a prepared statement were issued by the National Council to the press as an official answer to the Cardinal, it would be carried across Canada. These are things which we must say over and over again.

IX

What Kind of Peace Do We Want?

Scott's fear that Canadian involvement in a new European war would have as one result another crisis over conscription for military service, in turn leading to a serious and lasting division in the country, increasingly made him consider a policy of non-intervention to be the most suitable for Canada. His views on neutrality found full expression in his book Canada Today *(1938) and in an article that he published in* Foreign Affairs *in January 1939 ('A Policy of Neutrality for Canada'). It was Scott's view, however, that Canada would not be able to stay out of a war that involved Britain unless steps were taken to secure the right to neutrality in the way the Union of South Africa had done in 1934. In the Royal Seals and Signet Act the Parliament of that country had removed all limitations upon the delegation of the monarch's executive power, thus making it possible for his ministers in South Africa to advise his representative to declare neutrality even though the king's ministers in Britain were advising him to declare war. As Canada had not passed such an act Scott believed Mackenzie King's promise, that 'Parliament will decide' whether the country would go to war or not, to be misleading or mistaken. With this in mind, Scott thought it was important to discuss what our war aims should be. He thereby hoped to show that there was no logical argument for Canada's participation in the coming war.*

From *Saturday Night*, vol. 54, 15 July 1939, p. 3. Reprinted by permission of *Saturday Night*

Everyone is preparing for war. Armaments are piling up, economic systems are being made over for military purposes, foodstuffs are being stored away in quantity. Plans are ready for the evacuation of whole cities. Everywhere a feverish preparation for human slaughter – and not a word about the terms of peace.

Wars arise from various causes, but they end in peace treaties. European history is strewn with the result of forceful change written into peace treaties. Westphalia, Utrecht, Paris, Vienna, Versailles ...,[1] each represents a new start in Europe, based on a new equilibrium of forces. The durability of the peace which followed each treaty was dependent on the wisdom or the folly of the treaty-makers.

If war comes again in Europe, Canadians will be expected to join in with the democracies. They will be asked to fight – for what? Some say for democracy, some say for the British Commonwealth, some say for civilisation. But whatever be the motive of their endeavour, ultimately they will get a peace treaty. No more democracy or civilization will emerge from the conflict than is represented in the terms of that treaty. The noblest aspirations of millions of dying soldiers can be nullified by the stroke of a peace-treaty pen.

In the last war, the British government had made secret commitments with allies the terms of which were not known to the tommies dying for democracy in the trenches. These secret treaties bedevilled the whole Versailles settlement. Hence the demand for 'open diplomacy,' the value of which will have to be learned all over again.

Today, before another war has begun but when all are preparing for it, today is the time to take stock of our position and to define our war aims. If a fraction of the energy devoted to military preparedness were spent on clarifying the issues of the war and in discovering a permanent basis for a new peace, the national effort would be infinitely more useful to humanity. To leave such thinking till the last days of the war is to invite hatred, revenge and passion to the drafting of the treaty.

Now the war which Canadians are contemplating is a European war. It will start between European nations for reasons which are primarily European. If it is to provide a stable solution of the problems which gave rise to it, it must result in something more than a dictated power-politics peace. No such peace will do more than create another armed armistice such as we have experienced since 1919. It must lay the basis for the future peaceful settlement of European disputes. It must end in some form of League of Nations or Pan-European Union.

Is it likely that Canada, a minor North-American power, can help in the achievement of this result? Will she be able to write a peace treaty for a continent of 500,000,000? Or will she wait to hear the results of her war effort, as she waited for the results of Munich?[2]

The Canadian government has not said what sort of settlement it favours. It has no policy with regard to the colonial question, no policy on disarmament, no plan for a new League [of Nations], no offer of access to raw materials. It is preparing for destruction, but not for construction. It is expecting the Canadian people to make another blind sacrifice, another supreme act of faith in the eventual wisdom of European peacemakers.

This situation might be tolerable, if in Europe itself we saw some sign of a constructive policy. But where is it? Not in the British Government, certainly. Will the British Conservative Party suddenly be converted again to a genuine League policy? Will they attempt to re-create the instrument they failed to maintain? Would they make the necessary sacrifice of England's national sovereignty for a new European order? No one in his senses can believe that Mr. Chamberlain, Sir Samuel Hoare, Sir John Simon, or the other dominant personalities in and near the government[3] will completely change their established characters. Such men will deal, as they have always dealt, with European problems in terms of diplomatic manoeuvres, temporary arrangements, gentlemen's agreements, and military alliances. They still believe in the Concert of Europe – a continuous poker game periodically interrupted by bloodshed. Any idea of a super-state is to them utterly abhorrent.

As of England today, so of France and Poland. We are waiting for something more than a 'what we have we'll hold' policy from them. If Italy should be detached from the Axis alliance she would be equally in the power-politics game.[4] Russia is an unpredictable quantity, but after the cold-shouldering she received when she was offering general disarmament and collective security it is hardly likely that she will try that policy again. We may scan the European horizon in vain for leadership and vision, for something more than a scurry for cover. Sir Arthur Salter has attempted a solution in his recent book *Security: Can We Retrieve It*, but his is not an official voice. Clarence Streit's *Union Now* sets forth a bold plan for a World Federation of States, which sets the idealists talking and leaves the chancelleries cold. It seems that another generation of Europeans will have to pass through the fire before the lessons of the last war are rediscovered. Power politics based on independent sovereignties are as accepted and unchallenged today as in 1914, amongst all European major powers.

There is no point in Canadians waxing morally indignant over this situation. Seeing we have refused to join the only regional League of Nations in our own hemisphere, the Pan-American Union,[5] and seeing we have refused to assert our independence of policy from a military alliance based on race, the British Empire, we are certainly in no position to point a finger. But equally there is no excuse for our fooling ourselves. If we go into the expected war we shall not be fighting for a new world order. None of our leaders will be aiming at it. We shall not be fighting for a permanent solution of European problems. Neither of the two great European alliances has put forward any such plan. We shall simply be joining for racial and sentimental reasons in one more battle for a temporary domination of continental Europe. Morally we shall be on exactly the same footing as the Germans and Italians who will flock to Europe from overseas for identical reasons.

Democracy implies a government based on consent and equality of rights. There can be no democracy in world affairs until there is a world government based on these principles. No one is fighting for international democracy unless he is fighting for some form of world government. The most vocal imperialists in Canada have always opposed the surrender of Canadian or British interests to the needs of the League of Nations.

Because of the weakness of the moral case for joining in another European war, Canadian war-mongerers have fallen back on a last line of defence. Canada must fight in Europe, they say, to defend herself. If the Axis powers win the war, Canada will be the next to fall. The Canadian frontier is on the Rhine – or is it the Euphrates?

This is a weighty argument, if true. Let us examine it.

Note first that it postpones the invasion of Canada until after the next world war. This puts it a tidy way off. The war must start, be fought to a finish, peace must be made, the war-weary German people (surely the Italians do not intend to annex the Laurentians!) must be got ready for a second major offensive, across the Atlantic. By that time anything may have happened; the German government may have changed, Fascism may prefer to spread south and east. Clearing up the wreck of Europe will take half a generation. Most likely of all, Russia will sit on the side lines until she can walk in, like the USA in 1917, and direct the peace-making amongst exhausted powers.

But let us grant the case. Germany wins the war. She contemplates invading Canada. One small detail remains to be disposed of. The United States of America.[6] Merely another 140,000,000 people, more powerful than Britain and France together. To hear some of our military experts talk, one would think that this was nothing at all. A mere trifle to a Germany which has just used up all her reserves defeating 85,000,000 British and French!

The idea is preposterous, granting even the most favourable circumstances to Germany. Actually, a war between Britain and France versus Germany and Italy would most likely be long drawn out and end in stalemate or general revolution. If Russia were in from the start against Germany, the latter will almost certainly be defeated. Europe can handle the Fascist threat herself. The greatest danger of aggression to Canada, as the Abbé Groulx has said,[7] is from the imperialists in her midst.

Note another interesting point about this argument. It entirely leaves Asia out of the picture. Japan is doing in Asia exactly what is is said that Germany might do in Europe. Why do not all the same arguments apply? Why is Canada not in danger of invasion if Japan wins? Why is Canada's frontier not on the Yangtse? Why do not our military experts urge us to intervene in Asia? Why does the Canadian government permit Japan to arm herself with Canadian exports?

The only difference between the two situations is a difference of race. There is no Canadian difference. No greater national interest is at stake in one of these continents rather than another, such as to justify isolation in one instance and military intervention in the other. The bombing of London may hurt our feelings more than the bombing of Nanking, but it does not threaten our security any more. And for anyone who has risen in his thinking above the primitive pull of race, it will not even cause more pain. At least in London there will be some people who brought the holocaust upon their own heads.

Canadian foreign policy should be soundly based upon two main principles. One is the defence of Canadian territory from invasion. The other is the creation of a new world order, a real League that will supersede our petty national sovereignties. Neither of these principles will be at stake if war breaks out in Europe.

EDITOR'S NOTES

1 The treaty of Westphalia (1648) ended the Thirty Years' War; Utrecht (1713) ended the War of the Spanish Succession; Paris (1763) ended the Seven Years' War; Vienna (1815) ended the Napoleonic Wars; Versailles (1919) ended the war with Germany and thus, in a sense, the First World War.

2 At Munich, on 29 September 1938, the dictators of Germany and Italy, Adolf Hitler and Benito Mussolini, and the prime ministers of France and Great Britain, Edouard Daladier and Neville Chamberlain, settled the territorial concessions that Czechoslovakia would be instructed to make to Germany. Neither the Czechoslovak government nor that of the Soviet Union was consulted. The Munich agreement prevented a European war that had seemed imminent, and was received with enthusiasm in most countries affected, though not in Czechoslovakia.

3 Both Hoare and Simon were former foreign secretaries in the British government. When Scott was writing, Hoare was First Lord of the Admiralty and Simon was Chancellor of the Exchequer in the Chamberlain cabinet.

4 The Axis was a loose alliance, formed in 1936, linking Germany and Italy.

5 Forerunner of the present Organization of American States, to which Canada still does not adhere.

6 Scott did not refer to it, but on 18 August 1938 President F.D. Roosevelt, while receiving an honorary degree from Queen's University in Kingston, had said: 'The Dominion of Canada is part of the sisterhood of the British Empire. I give to you assurance that the people of the United States will not stand idly by if domination of Canadian soil is threatened by any other Empire.'

7 Lionel Groulx, nationalist historian and publicist. See above: 'French Canadian Nationalism,' note 1.

X

Social Planning and the War

*In wartime planning Scott saw proof of the contention by the LSR and CCF that
planning could achieve specific economic and social goals. The creation of large
armed forces, the management of war production, and the elimination of unemployment all seemed to point to the possibility of positive government action, in
peace as in war. Scott assumed that there would be popular support for such
action in peacetime. He stated his views repeatedly, as in* Make This YOUR
Canada *(1943), written with his friend and associate David Lewis, and* Canada
after the War *(1943), co-edited with a University of Toronto political economist,
Alexander Brady. Scott recognized, of course, that the War Measures Act, which
had come into effect in September 1939, made constitutionally possible in war
what afterwards would require amendments to the British North America Act.*
From *The Canadian Forum*, vol. 20, August 1940, pp. 138–9. Reprinted by
permission of *The Canadian Forum*

Five years ago the research committee of the League for Social Reconstruction
produced their book *Social Planning for Canada*. It set out to show why the
capitalist economy of Canada had become unable to provide steady employment
and an increasing standard of living for Canadians; how the growth of monopoly
had resulted in a concentration of wealth and economic power which constantly
threatened our democracy; and that the proper democratic solution of the problem
was for the people of Canada, through appropriate public bodies, to begin planning
their economic development so as to achieve social justice and economic security.
Laissez-faire capitalism being on the decline, the only choice lay between fascism
and a planned democracy.

The LSR book was well received by the general public. Though hard to read and
expensive to buy, it ran through two editions. A fortunate attack upon it by a
well-connected St. James Street pamphleteer gave it some sale even in financial
circles.[1] But its teaching fell on stony ground, for the depression was lifting and
the old controls in Canada were about to re-establish themselves through the
victory of the Liberal party. Governmental inaction was voted into office in 1935
– which meant that financial and monopolistic control carried on. Economic
planning for democratic purposes was postponed.

Now the situation has drastically changed. The lessons that sweet reason and
academic argument could not instil have been driven home by the grim necessities
of war. Two unplanned societies, France and England, found themselves

retreating before the sheer efficiency of a Nazi-planned Germany. To meet that challenge England, late in the day, has discarded her economic individualism, and entered upon a new phase of war socialism. Socialist members of the Labour party have entered the cabinet in key positions. All property in England is now liable to conscription by governmental decree. The excess profits tax has reached 100%, and more than 15,000 firms are now under government control. Much of the old system remains (too much, as the example of the holdup in tank production showed) but the inadequacy of capitalist methods of war production is fully recognized. National planning has taken their place, using the techniques of capitalist manufacture but supplying new centralized controls directed toward a national purpose. A new industrial revolution has begun.

In Canada, where the imitation of England is accentuated by war sentiment, the same process is underway. So far as the law is concenred, the War Measures Act and supplementary statutes already provide a greater accumulation of statutory authority in Ottawa than was ever contemplated by Canadian planners. The radical suggestions of five years ago are commonplace today. The constitutional difficulties have temporarily vanished through the coming into force of the dominion's residuary and emergency powers. Canada, like England, recognizes that if she wants the maximum wealth in war supplies she must use the methods of economic planning and not those of capitalism. Public bodies and government officials are now deciding what commodities are needed and in what quantities; they also decide where they can best be produced; men in factories then go ahead and produce them. The role of the private business man or corporation in these planned areas is to see that production is efficient – nothing more. Deciding where and what kind of new developments should come is a public responsibility.

This description doubtless over-simplifies the actual situation. We are running two systems side by side at the moment, and economic anarchy still exists in fields that badly need planning. The examples of Henry Ford and the British Columbia oil companies, both of whom sabotaged a governmental program,[2] sharply reveal the dangers that lie in private ownership of essential economic activities. And we are still allowing extra profits to be made by private persons out of the war emergency. The Liberal party swamped the CCF proposal in parliament to impose a 100% excess profits tax. Our war planning is shot through with traditional ideas of property rights derived from the laissez-faire period. This is scarcely to be wondered at when the composition of the planning boards is examined; to a great extent they consist of men with a necessary administrative experience, but with a social philosophy quite naturally belonging to another era. Nevertheless it remains true that the greatest lesson the public of Canada has ever had in national planning is now being given. And the simple fact emerges, that if this is the way to get more guns, it is also the way to get more butter. The methods used to save the country in time of war can be used to restore the country in time of peace.

Since this is the way our society is developing, the new problems confronting democracy in a planned society should now be faced. Such problems should, indeed, be investigated and dealt with by a special governmental board, which would report periodically to parliament on ways and means of safeguarding the maximum civil and personal liberties consistent with efficient planning. Liberty must be planned too, in the world we are entering. If the war is to be won in a spiritual as well as in a military sense such work cannot begin too soon. History can supply examples of countries which won wars and lost their domestic freedom at the same time. The effect of the present war upon Canada is to awaken a sense of social responsibility, a desire to serve the state and to face realities, out of which greater national unity and a more secure democracy may be born; but the war also stirs up passions and fears that hamper the free exchange of ideas on which democracy depends, and it gives reactionary elements an opportunity, often under the cover of a 'bloodshot patriotism,' to prepare the instruments of repression. The greater the number of social controls, the greater the danger of tyranny if they fall into the wrong hands; but the greater also is the opportunity of secure and ordered living if they are infused with a democratic purpose and made answerable to a democratic will.

Wars may be fought either by the methods of dictatorship or by the methods of democracy. Germany is using the former methods; we are attempting to make ourselves equally strong for self-defense without sacrifice of the democratic spirit. In adapting our existing institutions to the needs of defense we shall find that fewer limitations than we now imagine have to be placed on freedom of thought and discussion and more than we imagine on our existing rights of property and our present ways of producing goods. Yet most people will part with their freedom of thought before they will part with their investments, and therein lies our danger. The refusal of the oil producers in British Columbia to obey the law – was it not more subversive of democracy than anything that a harmless religious sect like the Witnesses of Jehovah have done? Yet we have proscribed the latter only.[3] Our interference with intellectual freedom in Canada so far has been greater than our interference with property. Our transition to a democratic planned society is going to be rendered more difficult because we have allowed wealth to accumulate to a dangerous degree, and from the owners of that wealth are bound to come most of the ideas and influences opposed to the changes we must undergo. Yet if we are to hold our own in the present world we must acquire the efficiency and strength that can come from the co-ordination of economic resources, and the ordered utilization of our productive capacity. We must plan as intelligently as our rivals, but more democratically.

Social Planning for Canada dealt very fully with the problem of how to keep a planned society democratic. But the planning under consideration there was for the peacetime purposes of social reconstruction, and the book presupposed a 'people's party,' fully representative of farmers, labor and consumers, as the motive power behind the planning. Today we are planning for wartime purposes, with primary emphasis on military organization, and without that kind of a people's party in control. The liberal party has a majority that justifies it in carrying on as Canada's war government, but even its members must admit that a party which has not held a convention in the past 20 years·still has something to learn about democracy. The need for organized thinking about democracy and wartime planning is thus particularly urgent. Here is a field of work, of immediate practical use for the attainment of the end for which the war is being fought, in which governments, the universities and other responsible bodies could co-operate. Nothing would strengthen this nation more than some official action that would symbolize an advance toward a more democratic social order, not after, but during the war. In war as in peace, democratic ideals can be attained, and a democratic war effort is still the most efficient, the most powerful and the most desirable.

EDITOR'S NOTES

1 P.C. Armstrong, a public relations executive for the CPR

2 Henry Ford, the American automobile manufacturer, hostile to unions, from 1937 to 1940 repeatedly offended against the terms of the National Labor Relations Act (Wagner-Connery Act) of 1935, which upheld the right of employees to organize and to bargain collectively through representatives of their own choosing. Ford's tactics included the use of company guards to beat up union organizers, and the firing of employees who were active in union organization.

   The multinational oil companies operating in British Columbia managed to subvert provincial government attempts in the 1930s to regulate the price of petroleum products. An effort in 1938–40 to set maximum pump prices for gasoline, though held by the courts to be legal, the companies managed to defeat by refusing to sell gasoline except for what they judged to be essential services.

3 On 4 July 1940 notice appeared in the *Canada Gazette* that the minister of justice, Ernest Lapointe, had caused an order in council to be passed which declared the Jehovah's Witnesses to be subversive. Prompted in part by the unwillingness of members of the sect to join in patriotic exercises or submit to military service, the action banning the Witnesses owed even more to the Roman Catholic hierarchy's intense hostility towards them. That hostility easily survived the end of the war, and persecution of the Witnesses reached a climax in Quebec in the late 1940s. This laid the basis for a well-known case that Scott pleaded before the Supreme Court of Canada and won, *Roncarelli* v. *Duplessis*. Damages were awarded in this case to a Montreal restaurant owner (and Jehovah's Witness) who had been deprived of his liquor licence because Premier Maurice Duplessis disapproved of his habit of providing bail for his co-religionists when these were arrested for trying to sell their literature.

XI

The Relationship of the White Collar Worker and Unions

The day after he delivered this address, Scott received a telephone call from Principal Cyril James of McGill. He asked for a copy of Scott's address. Scott replied that he did not have a prepared speech but spoke only from notes. James then asked him to write out the gist of his remarks. Scott agreed to this; the text reproduced here was the result.

The principal's interest was due to the annoyance of a member of the Board of Governors that a McGill professor should have been encouraging a union of bank clerks, and who had asked James to report on the matter. When he gave James a copy of the typescript of the address, Scott recalled: 'The principal asked me: "I suppose if I asked you to stop this kind of work you wouldn't, would you?" When I said no, he smiled wanly. I am sure he expected, and somewhat welcomed, the answer.' Soon afterwards Scott managed to secure distribution of the address in the form of a pamphlet distributed by the Steelworkers' Organizing Committee. However, unionism failed to make significant inroads among bank workers or other white collar workers at the time.
Address to Local No. 1, Royal Bank Division, Office and Professional Workers Organizing Committee, Montreal, 22 January 1942

... Tonight I am to speak to you about the relationship between the white collar workers and trades unions. It is a subject which, of course, concerns you directly. You are in the process of building a union. You know much more about that than I do. But perhaps I can give you a wider picture of the social and industrial relationships in Canada which will enable you to see your movement as part of a much bigger process of social evolution. I think you will understand better why unions are necessary to white collar workers when you approach the question from the broader point of view.

I want first of all to give you some figures on the class structure of Canada [see p. 50]. They are taken from Dr. Leonard Marsh's book *Canadians In and Out of Work* (p. 391) and are based on the census of 1931.[1]

You will note that the white collar worker is part of what Dr. Marsh calls the middle class. These workers, with the other types of workers in the middle class and in the working class proper, have a greater degree of common interest than have any other groups in the scale. The upper 0.6% need not concern us – they are the top ranking managers, financiers and industrialists, and can quite well take

SOCIAL CLASSES IN CANADA
Estimated distribution of families

Class	Number	Percent
Well-to-do	10,500	0.6
($10,000 a year or over)		
Middle classes	492,000	25.7
Smaller businessmen	(121,700)	(6.4)
Smaller professional men	(178,200)	(9.3)
White collar workers	(110,700)	(5.8)
Independent industrial workers	(81,400)	(4.2)
Working classes	815,000	42.5
Farm classes	598,700	31.2

care of themselves. The farmers are mostly owners of their farms and live on the sale of their goods, produced on the farm. They do not receive wages or salaries. But the white collar and other workers are all on wages and small salaries. They are a part of the wage system. This gives them a very special unity of status, whether they realize it or not. For wages and salaries are paid by employers, and employers, in our present economic system, have to run their businesses at a profit or else go bankrupt. Since all wages and salaries are part of the cost of production, and since profits are more likely to rise if costs are kept down, there is a constant pressure in the system itself to keep wages down. White collar and industrial workers are equally affected.

Now in an expanding economy, over a long period, other factors will tend to raise the level of wages. I will not pretend to go into the economics of the process. But the basic fact remains true of both the industrial and white collar worker, that in the adjustments of wages within the individual firm the search for profit tends to go opposed to the claim for higher wages. The distribution of profit each year, and the decision as to whether higher wages are possible or not, are always made by agents of the owners of industry, with no workers' representatives present. I have heard of one firm in Canada that put a worker on its board of directors, but this is certainly a rarity. A fundamental purpose of a union is to enable the workers – of all types – to have their proper claim on the earnings of a business duly presented. Otherwise, not being around when the profits are being shared they are all too likely to be overlooked.

From the point of view of modern cost-accounting, a business operation is 'successful' and 'efficient' if it shows a money profit. Some activities do not need to show a profit. The building of roads, for instance, however efficient, shows no profit. But we all know that the real profit comes in the contribution that roads make to the general well-being. This does not need to be estimated in money. The same is true of my business: education. It shows a dreadful loss in money every year, for which we tax ourselves. Yet is not education truly 'profitable'? Money profit, however necessary it is to measure it, is probably the poorest kind of profit there is. Yet in our present set-up this is what every business must strive for, and by this we judge it. Our scale of values is quite wrong. I have often thought it might be a good idea to compel every company in its annual statement to include figures showing the number of workers employed, the relation between this year's and last year's wages, numbers enjoying holidays with pay, and similar human items. Though not necessary to the financial showing of the company, it would be mighty interesting from the social viewpoint.

My first point, then, is that for the purpose of securing a fair division of the earnings of industry, it is just as valuable for the white collar as for the industrial workers to have an organization which can put their case effectively. This is what trades unions do. A good union will have a research department, studying its own industry, keeping track of developments, and enabling its members to speak with an authoritative voice. Possibly the white collar trades unions, because of their greater skill in bookkeeping and accounting, can perform this service not only for themselves but for the industrial unions as well.

Let us look further into the possibilities of trades unions, and ask ourselves whether they do not appear as useful for white collar workers as for others. That union is strength is a maxim too obvious to need proof. Can it be said that the white collar workers are strong today, in any sense of that word? Are they not just about the most silent partner there is in the whole industrial process? Farmers are often heard from. They have their organizations. They have even had their political parties. The Co-operative Commonwealth Federation is really the child of the Western Farmer Parties. The industrial workers are more and more being heard from, just exactly in proportion as they organize themselves. They are still not being heard from enough, for the great majority in Canada are still quite unorganized. The employing class is certainly heard from; it long ago learned the value of organization. Have you not heard of the Canadian Bankers Association? And what about the Canadian Manufacturers' Association, the Boards of Trade, the Chambers of Commerce? What indeed is the ordinary joint-stock company, except a sort of trades union of investors? Commercial corporations and their later progeny, the holding companies, are quite modern inventions. They enable groups of capitalists to act collectively together through agents of their own choosing. That is exactly what trades unions do for workers. Organization is the outstanding fact in modern society. If you do not put yourselves in that picture, you will be left out.

When I see all the fuss and bother that is made about unions by men who are more highly organized than any union can hope to be, I cannot help wondering at the blindness of those who are taken in by such talk. The case for unionism is so clear that the opposition to it takes on a more sinister aspect. Every employer who is genuinely interested in the welfare of his workers must want them organized. If he doesn't he cannot be genuinely interested in their welfare. His opposition must be intended to keep them suppressed and docile, or else it is based on an ignorance which in this day and age is quite inexcusable. It is not to be forgotten that the Dominion Government has proclaimed, as its official war policy, that unions should be recognized, and that it is now a crime for an employer to dismiss an employee for trades union activities.

Wherever we look around the world, we find that the happiest and most progressive democracies are also the ones where unions flourish. I have been in Sweden, for example, a country foremost in its freedom of the individual, its economic stability, its co-operative societies – and its unions. About 80% of Swedish workers are organized. In Canada, only about 20% are. In New Zealand, under the labour government, unionism is universal and compulsory. England, of course, is the natural home of unionism, with labour leaders prominent in the War Cabinet. The New Deal in the United States represented a tremendous social advance in that country, and it was accompanied by a great advance in trades unions. In Russia all workers are unionized, and the morale and strength of that country needs no reminder these days.[2] Conversely, the first thing that Hitler did in Germany was to destroy the unions. Pétain is trying to do the same thing now in France.[3] Fascism knows that unions are dangerous – to fascism. They are the heart of democracy.

This brings me to what I consider to be the greatest virtue of the union movement. It is not just a method of getting better working conditions and higher wages, though these benefits are not to be despised. It is not just a method by which workers, too, can join other organized groups in a battle for selfish advantage. It is a great movement for human freedom and emancipation. In its early stages, especially when employers oppose it, it causes conflict. You may have to stand fast against attack; if so, remember that others have done so and have won through. Be true to each other and to your great cause, and nothing can stop you. But not for conflict are you being formed; your aim is human advancement and social progress. You can be a creative force in society. You can give status to men and women who are merely cogs in a soulless machine; you can bring back human dignity to labour. Every great religion has taught the sanctity of labour; you can give expression to that truth. You will compel society to consider your rights and to include your claims in its calculations. You will give a broader base to our democracy, for none of us can be strong when some are weak. And from your ranks will come new leaders, able to make their contribution to the common cause.

I see one way in which white collar workers and industrial workers are united in a common interest. They both need the same kind of political representation. They both need a democratic political organization in which their interests will predominate in proportion to their numerical strength in society. If you take the farmers, workers and white collar groups together you have the great majority of the Canadian people. The true test of the success of our economic policies in the past is: What has it done for these classes? Unless they are well served and protected the system is a failure. Unless political parties put the interests of this great majority above all other interests, they are a failure. You can judge for yourselves how far you think our political parties have lived up to this test in the past few years. If you find the answer unsatisfactory, ask yourselves who runs these parties. How is their policy formulated? Can the ordinary man and woman participate in the party life between elections as well as during elections? Who pays the cost of elections? Do you? If somebody else controls [party life], that person will look after his interests before he looks after your own. You will find that with a union you will take a new interest in politics. You will train leaders who can step into public life from your own ranks. That is how labour and social-democratic governments rose to power in Sweden, Norway, Denmark, New Zealand, Australia and other countries. And that is why the laws of those countries have been more favourable to the common people than our laws have been.

Finally, let me warn you against an attitude of mind which has had much influence in the past in keeping white collar classes from getting organized. This is the belief, carefully fostered from outside, that white collar workers are 'above' unionism. They are flattered by being given a 'salary' instead of a 'wage.' Do not be fooled by this appeal to snobbery. Look the facts in the face. A low income remains low no matter what it is called. A supposedly higher social status is no substitute for freedom and influence. Real status comes from the possession of power, and this can be gained only by organization. In a true democracy, every man is the equal of every other man if he gives of his best. We do not want these false class divisions in Canada; we want a greater sense of unity of purpose and of effort. You will be contributing to our national unity if you co-operate with your fellow workers in the great task of securing to every man and woman their just reward for labour and their equal rank as fellow-citizens in an advancing democracy.

EDITOR'S NOTES

1 Leonard Marsh was a McGill economist who during the 1930s directed the McGill Social Sciences Research Committee. Funded by the Rockefeller Foundation, the committee sponsored the publication of approximately ten volumes in economics and sociology. Marsh succeeded Scott as national president of the LSR, serving in that capacity from 1937 to 1939.

2 In June 1941 Germany had invaded the Soviet Union, and by December had penetrated
close to the outskirts of Moscow. The Russians defended themselves tenaciously,
and early in 1942 were counter-attacking German forces that proved to be inadequately
equipped for the Russian winter.

3 Marshal Henri Philippe Pétain was a hero of the First World War who in 1940 became
chief of the collaborationist French government that had its capital in Vichy.

XII

A Decade of the League for Social Reconstruction

*By early 1942 the LSR had virtually ceased to exist. Only the branches in Toronto
and Montreal, always by far the largest, still showed faint signs of life. Some
members had gone into the armed forces or were working for the federal government. Others were devoting their spare time to the CCF, which by 1941 was
showing signs of increasing strength. Indeed, although the league expired quietly sometime in the later winter or early spring, it lived on in the CCF. Scott
himself served as something of a symbol of this development, for in 1942 he
became national chairman of the party.*

*In this article Scott looked back on the LSR's years of activity and on its
achievements.*

From *Saturday Night*, vol. 57, 24 January 1942. Reprinted by permission of
Saturday Night

Ten years ago, in January 1932, about eighteen people met in Toronto to draft a
manifesto for a new social order in Canada. So large an undertaking for so small a
group was undoubtedly presumptuous, the more so as most of them were
professors – men,[1] that is, whose ideas about practical affairs were by definition academic and hence untrustworthy. Those were days when the aura of
infallibility had not yet worn off the captains of industry, though in places it
was wearing thin; nor had 'brain trusts' yet become an acceptable institution of
government.[2]

However, the world was due for great changes, that was clear, and these
individuals were determined to create an organization through which to dissemi-
nate their views about the future. Thus was born the League for Social
Reconstruction. It defined itself as 'an association of men and women who are
working for the establishment in Canada of a social order in which the basic

principle regulating production, distribution and service will be the common good rather than private profit.' The substitution of democratic planning for capitalist anarchy was the central idea of the movement.

Ten years is a short time in the life of human communities. Great changes come slowly, perhaps particularly slowly in Canada, a country which has not yet fully awakened from the long sleep of colonialism. But future historians will probably consider the debate of the 1930s as being one of the most compressed periods of revolutionary change that the world has ever known. To gain some measure of how far we have moved, even in Canada, let the reader substitute the words 'war effort' for the words 'common good' in the LSR statement and then ask himself whether the amended declaration of purpose would not be accepted by 95% of Canadians today.

If, by subordinating private profit to 'war effort' we can produce the astonishing increase of physical goods and services now evident in Canada by comparison with 1932, why could we not have produced the same increase before the war by subordinating private profit to the 'common good'? The war effort needs ships, guns, planes, tanks. The common good needs houses, schools, hospitals, roads, libraries, museums and more goods and services of all kinds. One is as easy to supply as the other.

The only thing wrong with the LSR idea, it seems, was that we did not adopt it. Now we have been forced toward it by the war emergency. Mr. Hitler has been more persuasive than all the LSR publications. Changing the economic system, it becomes clear, is primarily a problem of changing our habits of mind.

The LSR achievements in the way of publications have not been spectacular. It took as its model the Fabian Society, the early tutor of the British Labour Party. Even Canadian radicals have their imperialist connections; or perhaps it would be truer to say that they must look outside the 'Tory Dominion,' as the *New Statesman* has called us, for their inspiration.[3] The American League for Industrial Democracy was another model consciously followed. But is is easier to copy an organization than to reproduce its personnel, and Canada could have used a Beatrice and a Sidney Webb. More particularly did we need a Bernard Shaw and an H.G. Wells: men, that is, who could inject new ideas with the needle of art rather than through an attempt to feed the patient with the tough meat of statistics and economic analysis.[4] But alas, all Canadian art has done for us is to teach us to admire our landscape through pictures; it has not yet opened our eyes to our social vices or portrayed for us a glorious future. Yet this seems the only way to reach the multitude.

Nevertheless the LSR did not perhaps do so badly, using such poor things as Frank Underhill, King Gordon, Eugene Forsey, Leonard Marsh, J.F. Parkinson, Graham Spry, George Grube and others.[5] Its major work was the preparation and, rather surprisingly to itself, the publication of *Social Planning for Canada*. Into

that cumbersome and rather disjointed volume went the arguments, the complaints, possibly the vision, of the planners. Though only seven men signed their
names as co-authors of the book, its actual writing and compilation was the result
of the joint effort of fully twenty-five individuals who might with some fairness be
classed as experts in their fields.

No doubt this collective cooking is evident in the broth. Still the book sold, thus
meeting the final test of capitalism. It ran through a second printing, and the
royalties financed the LSR for another two years. Not a little of the credit for this
success must be given to the anonymous pamphleteer ... who wrote a sixty page
attack on the volume and its pernicious ideas, and had his diatribe distributed from
the head office of his employers, one of the largest corporations of Canada,[6] to a
number of business men. That sent the sale up by the hundreds.

The only other book to be published by the LSR was *Democracy Needs
Socialism*, intended as a more popular version of *Social Planning for Canada*. It is
doubtful if the LSR could ever be popular in any sense of the term, and this second
venture received, as it deserved, less attention than its predecessor, though
managing to dispose of itself in time. Then there were a number of pamphlets
brought out during the decade: *Combines and the Consumer, Dividends and the
Depression, Social Reconstruction and the* B.N.A. *Act, Does Canada Need
Immigrants?, The Church and the Economic Order, Recovery – For Whom?,
Pioneers in Poverty, Rich Man, Poor Man*.

These did not achieve the wide scale that pamphlets must if they are to result in
political change, but no doubt helped to spread the LSR ideas. The LSR also
presented a brief to the Sirois Commission[7] ..., subsequently published under the
title *Canada – One or Nine?*, the proposals of which can truly be said to have found
a considerable degree of acceptance in the final recommendations of the
Commission. The LSR bought, and saved from bankruptcy, the *Canadian Forum*,
which it still owns. LSR members, too, have done their fair share of public
lecturing, both to their own and to other groups. At one time the organization had
as many as twelve branches.[8]

From the very first the relationship between the LSR and the CCF caused some
concern. Obviously both were aiming at the same kind of new social order. But the
LSR carefully refrained from affiliating with the CCF, so as to preserve its
independence and its right to criticize. Hence LSR publications are not official CCF
publications. The LSR, too, was first in the field, for the CCF was not formed till
July 1932. It is interesting to note, however, that the political party was formed
entirely independently of the intellectual movement, for no LSR members attended
the Calgary meeting at which the CCF was organized.[9] Mr. Woodsworth, it is true,
was president of both movements – but then nothing progressive and democratic
could occur in those days without J.S. Woodsworth being somewhere in the
picture.[10] It was not long before most LSR members became individual members of

the CCF, and a comparison between the Regina manifesto of the CCF in 1933 and the LSR manifesto of 1932 will indicate the degree of influence which the eastern theoreticians had upon the western political movement.

Persecution? Some, but perhaps not more than was to be expected in a movement starting where it did at the time it did. There were some near escapes from loss of positions, and one prominent member of the inner LSR group was deprived of his post in a Canadian college.[11] His exile to Siberia meant a new and successful career in the United States. Such things occur even in the best democracies. The Canadian touch was the later discovery that a prominent member of his Board of Trustees was connected with a corporation that had failed to fulfil all its obligations with respect to corporation taxes.

Today, after ten years, the LSR has virtually ceased to function as an organization. There has been a dispersal of leaders, and the actualities of politics, particularly since the new advances of the CCF, seem more attractive today than the pursuit of theoretic truth. This is perhaps a pity, for if ever Canadians should be concerned about their future it is now. Victory must be won, but it is going to require more than military victory to steer us through the coming years: the total elimination of Canada is more likely to occur through annexation to the United States than through occupation by Hitler. We shall only survive as a nation if we have a live ideal of ourselves as a nation. The LSR has contributed a great deal toward the formulation of that ideal.

EDITOR'S NOTES

1 Actually, at least two of the eighteen were women: Irene Biss, a lecturer in economics at the University of Toronto, and Isabel Thomas, a Toronto high school teacher of English.

2 In 1933 a Winnipeg newspaperman, G.V. Ferguson, referred to the LSR in print as the 'CCF brain trust.' The reference was to the group of academics and intellectuals who flocked to Washington in the early days of the 'New Deal' announced by President Franklin Delano Roosevelt.

3 The *New Statesman* was a prominent British political weekly with strong Labour sympathies.

4 Beatrice and Sidney Webb were important in amassing statistics and other information in support of the cause of social change. Like the playwright and essayist George Bernard Shaw and the novelist H.G. Wells, the Webbs were active in the Fabian Society, that organization of left-wing intellectuals which began in the 1880s to agitate for a more egalitarian and socialistic Britain. The League for Industrial Democracy was an analogous organization in the United States; associated with it in the 1920s and 1930s were socialists like Harry Laidler and Norman Thomas.

5 Underhill taught history at the University of Toronto; King Gordon was Professor of

Christian Ethics at United Theological Seminary in Montreal, and later travelling secretary for the Fellowship for a Christian Social Order; Forsey and Marsh taught economics at McGill and Parkinson at the University of Toronto; Spry was a journalist and political organizer; Grube taught classics at Trinity College, University of Toronto.

6 The author of this attack on the LSR book was P.C. Armstrong, a public relations executive employed by tne Canadian Pacific Railway company.

7 The Royal Commission on Dominion-Provincial Relations (1937–40)

8 In fact, at the beginning of 1933 the LSR had seventeen branches, from Montreal and Verdun to Vancouver and Victoria.

9 In fact, LSR members from branches in Alberta and British Columbia attended the Calgary conference as observers.

10 J.S. Woodsworth served as honorary national president of the LSR from 1932 until his death early in 1942.

11 King Gordon was dismissed from his position, ostensibly on budgetary grounds. Many believed that his outspoken Christian socialism was a more important reason. To this day no conclusive proof for this belief has been found. In 1937 Gordon moved to New York and joined a publishing house; in the early 1940s he was managing editor of the weekly *Nation*.

XIII

What Did 'No' Mean?

All Canadian political leaders entered the Second World War promising that there would be no conscription for overseas military service. The adoption of that policy in 1917 had created wounds that were by no means healed when in 1939 war broke out in Europe once more. By late 1941, however, English Canadians were increasingly demanding a stronger demonstration of Canadian commitment to the war. Conscription for overseas service – conscription for home service had been in effect since June 1940 – became the symbol of this demand. The Conservative party, once again led by Arthur Meighen, adopted a policy of conscription. Prime Minister Mackenzie King and most of his Cabinet did not think that conscription was necessary from a military point of view, but the change in Tory policy put them under considerable pressure. King found a means of channelling public opinion into a relatively harmless path: there was to be a plebiscite in which the voters would be asked whether they would release the government from its pledge not to introduce conscription. In the plebiscite, held on 27 April 1942, English Canadians voted mostly

*in favour, whereas French Canadians voted against. Scott's article is an
interpretation of that negative vote. It subsequently appeared in the form of a
pamphlet,* The Plebiscite Vote in Quebec, *which received wide circulation in
Quebec.*

*By the time the plebiscite took place, Meighen's attempt to return to the House
of Commons had met with failure. He ran in a by-election in the supposedly safe
Tory seat of York South. In accordance with tradition, the Liberals did not
nominate a candidate to oppose him. Less concerned with tradition, the ccF did
contest the constituency. With financial help from the Liberals, provided very
quietly, and backed by a good organization, the ccF candidate, a teacher named
Joseph Noseworthy, dealt Meighen a stunning defeat. Meighen soon afterwards
resigned the Tory leadership, and was succeeded by the premier of Manitoba,
John Bracken.*

From *The Canadian Forum*, vol. 22, June 1942, pp. 71–3. Reprinted by permission of *The Canadian Forum*

The important thing for Canadians to understand about the plebiscite of April 27th
is not what the 'Yes' vote meant, but what the 'No' vote meant.

The 'Yes' vote itself is obscure enough to satisfy even the most cunning
politician. It was not a vote for conscription, since the question was never asked
whether or not Canadians wanted conscription for overseas service. That simple
question would have been altogether too straightforward to suit our present
political habits. The question was whether or not the government was to be free to
use Canadian manpower as it saw fit for the future. But there can be no doubt that
many who voted 'Yes' meant that they wanted conscription, and wanted it now.
Many others who voted 'Yes' did so because Mr. King made it appear that a
negative vote would have indicated a want of confidence in himself; he thus neatly
converted the Conservative and ccF parties, which had urged a 'Yes' vote, into
Liberal election machines. Though at the last minute this intention was denied, the
impression was not eradicated, as any glance at the newspapers will show. So
people voted 'Yes' for many different and even contradictory reasons.

Nevertheless this does not confront the country with any great difficulty or
danger. The yes voters will for the most part approve of a more resolute war policy.
It is the 'No' votes which should be studied and weighed, because a misunder-
stand-ing of this vote, and action by the government based on that misunderstanding, could easily result in grave peril to our country. No man in his senses, even if
he is willing to sacrifice the whole future of Canada as a nation in order to increase
her present war effort, could wish to take a step which would immediately divide
our forces and so weaken the national will. It would be about as sensible as if the
English Tories were to start a major drive on trades unions in order to speed up war
production, or Chiang Kai-shek were to revive his former attacks upon the

Communist armies now fighting in his ranks.[1] Aggravating internal dissensions is a curious sort of loyalty to the United Nations.

Yet that is what certain groups in Canada have already done by their treatment of the conscription issue, and what these same groups are still doing by their misreading of the plebiscite vote. And though French Canada is not without her own groups who play politics with these vital matters, nevertheless the major responsibility for the difficulty lies with English Canada. It is English-speaking Canadians who have been in charge of the major domestic decisions in this as in past wars in which Canada has engaged. Seldom has an effort been made to get to the roots of what appears to be a peculiar reluctance on the part of Quebec to see things as Anglo-Saxons see them. Seldom has a sympathetic analysis been made of the currents of thought in French Canada. Every English-speaking Canadian knows that though Mr. Meighen and Tim Buck both urged a yes vote in the plebiscite, they did so for very different reasons.[2] Yet how many people can distinguish between those French-speaking Canadians who voted no because they like isolation, and those who voted no because they like Canada?

British people everywhere would do well to reflect on one fact that this war has brought strikingly to light, namely, that the non-British peoples who are supposed to enjoy the blessings of the British Empire do not seem to appreciate those blessings as much as we have been taught that they did. The Irish underwent British rule for 800 years, and in this crisis prefer not to fight with Britain at all. The Boer leader, Hertzog, advocated neutrality for South Africa in 1939, and though Smuts found enough support to defeat him there is still a dangerous anti-war element in that dominion.[3] The great Indian leader Nehru was in jail for a long time because he refused to fight for India on British terms, and recently rejected the Cripps offer of dominion status as inadequate.[4] The Burmese, after 100 years within the Empire, seem actually to have fought for the Japanese invaders. And now Quebec votes 'no' on the plebiscite. No doubt the Tories will say that this all goes to prove the superiority of the Anglo-Saxon over the 'native.' But people possessed of any intelligence and any concern for the cause of human freedom will be profoundly disturbed by these danger-signals, and will take time off for a little self-criticism. There obviously have been serious mistakes in policy. It may not be too late to rectify some of these mistakes.

Now there is one common factor that has been present in all these situations, and which may go a long way toward explaining them. It is the factor of British rule *over* these other races. These curious non-British people seem to like freedom so much that they want to be free even from British rule. Where this freedom has been most conceded, there is less difficulty in finding common ground in the war effort, and where it has been least conceded, there is more difficulty. There would never have been a General Smuts in South Africa if there had not been a grant of dominion status to his country. Perhaps if Premier U Saw of Burma had been granted the new status he was seeking conditions might have been different there.

The Irish do not yet feel they are really free, since Ulster is still under British rule. Yet though Mr. de Valera does not grant bases to the allies he nevertheless suppresses the IRA.[5] In other words, it is generally true to say that the unwillingness of certain parts of the British empire to fall in line with a British idea of 'total war' is at bottom due to a love of liberty. They want democracy at home before they begin dying for it abroad. This attitude can be pressed too far, no doubt, when the enemy is at the gate; nevertheless it is a very human attitude and at bottom a very proper attitude.

How does all this relate to Quebec and the plebiscite? It is very closely related. The large 'no' vote was chiefly a protest, not against the war, but against the idea of imperialism.

The people of Quebec have long memories. Is not the motto of the province *Je me souviens*? They look at each new political event from the point of view of their own special experience. No political issue in Canada is so surrounded by imperialist associations as conscription for overseas service. A country called Canada with European connections has existed for over four hundred years. When was the first expeditionary force of Canadians sent by a Canadian government to serve in an overseas war? Not till forty years ago, in the Boer War. Then Canadians went to assist the empire in imposing its rule upon a small nation against its will. That evil act has been dearly paid for in this century. Even those who may still think that it was justifiable will recognize that it started an association of ideas that has never yet been eradicated – the idea that Canadian armies go abroad only in the interests of British imperialism. And if any reader thinks this is opening up an old sore, let him remember that the Boer War produced Henri Bourassa, who was the founder of *Le Devoir*, and that both of these avowed enemies of imperialism are very much alive and active in this war.

The First World War added another complication in Quebec to the idea of imperialist expeditionary forces. It introduced the idea of compulsory overseas service for French Canadians at the insistence of the British majority in Canada. And mixed up with the conscription campaign of 1917 was a degree of political corruption and financial scheming (a Union government was needed as much to save railway investments as to impose conscription)[6] enough to obscure even the highest motives. During the interval between the two world wars most of English-speaking Canada came to the view that conscription for overseas service was a bad mistake which ought not to be repeated. That was the official view of every political party.

Then came World War II. From the point of view of Quebec, what had changed? At the outset, very little. The conflict started as a European war: England and France against Germany. The Tories were running England. Should Canadians be conscripted for that? Everyone agreed they should not. Not another country in this hemisphere considered the issue at that time a life and death struggle between democracy and tyranny. Quebec accepted Canada's immediate participation, and certainly cannot be blamed if she was not immediately caught up with the idea of a great crusade. And for all the talk there has been about our free entry into the war, the fact remains that from Quebec's point of view we had no right to neutrality – had not Mr. Lapointe said so? – and therefore there was no choice in the matter.[7] In the same way the sending of the expeditionary force to England was accepted as inevitable, even though there was no vote in the Canadian Parliament on the question. But when Quebec saw the conscription issue being raised once again by a group of Toronto imperialists and a small clique in the Conservative party, and being used once more as a weapon with which to defeat a Liberal premier and the Liberal party, then Quebec closed its ranks. This was something they all knew about; this was what Mayor Houde had predicted when he marched off to the concentration camp.[8] And no new factors in the world situation, such as Pearl Harbor, the United States entry into the war, or the sweeping Japanese victories, even when added to the fall of France, had altered the internal appearance of the conscription issue in Quebec. Undoubtedly to many English-speaking Canadians these new dangers justified a change of policy about manpower; French Canada must realise that the yes vote in the eight provinces cannot be simply explained as a result of the imperial connection. The fact remains, however, that Quebec opinion was different, and saw the old familiar features in the conscription drive. Along both shores of the St. Lawrence it still looked like conscription imposed by imperialists, run by imperialists and utilized by imperialists. The ill-considered Canadian expedition sent to Hong Kong at British request did not improve matters.[9] Besides, were not Canadian troops really needed now at home, and had not Australia, South Africa and Northern Ireland refused conscription? So history repeated itself. Quebec voted on April 27 not on the question as to whether the government's hands should be freed, but on the question as to whether Canadians should be forced to defend England and the British Empire. It emerged surprised and strengthened by its own unanimity.

Surely all English-speaking Canadians, and people outside Canada, can understand such a result even if they regret it? Surely, if one grants the premises from which Quebec's thinking started, there was no other vote that could have been given by any self-respecting people? There did not seem to be any need for Canada to have any more conscription for her own defence. Not lack of manpower, but lack of machines, has always been stressed as the chief Allied difficulty. And surely for all Canadians the remedy is fairly clear. As Mr. Leslie Roberts has so well expressed it,[10] Canada has to make up her mind whether she is fighting this war as a British Colony or as one of the United Nations. It is the continuing element of colonialism in Canada's war effort, real or apparent, that is causing so much trouble. We have not made up our minds to be an independent nation in world affairs, thinking out our own policy and making whatever contribution that policy requires, and consequently everything we do looks as though it were done for somebody else and not for ourselves. We have failed even to provide ourselves with the symbols of nationhood. Our war posters and publicity are filled with suggestions that we are just a little lion alongside a Big Lion. We pretend that the bravery of Londoners is greater than that of the people in Chungking or Leningrad. We have been guilty of forms of racial pride that are naturally obstacles to co-operation with other races. There is a close parallel between certain difficulties in Canada and certain others in India.

The French Canadians mean what they say when they say they will do everything necessary for the defence of Canada. They have already accepted conscription of manpower for this purpose, and they do not mind whether this means going to Alaska, Greenland or Panama. It is a good deal farther from Quebec City to Alaska than from Quebec City to London. Why the difference in attitude toward compulsory service in the two places? Solely because service across the Atlantic represents the imperialist tie, and looks like defence of the British Empire rather than defence of Canada or Canadian interests. Who will decide the use of Canadian troops overseas? Who really decides when they are to go and where they are to go? These questions touch the realities of the problem in Quebec. The more Canada insists on having a voice of her own in the joint Allied Councils, the more she gets away from the old military tradition that her part is just to 'offer' troops for Britain to use where Britain wants them, the easier it will be to bridge the gulf between Quebec and the other provinces. All that Quebec means by the 'no' vote is that she does not wish her children to die for any country other than their own. This is nothing very startling.

A fair assessment of the whole situation, of course, must include the small vocal element in Quebec that is trying to capitalize on the present discontent in order to gain power and prestige, and that has leanings toward a clerical-fascism of a Spanish or Italian type. There are such people, but they are no more Quebec than Mr. Meighen is Canada. There are, shall we say, imperfect democrats in all parts of Canada, but the ones in Quebec are much less powerful than those outside Quebec, and less misleading because they do not beat the patriotic drum so loudly. The same people who voted 'no' so overwhelmingly in Mr. St. Laurent's constituency, only a short time ago preferred Mr. St. Laurent to a nationalist candidate who posed as the 'De Valera of Canada.'[11] A war effort planned by Canadians for Canadians, in conjunction with all our Allies, respecting minority points of view and deeply concerned for the common man in office, field and factory, will receive all the support that is needed from Quebec no matter where the battlefields may be. But it must be a war effort free from the restricting concepts of race and empire, free from control by vested interests at home, and devoted in deeds as well as in words to the great principles of human liberty and human brotherhood which it professes to be serving.

EDITOR'S NOTES

1 Chiang Kai-shek was a Chinese general and leader of the Kuomintang or Nationalists. His claim to govern all of China was effectively challenged in the immediate post-war period by Mao Tse-tung's Communist forces, and Chiang was forced to take refuge on the island of Taiwan, the only part of China to remain in Nationalist hands.

2 Tim Buck was leader of the Communist Party of Canada. Banned since 1940 under the War Measures Act, it re-emerged late in 1942 as the Labor Progressive Party.

3 General James B.M. Hertzog was an Afrikaner leader and Nationalist prime minister of South Africa from 1924 to 1939. General Jan C. Smuts, leader of the Unionist party, was prime minister from 1921 to 1924 and again from 1939 to 1948.

4 Jawaharlal Nehru was after Mahatma Gandi the most important Hindu political leader in the 1940s, and in 1947 became prime minister of independent India. Sir Stafford Cripps was a Labour member of Winston Churchill's War Cabinet, and leader of a British mission to India during the war.

5 Eamon de Valera was prime minister of the Irish Free State, later the Republic of Eire, for most of the years from 1932 to 1959. Although committed in principle to the unification of Ireland, his government suppressed the Irish Republican Army (IRA), which sought (and seeks) to secure the goal of unification by terrorist means. De Valera did so because the IRA challenged the power and policies of Dublin as well as those of London.

6 The Union government, led by Sir Robert Borden, consisted of Conservatives and conscriptionist Liberals, mainly from Ontario and the West, who had abandoned Sir Wilfrid Laurier over the conscription issue. The railway investments referred to were particularly those in the Canadian Northern Railway and the Grand Trunk Pacific Railway. Both, with several other lines, became components of the Canadian National Railway system.

7 Ernest Lapointe was in 1939 minister of justice and King's Quebec lieutenant. He died in November 1941. It was certainly Scott's opinion in 1939 that Canada had no legal right to neutrality.

8 Camillien Houde, Mayor of Montreal, was interned from 1940 to 1944 for opposing the registration of manpower under the National Resources Mobilization Act of June 1940.

9 Two battalions, the Royal Rifles of Canada and the Winnipeg Grenadiers, arrived in Hong Kong scant weeks before the outbreak of general war in the Pacific on 7 December 1941. They had not reached an advanced level of training and still lacked some of their equipment when the Japanese attack came. Those who did not die in action were made prisoners of war.

10 Leslie Roberts was a Canadian journalist, author of *We Must Be Free* (Toronto 1939) and other works.

11 Louis St Laurent, who succeeded Ernest Lapointe as minister of justice, won a by-election in Quebec East in February 1942. His opponent was the right-wing Quebec nationalist Paul Bouchard, who ran under the banner of the new Parti Canadien.

XIV

A Note on Canadian War Poetry

This article is included here not because of what it says about poetry, but because of what it says about a frame of mind which Scott called 'our Canadian colonialism.' He believed this colonialism had led many Canadians into unthinking acceptance of the war in 1939, and still ruled their minds three years later. He captured this colonialism in some lines from his poem about Prime Minister R.B. Bennett, 'Ode to a Politician':

At school he learns the three Canadian things:
Obedience, Loyalty and Love of Kings.

To serve a country other than his own
Becomes for him the highest duty known,

To keep antiquity alive forever
The proper object of his young endeavour.

Hence though the Northland calls him to be free
He never sheds this first servility.

When asked whether and when this colonialism had disappeared, Scott said to me that vestiges of it were still alive at the time of the debate over the new Canadian flag in 1964, but that since then it seemed to have faded away.
From *Preview*, no. 9, December 1942, pp. 3–5

A live movement in poetry will reflect and often foreshadow the creative movements in its social environment. Poets sensitive to the growing forces of their age will give symbolic expression to those forces and will become a potent instrument of social change. The more revolutionary their epoch the more markedly will their writing differ from that of their predecessors, for they will be obliged to experiment with new form and imagery in order to convey their new ideas. Their style will thus at first appear crude and unpolished, and will shock the established taste. They will be laughed at for their clumsiness and obscurity. So the poets of the Romantic Revival absorbed the revolutionary fervour of regicidal France, threw overboard the outmoded classicism of the 18th century, and faced misunderstanding and sharp criticism until time had carried their contemporaries forward to the new positions. So too the American poetry revival in the first quarter of this century, with its greater freedom, variety and humanism, prepared the way for the new social thinking which emerged politically through the New Deal.[1] Carl Sandburg's robust popular verse heralded the 'forgotten man' of the new politics and broke ground for the CIO.[2] The English revival of the 1930's showed at least a deep dissatisfaction with the pre-war English society.

A dead tradition of poetic writing, on the other hand, reflects nothing but the attitudes of the past, expressed in the clichés of the past. It will fear and oppose the new in literature because the new spells death to itself. In Canada, where so much tradition, deprived of content, has become mere habit, this influence produces the kind of poem with which we are all too painfully familiar – neat, accurate, unambiguous, earnest and ordinary. The surprising thing is how long such sterility can live and go on reproducing itself. Ultimately, however, the gap between itself and life grows so wide that collapse occurs. Usually the well-established tradition is sanctified by state approval in some form. At meetings of its devotees medals are given, the 'moderns' are scorned, and tea is poured.

To read *Voices of Victory*, described as 'Representative Poetry of Canada in Wartime' (Macmillan, 1941), is to find oneself buried in just this kind of tradition. In other days the inclination would have been to throw the book aside and waste no more time over it. In these days of critical choices for humanity, and for Canada as part of humanity, such a phenomenon as this anthology is perhaps worth a moment's analysis. We can all feel the uncertainty of the present world situation, poised as we are on a political watershed. Our doubt is not with regard to military victory, which we believe can be won, but with regard to the peace, which can so easily be lost. There has clearly been too little change since the war began in the social outlook of some of the principal Allied powers, and least of all in Canada. Perhaps in Canada more than anywhere else the old traditions are still with us, as dominant as before. Wherever we look – in politics, in the churches, in education, in business, in the press – the pre-war Canadian social order survives, slightly modified but basically unreformed. Yet there are new forces stirring underneath the old crust, moving deeply in the hearts and minds of men, giving us common cause with other races and nations. Of these forces a vital poetic movement might be made. *Voices of Victory* does not seem to be aware that they exist. It is bad enough to have so little external sign of these new impulses in Canadian politics, but this is partly understandable since the primacy of military effort over social reform appeals to many. What is more discouraging is the utter lack on the part of these Canadian writers of the sense of impending change, of the need for democratic advance, and of any new outlook on the contemporary world. Judging by this volume, nothing has altered in the realm of poetry or politics since 1914. Needless to say there is no new style or diction, no venture in original modes of expression.

These poems were selected from 766 entries to a contest organised by the Poetry Group of the Toronto Branch of the Canadian Authors Association. The purpose of the contest, we are told, was twofold: first, to contribute the proceeds of sales to the Canadian Red Cross British Bomb Victims Fund, and secondly, to 'let the poetic genius of Canada and the Canadian people sound a spiritual challenge to the brutality of enemy despots and tyrants.' The frontispiece, a reproduction of a prize medal donated by the Athlones[3] and containing their effigy, prepares the reader for this priority of ideas. Then comes Charles G.D. Roberts' 'Canada Speaks to Britain': 'She calls. And we will answer to our last breath.' This sets the tone for what follows. Canada's essential colonialism stands out everywhere in this answer to England's call. One would gather that before the call came all was right with the world, and after the call ceases no doubt the poets will return to their non-American nightingales. The prize poem, 'Recompense,' leads us through the 'faery foam / of blackthorn blossoms breaking' to 'England's dower / of deathless loveliness.' It has the lush glamour of a cricket match: all Gentlemen and no Players. The second prize goes to 'Canadian Crusade,' a poem which is at least free from nostalgia; its sentimentality is local rather than transatlantic. The third prize is given to a eulogy of Churchill.[4]

There follow twenty poems receiving honourable mention, 'in order of merit.' After this the contributors are unranked. Most of the poems deal in traditional manner with the standard themes of sacrifice, suffering, death, with special reference to torpedoed children. Nowhere in the entire volume is there an echo, even faint, of a people's war or a people's peace, or of the war within the war represented by the great cry of exploited humanity for the promised four freedoms. Exception should be made for a poem by Kenneth Leslie (unranked) who has at least perceived the significance of Russia's part in the struggle. Nor is there any evidence that these writers perceive the profound drama of man's attempt to purge himself through suffering of his own making, or that they feel the profound tragedies of an age that threw away its last victory and hesitates now to make vital its war aims by an immediate application of their principles. All is apparently quiet on the philosophic front. So we get sentiment but no passion, loyalty but no dynamic assertion, Ministry of Information leaflets but very little poetry.

Of all the contributing factors that go to make up the state of mind reflected here the deepest and most dominant, in my opinion, is our Canadian colonialism. This has little (though some) relationship with outward governmental forms. It is more a cast of thought, a mental climate. The colonial is an incomplete person. He must look to others for his guidance, and far away for his criterion of value. He copies the parental style instead of incorporating what is best in something of his own. He undervalues his own contribution and overestimates what others can do for him. Old greatness is more to him than new truth. Above all he fears originality, which might cut him off from his secure base. The outside world of men seems foreign and hostile to him, and he will cling to the ancient traditions long after they have been abandoned in his metropolis. No matter how great his sincerity or how devoted his attachment, he is incapable, while suffering from this political Oedipus complex, of rising above the ordinary. For the most perfect copy is second-rate, while the least originality is unique. And when the wave of any future reaches him, it is but a ripple. How a country can shake itself out of this state of mind I do not know, but the duty of the poet is to help in the enfranchisement, not to decorate the ancient chariot.

EDITOR'S NOTES

1 New Deal was the name given to the reformist legislative program associated with the first term of President Franklin Delano Roosevelt (1933–37).
2 The Congress of Industrial Organizations. See above, letter to David Lewis, 11 July 1937, note 1.
3 The Earl of Athlone was governor-general of Canada at this time.
4 Winston Churchill was prime minister of Great Britain from 1940 to 1945.

XV

Canadian Federalism and the Provinces: Some Lessons from the War

The war brought economic controls, imposed by the federal government under the authority of the War Measures Act, that were constitutionally impossible in time of peace. In this address to young lawyers in Quebec City, Scott pointed out what he believed to be the positive aspects of these controls and argued that some of them would be desirable and even necessary after the war ended. He noted that changes in the British North America Act would be necessary to retain these controls.

Abridged version of an address delivered in French to the Junior Bar Association, Quebec City, 27 November 1943

We Canadians cannot ignore the BNA Act; our present is based on it and our future depends on it. We either modify it to suit our present needs, or we leave it alone and let events dictate its future shape. It is evident that we live in a changing world, and to this inevitability of change constitutions are no exception.

Today, because of the war, we have a very centralized government; federal authority touches every aspect of provincial affairs. So much so that it may truly be said that Canadians living in Central Canada have not known so much centralization since the Act of Union of 1841. Nevertheless, despite the growth of federal power since the beginning of the war, we see that the provinces are surviving and in fact are getting along very well. They have temporarily given up their right to impose income and corporation taxes, yet their revenues have never been so high. Within the accepted areas of provincial jurisdiction, such as education, municipal affairs, control of natural resources and civil law, provincial authority remains substantially the same.

The role of provincial governments, while reduced in certain respects by federal intervention, seems to increase in other ways. Similarly the functions of municipal governments are also growing, and our cities and towns tend to develop in the same rhythm as provincial and federal institutions.

What we are observing in Canada is not only an enlargement of federal power. No doubt this is taking place; the demands of the war effort force us to accept controls which could scarcely have been anticipated in 1939.

But along with federal centralization we are witnessing a growth of governmental functions everywhere, and I think it more correct to say that State power has increased than to say only that central government power has increased.

If we look at the international scene we observe the same tendency; various central agencies of the Allied Powers can issue directives that control member governments and their populations. Bodies like the Joint Food Board, the Joint War Aid Committee, and similar authorities make decisions which form part of Canadian policy.[1] The nations of today will only be the provinces of the future world order.

All this points to the fact that the old economic doctrine of laissez-faire is no longer dominant. The classic capitalist doctrine is in decline; dead, some caustic souls would say. To replace it a more organic and structured society seems to be forming. The individual is becoming less of a nameless being, an atom, and more an active member of an organic whole. Today, we speak less of the single worker and more of trade-unions. We think less in terms of the individual farmer and more of the agricultural class and of plans to raise its standard of living. We see the small shopkeeper struggling to avoid bankruptcy and we become interested in co-operation movements which protect their members through self-help. We talk about nationalizing public utilities but we never suggest that those already taken over by the state should be given back to private interests. If free enterprise is supposed to be suited to modern man, how can we explain the forces all leading today toward the same end: a more planned society with more public ownership?

As this audience doubtless appreciates, I am not one who fears this tendency. I know there are grave dangers we shall meet and some we are already meeting. The powers of the state might become so great that they would completely crush the individual. There is a danger for minorities that the majority will arbitrarily impose its will and allow little freedom for a different culture.

I shall elaborate on these dangers in a moment, but let me say that in general I am happy at this decline of laissez-faire. Individualism had been pushed too far. And if I understand correctly the teaching of the [Roman Catholic] Church on this point, I know that it has always condemned the excesses of economic liberalism. Other churches have held similar views. The growth of a larger sense of responsibility toward the less fortunate members of our society, the desire to provide systems of social security which will protect the weak and unfortunate, seem to me to represent a great advance over that other kind of society in which the individual seeks only his private profit and leaves his brother to suffer his fate alone.

You may think I am getting far away from the BNA Act! Not really, because I do not think that any constitution, no matter its type, is an end in itself but only a means to an end. The principal organs of our government are intended to produce peace, security and welfare for our people, and their functions are defined by legal rules. The efficiency of this constitutional structure is measured by the amount of happiness and freedom it assures to the citizens. If Canadians agree on the basic principles on which they wish to construct their society, then they will agree on the broad lines of the constitution which will attain these ends; on the other hand, if they are divided as to their national aspirations, no discussion of the constitution will bring them together.

Our first need is to carry in our hearts and minds the image of a Canada to which we all wish to belong and to whose greatness we all want to contribute. But this image must be realistic: it must take into account the distances, the various ethnic groups, the different religions. A purely theoretic constitution is out of the question; it must be essentially Canadian, respecting past traditions as well as looking to future needs. We must remain a federal state, bilingual and democratic. We must be ready to assume our place among the big industrial nations of the modern world.

In 1867 our grandfathers agreed upon the constitution of Canada. They united several provinces into a single state. There were disagreements – more serious in the maritime provinces than in Quebec – but in general the solution reached for the past problems was reasonable, and looking back it is hard to imagine what better solution could have been found. I believe that with all its weaknesses the BNA Act was a constructive work which has permitted both English- and French-speaking Canadians to develop themselves better than had till then been possible.

It is clear that far from moving toward the unification of our two dominant cultures, we have come to a full recognition of their respective values. I would like to believe that with time we shall come to realize that we are all citizens of the same country, first and foremost Canadians; after that we are members of an ethnic and cultural group. Until we learn to feel ourselves part of a single country to which we owe our political allegiance, we shall never be able to make full use of our opportunities and we shall continue to waste our time in nationalist disputes and internal conflicts.

The BNA Act was conceived and drafted when the philosophy of laissez-faire was at its height. Great changes have taken place since then, and new situations have arisen requiring state control. We must re-examine the constitution not just because we want to change our society but because it has already changed. It is, in fact, adapting itself to new social needs deriving from extra-legal sources.

No one in 1867 could have foreseen the extent of the commercial and manufacturing growth that would occur in Canada. Today a large corporation may carry on business in several provinces, a single company may have factories in every part of the country controlled from one head office. The workers in one union can call a strike which will start simultaneously in every province. The welfare and income of thousands of Canadians depend today on the decisions of a few individuals in Montreal or Toronto, or on the price of a product in the world market.

Thus to provide employment for the thousands of workers now in war-industries we must find foreign markets to absorb their production after the war. Finding jobs for Quebec workers requires more than provincial efforts and provincial laws. Wage levels in Quebec are affected by those paid in Ontario and New Brunswick as well as by those in force in the United States and other countries. We are compelled to become citizens of a much larger world than the one our fathers lived in. The growth of industrialism, which so many fear in Quebec, obliges us to unite and co-operate if we wish to avoid economic depression. The aeroplane, the telephone, the radio and the automobile have so reduced the size of Canada that national or international isolation for any part of the country is impossible.

One of the most striking characteristics of the modern state is the development, at both the federal and provincial level, of new agencies of government and new administrative laws. There is a corresponding decline in the domain of the civil law in Quebec. The Legislature is continuously enacting special statutes to govern activities formerly ruled by the Civil Code. So we have minimum wage laws, collective bargaining laws, compulsory insurance for industrial accidents, health regulations, all of which affect the individual's freedom of contract and rights as owner of property. Individual rights decline while social obligations increase. Recognizing this tendency, the Faculty of Law at McGill has increased its teaching of public and administrative law, as have so many other law faculties on this continent.

The constitutional problem is but one expression of the changes that are taking place in our social relations. If the increasing forms of control over the economy are to continue they must derive their powers from the constitution. But will these be federal or provincial powers? That is the great question. The needs of the present war effort have brought a sudden increase in federal power; these have grown much more rapidly than provincial powers, but will this trend continue or should we look for a return to the pre-war situation when peace comes?

The word 'centralization,' in itself, means little; it is the actualities that matter. Every federal state must have some centralization. No one would suggest that Ottawa have no power at all.

Today the central government plans and directs all military, air and naval operations, recruits, equips and supplies the armed forces. To provide the necessary supplies, the federal authorities are obliged to see that these are produced and distributed on a large scale. Already some 800 millions of taxpayers' money are invested in war industries. This centralization is exclusively for war purposes and can only be undertaken by the federal government. If we wish to end it, we must not only win the war but win the peace to follow.

The best way to avoid future wars is to create an international organization which can preserve peace. By their nature military regimes are centralizers. We can be sure that if Canada ever becomes engaged in another world war we will be subjected to an even more extreme centralization than that which now exists. When peace comes, all these functions of the federal government will resume their normal proportions. On the other hand, they will continue for some time after the end of hostilities to provide employment for the discharged men and women and to take care of their financial needs.

Besides this, Ottawa must have certain controls to prevent inflation. Thus we have now price and wage controls, priorities in production and rationing of consumer goods and services. These are all new experiences for Canadians, affecting us all personally. It must be noted that none of these powers have ever been used by provinces, with few exceptions. Before the war no province was attempting to plan its economy, and Ottawa by its controls has restricted the powers of private corporations much more than those of provinces. Formerly, corporations and trusts decided questions of price, wages and production, save for minimum wages. Federal policy was to be expected; it would have been impossible to prevent inflation by separate provincial laws. Had we relied on these, we should have witnessed the uncontrolled price rise that occurred after World War I.

When peace comes and the emergency ends, I do not think federal powers will be sufficient to support the present system of controls. The 'regulation of trade and commerce' has been interpreted narrowly to cover only international and perhaps interprovincial trade. Price fixing seems beyond federal jurisdiction. Prices cannot be frozen without wage controls since wages form a large part of the price; this too goes beyond federal authority in peacetime.

Unless we change the constitution, or the courts interpret it differently, Ottawa will have to abandon most of its controls after the war. This means that the trusts, the banks and the private corporations will regain the powers which they exercised previously. In the 1930's we learned what can happen when the state abandons its functions to private interests. We might face another crisis because even the most powerful corporations are incapable of controlling inflation. We may have to choose between centralization or economic disaster. I believe that controls which no province can exercise effectively and on which the health of the whole economy depends must belong to the federal government.

There is concern in Quebec about federal intervention in the field of social welfare. I think these fears are exaggerated, because no one is proposing an exclusive federal authority here. Laws dealing with the family, education, aid to needy mothers and widows, where cultural differences are involved, are best adopted and administered by provinces or, in some cases, by municipalities. I want to see provincial welfare services develop and not decrease. This does not mean the federal government has no responsibility in such matters. The promotion of public health, the provision of homes and equal opportunities for children to develop their full capacities must be the aim of national as well as provincial policies. I would like a principle of co-operation to prevail here, all agencies of government working to achieve social justice while maintaining the equilibrium of the federal system.

After this brief analysis of the nature of the present centralization in Canada, I have allowed myself to look into the future and I have suggested that there are areas in which we can anticipate that the federal Parliament will act and assume new responsibilities. But I hope to have said enough to remove from your minds the fears and apprehensions which some prophets of doom keep repeating, namely that the provinces are destined to disappear.

Very much on the contrary, the above changes will reaffirm the role of the provinces and will allow us to restore and consolidate our economic security, so that the provinces and local governments can function with ease and efficacy. The federal system must not be abolished, but we must seek to adapt it to our present needs. The constant goal of any future system of laws which we must adopt must always be, in the last analysis, the preservation of the cultural and spiritual values of our two great civilizations.

EDITOR'S NOTE

1 These joint or combined boards were the creation of the United States and Great Britain in 1942. Canada was not consulted in their formation, but co-operated within them.

XVI

The Montreal Star and the CCF: Another Monopoly at Work

Scott wrote this pamphlet in 1944 in protest against the policy followed by the
Montreal Star of pretending that the CCF did not exist except when it wished to
attack the party editorially. The policy was reportedly dictated by the news-
paper's owner, J.W. McConnell, a member of the McGill Board of Governors
since 1928 and a determined anti-socialist. Annoying at the best of times, the
policy struck Scott and other CCFers as particularly outrageous when the Star
charged that the CCF refused to answer editorial attacks. As Scott was in 1944
national chairman of the CCF as well as president of the Quebec section, he
undertook to reply on behalf of the party. In order to secure distribution of the
pamphlet, Scott organized a committee to address copies to every professional
man in Montreal who was listed in the yellow pages of the telephone directory.
He personally addressed copies to each member of the Board of Governors,
including J.W. McConnell himself.

Having failed to print the letter of 18 February 1944, incorporated in Scott's
pamphlet, the Star's editors banned Scott's name from their columns for years.

Everyone has read the vicious attacks upon the CCF conducted by the *Montreal*
Star. Nearly every day, sometimes twice a day, it has been accusing the CCF of
plans to establish a dictatorship in Canada, and of a desire to abolish democratic
processes including freedom of the press. Everyone of these charges is
demonstrably false.

All the time this campaign has been going on, the *Star* has itself been guilty of
the most flagrant abuses of monopoly power. It is important that the citizens of
Canada should know just what is happening. Here is the story.

OWNERSHIP OF THE STAR

The *Star*, along with its subsidiaries the *Herald*, the *Family Herald & Weekly*
Star and the *Standard*, was bought some years ago by Mr. J.W. McConnell. Mr.
McConnell is a multi-millionaire, who has been closely connected with many of
Canada's most powerful corporations. He is the big financier turned newspaper
owner, and has never before been in the newspaper business.

By the purchase of these various papers, Mr. McConnell acquired a monopoly control over the evening news distribution in English in the Montreal area. With his franchise from the Canadian Press, which in turn holds exclusive rights for Associated Press and Reuter's, he has the exclusive use of these press services between the hours of 9:30 AM and 9:30 PM. He alone receives the news of the world from these sources during these hours; he alone is able to decide what part of this news to release to the Montreal public and what to withhold from them. He also controls the only English outlets during these hours for the British United Press and the United Press. His money has thus placed him in the position of district controller of public information. He is responsible only to himself.

HOW THE NEWS IS DOCTORED

If a man produces adulterated food, he can be prosecuted under the Pure Food laws. We protect the physical health of our people against food poisons. If a man utters seditious words he can be sent to gaol; if he publishes defamatory matter he can be sued for damages. But if he is a newspaper owner and distorts, colours or prohibits the publication of news that the people have a right to look for in a great metropolitan daily, there is no law to stop him. We rely upon the ethics and standards of the newspaper editors themselves to see that we get fair and faithful reporting of all the news that is current at any time. Nearly all newspapers in Canada, true to this tradition of a free press, take care to see that, no matter what their editorial policy may be, the news columns are not tampered with.

For some time past the Montreal Star, under Mr. McConnell's direction, has followed a different policy with respect to the CCF party. It has barred all news about CCF activities in Montreal. It will not report CCF meetings. It will not accept paid CCF advertisements. It will not print official letters from CCF leaders. Meanwhile it carries on its attacks upon the CCF and gives full reports to CCF opponents. Mr. McConnell is using his monopoly power to prevent his readers from learning the truth about one of Canada's major parties.

In a last effort to bring the *Star* to recognise its responsibilities to the Montreal public, the following letter was delivered to Mr. S. Morgan Powell, Editor-in-chief of the *Star*, on February 18th.

February 18, 1944

The Editor,
The Montreal Star,
Montreal

Dear Sir:
In your editorial of Monday, Feb. 14th, after repeating the now tiresome misrepresentations of the Hon. Angus L. Macdonald about the CCF and 'dictatorship,'[1] you go on to

say that the CCF 'is not endeavouring to answer those who have unmasked it. Its very failure to do so may be taken either as a confession of weakness or an admission of the truth of the charges that are laid against it.'

Since you emphasize our silence, I think I am justified in assuming you wish a reply.

For sometime past your paper has refused to publish official letters from officers of the Quebec CCF in answer to the campaign of vilification against our movement. In addition, you have on more than one occasion refused to accept paid advertisements for CCF meetings; though as recently as February 16th you accepted an advertisement for Mr. Stanley Ryerson, a well known Communist.[2] The last time you refused us was on February 4th, when Mr. Eugene Forsey, a former McGill professor and an economist of repute, was speaking in the Montreal High School; you would not let us advertise that he was going to speak, nor did you report a word of what he said. Thus you have barred your letter columns, your advertising columns and your news columns to the CCF, and you now have the effrontery to accuse it of a silence which is an admission of guilt.

In order that you may have one more opportunity of showing that you can still live up to the traditions of a free press, I am writing this letter and delivering it in person to your editorial staff. I am not so much concerned at the moment with Mr. Macdonald's mud-slinging, though that would be easy to dispose of. The democratic structure, financing and policy of the CCF are too well known to be hurt by this nonsense, and I doubt whether there are many Canadians who are foolish enough to believe that dictatorship threatens from a democratic people's party rather than from reactionary big business. What I am concerned about is the behaviour of the press of Canada and of your paper in particular. While you preach democracy, you violate democratic principles and break the best traditions of your profession.

I wish to make our position clear with regard to the freedom of the press. We in the CCF are the strongest defenders of freedom of speech, of association and of the press. Your right to criticise us in your editorials we freely admit. We only regret that you prefer consistent misrepresentation to constructive criticism of policy; however, we are content to let the public draw their own conclusions from your preference. But we maintain that with your right to criticise goes a correlative duty which you owe to the public, and that is the duty of fair reporting of public meetings, including CCF meetings, and of equal access to all political parties to your advertising and letter columns on equal terms. If you fail in this duty, it is hypocritical to preach democracy in your editorials, or to claim that you are defenders of a 'free' press.

Yours very truly,

F.R. SCOTT

National Chairman, CCF Party, and President, Quebec Section of the CCF

The above letter was refused publication. Further, on February 24th the *Star* refused a paid advèrtisement for a CCF meeting in Notre Dame de Grace, and did not report the meeting although its reporter was present.

HELP THE CCF FIGHT MONOPOLY

The CCF has only limited resources with which to fight the monopolies who are using the war opportunity to increase their stranglehold over Canadian industry and the Canadian people. Even so, the success of the CCF campaign is evidenced by the desperate measures which the power-groups are using to stem the rising tide. Even though you may not be wholly in sympathy with the CCF, we trust that you will at least aid us in carrying on this particular battle against the Star and in favour of a free Canadian press. This matter goes far deeper than party politics; it touches the roots of our civil liberties. Anything you contribute in response to this appeal will be set aside for this local campaign. If you do not care to send us money, we hope that you will at least write to the Star indicating your profound disagreement with its present policy.

EDITOR'S NOTES

1 Angus L. Macdonald was a former premier of Nova Scotia who during the war served as Mackenzie King's minister of national defence for naval services.
2 At the time, the publications of Stanley B. Ryerson, a Marxist historian, included *1837: The Birth of Canadian Democracy* (1937) and *French Canada* (1943). Scott recalled that a *Star* editor told him privately that the newspaper was willing to carry Communist ads while banning those for the CCF because 'they aren't dangerous; the CCF is.'

XVII

Gare aux mots!

Neither the LSR nor the CCF described itself as a 'socialist' movement in its original manifesto. The CCF was formed as a federation of farmer, labour, and socialist groups, which also soon attracted support from middle-class people who organized themselves in 'CCF Clubs.' Many of those who joined the CCF would not have accepted the term 'socialist' as describing their ideas. Nevertheless the term did come into increasingly general use in the LSR and CCF during the 1930s. It continued to mean different things to different people, however. Scott warned

in 1945 against its exclusive identification with materialism and collectivism,
something that continued to be common particularly in Quebec.
From *Culture*, vol. 6, no. 3 (September 1945), pp. 319–22

One of the great difficulties in establishing a better understanding between the two cultural groups in Canada (Anglo-Protestant and French-Catholic) arises from the fact that words are often used in quite a different sense in the two languages. Thus even when two writers or speakers understand both French and English, they do not always understand the meaning that each seeks to convey to the other. A disagreement that appears on the surface often turns out to be no more than a verbal dispute.

As an illustration of this difficulty, involving the use of a word which is everywhere being discussed today, I would refer to the recent article in *Culture* by Louis-Philippe Pigeon entitled 'Gare aux infiltrations de socialisme.'[1]

Mr. Pigeon, as a good writer should, defines what he means by the term 'socialism.' He says: 'Cette doctrine consiste essentiellement à affirmer que l'activité économique doit être menée socialement, c'est-à-dire par l'état. En effet, dès que l'on nie totalement le principe capitaliste d'après lequel le propriétaire d'un bien est libre d'en régler l'usage, on est obligé d'instaurer comme seul principe d'ordre économique dans la société le pouvoir de l'état.'

He goes on to point out that the socialisation of human activity signifies in reality its complete subordination to the state, in other words, totalitarianism. Not unnaturally, Mr. Pigeon is opposed 'socialism.' So would be every other decent individual – if that is what socialism means.

From considerable reading of the literature in French-speaking Canada I am convinced that Mr. Pigeon's concept of socialism is very widely held. Socialism is thought to be an order of society in which the individual is subordinated to the state, in which all right of private property is abolished, and in which a materialist philosophy is enthroned.

The right to define the meaning of a word is, I suppose, a right that belongs to everybody. There is not yet in evidence a single authoritative universal dictionary. But in general I think it is always fair to consider what the supporters and believers in any creed or policy mean by their terms before condemning them outright. It would be scarcely reasonable, for example, to base one's attitude toward Catholicism on a definition given by a violent anti-Catholic ... It was Aristotle who said that to understand anything one must examine it in its highest and best expression. If one turns to the writings of Canadian socialists, or to the best writings of labour and socialist leaders in other democratic countries, the concept of socialism which emerges is almost the exact opposite of that in Mr. Pigeon's article.

Democratic socialism – and that is the only form of socialism which has any strength or importance in Canada or the British Commonwealth – places a respect for human personality first in its thought. Its avowed purpose is to secure the welfare of every family and individual in society, and its chief criticism of modern capitalism is precisely that profit, measured in money, is placed before people and their needs. It does not seek to make the state the sole arbiter of human destiny; it seeks to use the power of the state, by democratic means and under democratic controls, to compel the great centres of economic power to serve human needs instead of private privilege. The state is viewed as the agent of the people, not as their master. Moreover the socialist does not think of society as composed solely of individuals on the one hand and a huge state machine on the other; he thinks of it as containing, besides the individual and the family, a large number of other organisms like co-operatives, trade unions, churches, cultural and educational groups, each of which has an important role to play and each of which is free to select its own membership and pursue its own interest under the general law. He most assuredly does not conceive of socialism as abolishing the right of private property; on the contrary he sees it as greatly increasing the amount of personal private property in the hands of every citizen, without which the full development of personality is not possible. But it need scarcely be pointed out that human personality is more dependent on the right to own a home than on the right to own a piece of paper on which are printed the magic words 'Ten Shares of CPR Preferred Stock.'

It is not my purpose to enter upon a description of socialism in this article. What I wish to bring out is the danger of misunderstanding that arises from the varying contents given to the same word by different people. It is the desire of vested interests in Canada to maintain as much confusion and as much misunderstanding as possible in order to apply the principle 'divide et impera.' It should be the desire of every writer and journal aiming at greater understanding to bridge the gulf between the cultural groups in Canada, and between Canadians and the outside world, by seeking out the common ideas that usually underlie the various points of view, and by bringing to the surface the purely verbal conflicts which arise through differences of terminology.

When this verbal confusion is cleared away it does not mean that all differences of opinion will disappear, or that all our multifarious groups and races in Canada are going to think alike. We need not fear a consequence so boring! What we may hope is that we may differ and discuss on real issues and not on false ones. To take the practical example of the word 'socialism' again, if the socialism condemned by the Papal Encyclicals[2] bears no relation to the socialism preached by Canadian socialists, then there is really no debate, no issue joined. To say that a man cannot be a Catholic and a socialist (in the Catholic sense) does not mean that he cannot be a Catholic and a socialist (in the usual Canadian or English sense). The new government in England frankly states that it intends to establish a Socialist Commonwealth in Great Britain, yet it has many Catholic members and obviously is not barred to Catholics. I call myself a socialist, yet I agree with Mr. Pigeon that his form of socialism is to be condemned. Unless these different uses of the word are understood, we shall have much unnecessary bickering in Canada.

Sometimes it is admitted that some forms of socialism are 'mitigated,' but the fear is expressed that these will degenerate into excesses. Thus Mr. Pigeon says: 'Ce n'est donc pas par accident que tous les pays *convertis* au socialisme ont abouti au totalitarisme.' With all respect, I suggest this is false history. Sweden and New Zealand have had socialist governments for some years, and are among the best governed countries. Would it be fair to argue that, because Italy and Spain turned fascist, Catholicism inevitably leads to fascism? Surely the truth is that any country may suffer the scourge of totalitarianism, and that we must all be on our guard.

If we admit good faith on both sides, then the discussion between the socialist and the anti-socialist can centre on the real issue, namely: what degree of state control and public or co-operative ownership is necessary in order to secure the economic well-being of our people and an orderly development of our resources? At present we are moving toward an ever-increasing concentration of industrial and financial power in private hands. To the socialist, this is the real *Road to Serfdom*, not an imaginary one like that of that academic survival, Professor Hayek.[3] Everyone will admit that some state control and some state ownership are necessary. As I understand Catholic thought, it agrees with the socialist that the development of producers' and consumers' co-operatives is a desirable thing. Both are agreed that individual private property must be secured. The conflict of ideas rages principally round the ownership of the instruments of production. I see no evidence that Canadian socialism, outside the small communist sect which follows Moscow, is tending to develop a rigid philosophy which excludes Christianity; on the contrary, here as in other democratic countries the socialist movement includes people of every faith and creed, and draws many of its leaders from the churches. Democratic socialism, like its predecessor economic liberalism from whose type of society we are surely passing, will reach across the barriers of race and creed, and will permit the individual to follow his faith without interference.

The enemies of freedom in Canada and elsewhere, the paid propagandists of economic privilege who flood our country at election time with abuse and misrepresentation in order to defend the *status quo*, are making more difficult the dissemination of understanding and good will. Let us not add to this confusion by a failure to appreciate the true thought and meaning that is contained in our terms and phrases. Let us agree to overthrow the tyranny of words.

EDITOR'S NOTES

1 *Culture*, June 1945, pp. 141–6. The author later became Mr Justice Pigeon of the Supreme Court of Canada.

2 Notably in *Rerum Novarum* (1891) and *Quadragesimo Anno* (1931)
3 Friedrich von Hayek, a leading apologist for capitalism, published his book *The Road to Serfdom* in 1944 as a warning against socialism and collectivism in all their forms.

XVIII

Social Medicine

In the light of current disputes about the remuneration of the medical profession, this address makes for particularly interesting reading. Originally delivered in French, it was subsequently published in the Bulletin *of the Canadian Association of Medical Students and Interns. No invitation to address the medical students at McGill ever came to Scott.*

Scott's discussion of the recent developments and experiments in Saskatchewan takes on added significance because that province was the first to introduce a full system of social medical care. In 1960 the CCF government led by T.C. Douglas set out on the road to a plan for prepaid medical services. In spite of opposition from the College of Physicians and Surgeons, the majority of a government-appointed committee recommended that a universal and comprehensive medical care insurance program be established, to be financed through taxes, and paying the doctors on a fee-for-service basis. A special session of the Legislature in November 1961 passed the Saskatchewan Medical Care Insurance Act, to come into effect on 1 April 1962. Douglas's successor as premier, Woodrow Lloyd, conscious of the hostility of many physicians, delayed implementation of the plan to 1 July in the hope of achieving some kind of compromise. This proved impossible, and in spite of the threat of a doctors' strike the plan took effect on 1 July. Doctors continued to provide emergency services, and approximately 10 per cent of them refused to join the strike. In addition the government recruited approximately 100 British physicians on short-term contracts. The strike was only partially effective, therefore, and after eighteen days the doctors agreed to negotiate with the government, using the services of a British mediator, Lord Taylor, a physician and Labour parliamentarian. On 23 July the parties reached a settlement which modified the plan somewhat while maintaining its compulsory, comprehensive, and state-run nature.

To their surprise, doctors found that their incomes increased as a result of the plan. A poll of approximately half of the province's physicians in 1965 found that more than two-thirds judged it to be a success, with a large majority believ-

ing it to provide services which were as good as or better than those available before the plan came into effect.
Abridged and translated version of an address delivered in French to the medical students of the University of Montreal, 19 January 1949

I am conscious that it may seem presumptuous for me, a layman, to address a group of aspiring doctors on any aspect of their professional life. I make no apology for so doing, however, for two reasons: first, because, to quote an old proverb, 'the best judge of a dinner is not the cook but the diner,' and I, as quite an experienced patient, a too frequent guest at your operating table, have a right to say what I think of the services you render; and secondly, because the subject of my paper belongs almost as much to the field of law and public administration, which is my professional field, as to that of medicine. For I intend to discuss what I shall call Social Medicine, and whatever else that much misunderstood phrase may mean, it undoubtedly suggests some form of prepaid medical care organized by the state for the benefit of all the citizens, and therefore involves my profession as well as yours.

THE CONTRAST

In our modern society we face two situations which stand in sharp contrast. On the one hand are the advances and discoveries of medical science, on the other are the great number of people needing more medical care. How do we bring the science to the people? That is the heart of the matter. Clearly the medical profession is not doing it at the moment, and indeed cannot do it. There are too few doctors, dentists, nurses and specialists. There are too few hospitals. Above all, the cost of medical services, which has increased in proportion as the skills have improved, has gone far beyond what the average individual citizen can afford. It is in the face of these facts that the private practice of medicine, as we have known it in the past, has been measured and found wanting. The individual doctor is more skilled, better trained and equipped than ever. But the need for his services is beyond his capacity to meet. We have produced good medicine, but we have not distributed it to all our people.

A DUAL RELATIONSHIP

This brings me to a fundamental distinction which must be the starting point of our discussion. The science, the art of medicine if you will, is one thing. The organization of the medical profession and its relation to the public is another. The art of medicine is your specialty and your privilege: no layman can tell you how to diagnose a case of typhoid or what treatment to recommend for pneumonia. But the layman can and does have an opinion on the organization of the medical profession and on the manner in which he, the patient, is to pay for the services he receives. Indeed, a social scientist who has studied the matter is as fully capable as a doctor to decide upon the merits of a particular plan of public health. The relation between doctor and patient is dual, not unilateral.

Many years ago in all parts of Canada, and even today in the rural communities, sickness was something which could be taken care of by the family with the aid of the family doctor. The patient stayed in bed at home. He required no specialists, no expensive drugs, and probably no hospitalization Moreover, the family income did not stop when the father was ill, for the potatoes went on growing in the fields, the corn ripened, the hens laid eggs, and the wife or children could milk the cows. Today consider the position of the average Canadian worker in the towns – and do not forget that most people are now wage or salary earners and not farmers. If the industrial worker becomes ill his income and that of his family stops immediately. He cannot send his wife or son down to the factory to replace him. The doctor may treat him at home if the case is a mild one, but he may have to be sent to the hospital. It is true there is much free medical care given to poor people, but those with some means of payment, the middle class, must try to meet their doctor's bills. It is they who are hardest hit, and they are in effect taxed to pay the cost of the free services. I can assure you from my personal experience that my greatest sense of economic insecurity today comes from the fear of unexpected medical costs. I could be financially destroyed by one serious illness in my family. I have protected myself against most other hazards, but this I cannot cope with unless the state comes to my aid. And since it is quite easy for the state to undertake this responsibility, since there are proven schemes in existence in other countries, even in other parts of Canada, I and many others like me see no reason why we should remain in this condition of insecurity just to satisfy the conservative traditions of certain members of the medical profession.

This means, of course, that our salvation can only come through political action. When we ask the state to do something for the welfare of the citizens, we are really asking some political party to enact the legislation through parliament or provincial legislature. The medical profession cannot do it. So I must turn to some political party for help in my trouble. On the other hand the political party cannot help me unless you agree to co-operate, for you alone possess the skill, the science and the art of healing. If we, the public, should stifle your science by our legislation, we shall not solve the problem, just as you cannot solve the problem unless your science is assisted by our legislation. We must work together, you and I, each contributing our share to the achievement of our common aim. Nevertheless as your science is today ahead of my legislation I do not hesitate to predict that the next great advance in the practice of medicine is going to come from the legislators rather than from the physicians, surgeons, or bacteriologists. I dare to suggest to you that the British National Health Service Act of 1947, by which prepaid and total medical and dental care was provided for 50,000,000 people from the cradle to the grave, will rank in medical history as being fully as great a triumph as the work of a Jenner, a Banting or a Florey.[1]

A VARIETY OF PLANS

All that I have said so far is by way of introduction to my subject. Now let me turn to an examination of some of the plans that are being studied and introduced. These vary from province to province, and from country to country. There is no single plan, no standard scheme suitable for all people. For that reason the terminology in this field is very inexact. What is 'state medicine'? What is 'socialized medicine'? There is no precise answer. For that matter what is 'private practice'? Is the Blue Cross Plan private practice? Everywhere we find changes occurring in the position of the medical practitioner, and he is far removed from the simple private practice of the family doctor of olden days. Therefore it is wrong to suppose that there is a choice between only two alternatives: private practice and state medicine. I see a choice between many possible plans.

Among the various plans now being proposed, I know of none which would turn all doctors into salaried officials of the state and all hospitals into state institutions. If that is what you understand by state medicine, then rest assured that this dreadful fate is not in store for you in any foreseeable future. Let me say a word, however, about working on salary. The whole trend of modern society is to convert incomes into salaries. Of the 148,000,000 people in the United States some 80% live off wages or salaries. I have lived off a salary all my working life, and I do not feel that my initiative has been destroyed or my personal relations with my students in any way hampered. Our judges are salaried state officials and surely the dispensing of justice is as high a function as the dispensing of health. So too our school teachers receive state salaries for work performed in public schools. Sometimes I wonder whether the doctor's fear for a salary is not due rather to the fear of losing those higher incomes which a few successful practitioners can make by charging each unfortunate patient as much as he can afford to pay. But I am your guest today and must not entertain such thoughts. Suffice it to say that the plans for public health which I shall discuss with you do not involve such drastic proposals.

1. *Voluntary Group Insurance*
The first plans which we have begun to make to meet the problem of medical costs are the various group schemes for hospitalization and medical care. The Blue Cross plan is locally the best known. Many industries are developing their own group plans. Private insurance companies now sell group policies covering all employees of particular employers. These schemes vary in the amount of

protection they afford, but they are all alike in their aim to introduce the insurance principle into medical practice. They are, however, a very small step toward the goal. Apart from other criticism that can be levelled against them, they have one fatal defect. They do not cover enough people. Therefore the costs are inevitably higher than they would be under a state scheme. The risks are not spread wide enough. Each of these groups has its own administration staff and expenses, and they can never reach out to the large numbers of people who do not fall within the categories covered. Moreover the number of days in hospital is usually strictly limited, so that the very severe illness, the calamity which can ruin a family, is not provided for; and the doctor is permitted to charge more than the fee paid by the association, so that the patient may find he is no better off than he was before. These voluntary schemes are poor and costly attempts to deal with a problem which is much too big for such half-hearted measures. Sometimes I suspect they are designed more to head off a proper national scheme rather than to meet the demand for health services.

2. *State Hospital Insurance*
Contrast with such group hospitalization plans the scheme which was introduced into Saskatchewan on January 1st, 1947. On that day the first compulsory hospitalization plan in North America went into effect. Very nearly every man, woman and child in Saskatchewan is covered: about 780,000 people. Everyone has the right to free hospital services, not just for a limited number of days but for as long as their medical adviser recommends. There is no exclusion for pre-existing conditions, no waiting period for maternity care. The patient also receives free use of operating and delivery rooms, free x-ray and laboratory examinations, and free drugs. The cost of the service was borne by a contribution of $10.00 per adult and $5.00 for each minor child, with a maximum of $30.00 per family. The administration costs in the first year were only 8.1% compared with an average of 13% for Blue Cross plans. To meet the increased demand for hospitals the provincial government has assisted in building new hospitals and has raised the number of beds from 3.9 per 1,000 to 5.8 per 1,000, and will soon have 7.8 per 1,000 people, which is considered to be adequate.

The Saskatchewan experiment has been an outstanding success. It is popular with the people. It has solved the financial problems of the hospitals. British Columbia is now embarking on a similar scheme. How long must we wait in other provinces? Remember that every delay costs human lives.

3. *Socialized Health Services*
The Hospital Services Plan is, however, only one of the successful experiments in Saskatchewan. There is another scheme now operating there which goes even farther. The Hospital Plan does not cover medical and surgical fees. It provides

hospital but not medical insurance. The Saskatchewan government is determined to carry out its whole program of social medicine, but without federal financial aid it cannot go beyond hospital insurance. However, it has provided a basis for the voluntary adoption of prepaid medical and surgical care and has taken the initiative in organizing Health Regions in the province where the people can voluntarily tax themselves to pay for the additional cost. One such region has adopted the plan, and I think you will be interested in hearing how it works.

This is Health Region No. 1 around Swift Current, in the south-west corner of Saskatchewan. The population of the region is 55,000 scattered over a wide area of rather poor land – not a good place in which to start a health experiment. Yet the voters decided to establish a scheme of their own, and it came into effect on July 1, 1946. Apart from a few persons covered by other plans, everybody in the region is given complete medical, surgical and obstetrical care – about 51,000 people in all. There is also a program of dental care for children under 16. The plan is financed by a personal tax, a land tax, and by provincial grants. The compulsory tax is $15.00 a year for one person, $24.00 for 2, $30.00 for 3 and $35.00 for a family of four or more. Property owners pay an additional land tax of 2.2 mills. The province pays 9% of the total revenue.

How does this plan affect the doctors, you will ask? Every general practitioner in the region, and there are 34 of them, has joined the plan. These men were paid out of a fund which amounted in 1947 to $410,850 so the average annual gross income was $12,739. Not bad for a poor region in Saskatchewan! The patient is free to choose his own doctor: if specialists are needed, the patient is referred to someone outside the region and his fees are paid by the fund. The doctor is paid a fee for every service rendered, the amount of the fee being worked out by agreement with the College of Physicians and Surgeons of Saskatchewan. The doctor's bills, however, are paid out of the regional funds and not directly by the patient.

This Swift Current Scheme has been investigated by Dr. A.D. Kelly, who has described his visit to the region in the *Canadian Medical Association Journal* for 1948 (pp. 506–11). His comments may be summarized in this quotation from his article:

An observer visiting the Swift Current headquarters of Health Region No. 1 gathers the impression that here is a successful experiment in the large scale provision of medical care, courageously applied, efficiently managed and remarkably free from attempts to make the facts fit preconceived ideas, financial or otherwise ...

The participating physicians appear to be satisfied with the operation of the plan which differs so little from conditions of private practice.

Dr. Kelly found only very minor differences between the principles on which this plan operated and the principles laid down by the CMA. It is too soon yet to draw any final conclusions from the Swift Current experiment, but it is obviously one possible way of setting up a new relationship between doctor and patient, which enables the patient to cover all his medical costs for a fixed payment, while leaving the doctor free to choose the number of patients he will serve and to treat them exactly as he did before the plan was set up.

If we add the cost of hospitalization to the cost of medical care in the Swift Current Region, it means that an individual pays only about $25.00 for the entire protection ($10.00 for hospitalization, $15.00 for medical care, plus a small land tax if he is also a property owner) while an entire family pays a maximum of $65.00 ($30.00 for hospitalization and $35.00 for medical care). In thus providing us in Canada with the first reliable statistics about the cost of organized health services, Saskatchewan is making a very valuable contribution to the solution of this problem. When Premier Douglas[2] started his pioneering experiments he had to rely on estimates that were based on guesswork.

The administration of the Saskatchewan Health Region No. 1 is fully democratic. The Region is divided into Districts, and the municipalities in each District appoint a District Health Council. These District Councils elect two or more representatives to the Regional Board, which has the general power of supervising the operation of the plan. A medical advisory committee appointed by the District Medical Society advises the Regional Board on matters relating to medical services which may be referred to it. An assessment committee of doctors scrutinizes, adjusts and recommends for payment the accounts received from all participating physicians.

One of the most popular aspects of this plan is the program of dental care for children under 16. There are four full-time dentists with assistants, who make use of both fixed and mobile clinics. By this means thousands of children who never had and never would have had proper dental care are now being looked after.

Already as a result of 18 months' experience new ideas for the future are being considered at Swift Current. At present patients who need specialists are sent outside the Region by the advice of the local doctor, and this expense is carried by the fund. It was found that in one year about $75,000 was spent outside the Region. With this amount of money, perhaps it would be possible to engage specialists who would live inside the Region, taking patients sent them by the general practitioners, and visiting the district health centres regularly to give counsel and advice. In other words, the scheme now operating is not static, but will grow and change as obstacles are overcome and new experience is gained. The medical philosophy, if I may use that term, which is suitable for the private practice of medicine is not entirely suitable for the conditions which the doctors will meet under a system of social medicine. There is a danger in the older medical schools, not that they will fail to give good technical training, but that they may turn out men and women who will not be prepared for the new social obligations of the medical profession, and who will therefore tend to place themselves in negative opposition to a community which is demanding some better method of providing health services. ... To make a success of any state-aided scheme the utmost co-operation between the profession and the community is required.

STRAINING AT GNATS

You will have to beware of two kinds of propagandists, those who tell you that the plan is perfect, and those who tell you that it is ruining the practice of medicine. Beware also of a more subtle kind of misrepresentation, the kind which selects a small defect and makes it appear as the chief result of social medicine. Let me give an example. In New Zealand where a complete socialized scheme rather like that in England has been operating for some eight years, it has been found that a certain number of people visit the doctor too often and on very slight pretext. It costs them no more; their bills are paid anyway. The doctors, in some cases, get rid of these troublesome patients by prescribing some harmless drug; the cost of this too is paid by the state. Thus abuses have been found and these be corrected. Yet I have heard a prominent physician, in talking about socialized medicine, tell this story about New Zealand without mentioning anything else about the success or failure of their plan! It reminds me of those people who opposed family allowances because, it was argued, some parents would spend the money on drink, or of those other people who used to say that it was no use providing good houses for the poor, since they would only fill their bathtubs with coal! Which is the greater abuse, the present system of medicine in Canada where literally thousands of people cannot get enough in the way of medical advice and drugs, or the New Zealand system where a tiny fraction of the people get a little too much? Must the great majority be sacrificed in order to prevent the few from abusing their privileges? Beware, I say, of those who keep silent about the grave abuses of our present system of private practice, and spend all their time warning you of the minor difficulties of some experimental scheme. Truly they strain at gnats and swallow camels.

Of course there will be difficulties and dangers in socialized medicine. Of course we shall make some mistakes. No human organization is perfect. We shall have to learn as we go along, testing each development by its results, not tying ourselves too closely to any one theory but being willing to allow criticism from all sides and to make the adaptations that experience suggests. There is no need, however, to continue interminably the debate as to the principle of social medicine itself; this issue has been settled in the minds of all but a few. The right to health has today become a human right, like the right to education. The question we must face now is not whether we shall have some form of socialized health services, but what form we shall have. And here we need not waste as much time as the opponents of change would like, since other countries and jurisdictions have already given us practical examples that we may choose from.

Once we establish the basis for prepaid medical care for our population, then we have another task ahead of us. We shall have then to concentrate upon improving the quality of service that is rendered. We shall have to train more medical students. We shall have to build and equip not only more hospitals, but health centres for every community. We shall have to concentrate more on preventive medicine. When a new state plan first goes into effect it opens the existing hospitals to a much greater number of patients, and places more work on the limited number of doctors now available; people will have to wait to get into hospitals. There will be criticism that the service is poor. This has happened everywhere. The reason for the decline in service, however, if there is a decline, is to be found in the shortage of personnel and equipment, rather than in the nature of the state scheme. We must not expect miracles at the start. It will take from five to ten years for any large-scale public health plan to discover and to remedy its initial defects. This is not an argument against starting, but rather against further delay. We shall not be better able to start five years from now than we are today. The federal government has done something in Canada to stimulate hospital building, but has failed to commit itself and the nation to an overall plan.

SOME CONCLUSIONS

It is not my purpose to argue in favour of one or other of the various alternatives that are available to us. I hope you will agree with me, however, that the following conclusions may be safely drawn from the experience of recent years:

1 Some form of socialized medicine is coming; what we must choose is the best form for our Canadian conditions. It follows that blind opposition to the idea is useless and merely hinders the development of the right system.
2 No scheme will work satisfactorily unless there is close co-operation between the public authorities and the medical profession. It is for the profession to concern itself primarily with the science of medicine and with standards of service; the responsibility of the public authorities, representing the citizen-patient, is primarily with organization and administration.
3 It is quite possible to provide a system in which the freedom of the patient to choose his doctor is preserved, and in which a doctor may refuse to take a patient.
4 It is quite possible in Canada to devise a system in which the legitimate autonomy of the provinces in this field is not destroyed.
5 There is a danger, particularly in the early stages of a new system, that doctors and hospitals will find it difficult to cope with the number of new patients they will be meeting. For this reason special attention must be given to the training of new personnel and the provision of new equipment.

Finally, ... you need have no fear about your future financial position under socialized medicine. I know of no scheme which does not increase the general income of the medical profession. Indeed, this increase has been so great in some cases that the public are beginning to wonder whether the doctor deserves to be paid so much more than other professional men. I am sure that if your profession insists on excessively high fees the public will retaliate by insisting that you be treated like school teachers and placed upon salary. Medicine is not a commercial business, but a service.

If the subject of social medicine is approached in the right spirit by the government, the public and the profession, there is a magnificent opportunity for great achievements in the future. Social medicine, far from being a barrier to progress, is an open road leading to new success in the eternal warfare of mankind against disease. Ultimately of course we shall need more than merely medical changes to bring general public health. The individual cannot be fully healthy unless his whole social environment is healthy. We must have not only social security, full employment, good education, and good housing, but art, culture, a spirit of co-operation and social justice if man is to be fully developed in all his faculties. Social medicine is not the whole answer to public health, but in my opinion it will represent a great step toward a healthier and happier society.

EDITOR'S NOTES

1 Edward Jenner was a British physician who invented the smallpox vaccine; Sir Frederick Banting was a Canadian scientist who in 1923 shared the Nobel Prize for physiology and medicine for his work on the discovery of insulin; Howard Walter Florey was an Australian pathologist who in 1945 shared the Nobel Prize for physiology and medicine for his work on the discovery of penicillin.
2 T.C. 'Tommy' Douglas came into office in 1944 at the head of the first CCF government in Canada. He served until 1961, when he resigned to become the first national leader of the NDP.

XIX

The Fundamentals of Socialism

At the eleventh national convention of the CCF, held in Vancouver in July 1950, Scott offered his final address as national chairman. He had served the party in that capacity for eight years. In his remarks he indicated the party's changing

view of international affairs to one largely supporting the Canadian govern-ment's cold war stance. He also signalled a change in the CCF's domestic pro-gram and tactics. Like other social democratic parties in the western world, the CCF was re-examining the means to achieve its goals as well as those goals themselves. In the case of the CCF, the dismal outcome of the 1949 federal election was a major reason for re-examination.
Opening Address of the National Chairman, Co-operative Commonwealth Federation, National Convention, Vancouver, 26 July 1950

It is my happy duty to open this Parliament of our Party, and to welcome you all to the sessions of the eleventh National CCF Convention. This is the first occasion on which we have met in Vancouver, and those of us who have come from afar are delighted to be meeting old friends and making new ones among the CCF members in British Columbia – a province which from the earliest days of the CCF, ... and even long before the CCF was formed, has contributed to the socialist and labour movement of Canada men and women of such vitality, such loyalty, and such variety. We are conscious too of the fact that our first visit to the West Coast takes place when so much that is fateful for humanity is being enacted across the ocean that washes these shores.[1] The time has passed when Vancouver seemed a distant outpost far removed from world events; in these days of oceanic pacts and new strate-gic relationships the Pacific matches the Atlantic as a centre of politics and power.

With your permission this morning I should like to discuss with you, by way of introduction to our deliberations, some questions that go rather deeply into our socialist philosophy. It is now seventeen years since we adopted the Regina Manifesto. Do we view any differently our fundamental task of creating a society in which the principle regulating production, distribution and exchange will be the supplying of human needs and not the making of profits? Is there any validity to the charge that we are just Liberals in a hurry, or is the nature of our program one which still divides us sharply from the slow Liberals and the retrogressive Conservatives? I raise these questions at this time for two reasons. First, socialists everywhere are taking stock of their position in the light of post-war experiences. Never before have so many democratic socialists been in power in so many countries; never before have such opportunities for experiment been available. On the other hand, the absence of serious economic hardship has slackened the interest of the ordinary Canadian in politics, and we have felt this inside our movement. The workers feel more sure of their jobs next week than they do of peace next week, more afraid of world war than of world depression. Indeed, we face the likelihood that liberal capitalism has learned enough from Mr. Keynes and from war planning to be able to avoid any economical crisis as severe as that which gave birth to the CCF.[2] I very much hope this is true, but I do not see that it makes any difference to the validity of the socialist case. Socialism is as valid a creed for a prosperous nation as for a depressed one, for it is concerned with the quality of social life, not just with the amount of wealth produced. A country like Canada can be prosperous, after a fashion, when it is building homes for the rich and none for the poor, when it is exploiting natural resources for the private profit of private monopolies, and when it is measuring social security by the least that is politically tolerable rather than by the utmost that our resources would justify. Full employment is not the same as social justice. Democracy needs socialism; this is plainer than ever before. Nevertheless, the world is rapidly changing. The socialist must be aware of world trends, and must realize that he is no more free than anyone else from the danger of becoming old-fashioned. If there is one way in which our socialism must be scientific, it is that we must learn from experiment and must keep our minds ever open to new truth.

The second reason why I should like to discuss these basic questions is purely personal. I saw the birth of the CCF at Regina in 1933; I have been closely connected with it ever since. I have held the office of National Chairman for four consecutive terms. I have decided not to stand again, so this is the last time I shall have the honour of opening a National Convention. I do not think the CCF need try to copy the British Labour Party and elect a new National Chairman every convention, but I feel there should be a reasonable rotation in the office and this seems a reasonable time for me to retire. I am not, however, to be taken as singing my CCF swan-song. I am not a swan, I don't sing, and I am not dying. I shall be happy to serve the Party in some other capacity if I am wanted. My association with this great movement for the betterment of Canada and of humanity, the friendships it has given me both here and abroad, and the sense of reality and purpose it has contributed to my life are experiences which to fellow socialists I need only mention to have understood. I am sure there is not one of you who does not feel the same way.

What then are some of the developments that have taken place in socialist thought since we drafted the Regina Manifesto? You will realize that I am giving my personal impressions, and I can only touch upon a few salient points. One trend that seems to me obvious is that the political aspects of socialism, its reliance on democratic procedures and its respect for human rights, have acquired a fresh importance in the light of recent world events. This is the result of our experiences with both Fascism and Communism. Both these movements illustrate the inherent evils in absolute power, regardless of its avowed goals. The Communist Party has no right to the word socialist, since what it calls 'scientific socialism' is the negation of the most fundamental part of socialism, namely its respect for the individual human being. As Deutscher points out in his remarkable biography of Stalin,[3] whereas the original Russian revolution of 1917 represented the victory of western political ideas over Russia, for Marx was a product of the west, the later revolution by which Stalin emerged as dictator represented the recapture of Russia by a powerful form of oriental despotism. The revolution was lost in Russia, not in the sense that capitalism returned, but because Czarism was strengthened. We now see that it is possible for a country to nationalize all the means of production and still be as far from socialism as ever. On the other hand, England today, despite her continuing private ownership, is evolving rapidly toward the co-operative commonwealth; in the former centre of world capitalism sits a Labour government which cares for the welfare of the masses, has an infinitely great respect for human rights, a keen desire for peace, and which has achieved commendable approxima- tion to economic equality.

It is evident that this thing we may call the spirit of man, this light of faith and conscience on which all civilization depends, is not primarily dependent on the ownership of property, essential though it is to subject all forms of ownership to social controls. Socialism is most concerned with the human spirit, with its freedom, its growth, its emancipation, and with ownership only in so far as some of its forms are obstacles to this freedom just as other forms seem essential to it. Socialism expresses in the fullest degree the great traditions of political democracy, traditions which are still very much alive even in the country where capitalism is most powerful, namely the United States. For that reason socialists will not hesitate to defend their political freedom should it be threatened by communist aggressors as it was recently threatened by fascist powers, and they will not let the strangeness of some of their capitalist bedfellows deflect them from this fundamental purpose. Any notion that we might creep into some neutral never-never land in such a conflict is not only utterly unrealistic, it is a denial of socialist responsibility. For socialists must fight to preserve those conditions under which socialism may live.

Having said so much, let me go on to say that I disagree with those who say that the issue today is not between capitalism and socialism, but between freedom and totalitarianism. That statement oversimplifies the facts. Freedom is endangered by certain capitalist practices and tendencies as well as by totalitarian movements, and the evils of capitalism help to create those movements. Capitalist forces, particularly in Canada and the United States, are still bitter enemies of social progress, still potent sources of reaction. They are offset by other forces of many kinds, but they exist and they must be mastered along with external enemies if freedom is to expand and be secure. This is a job that none but a socialist party can accomplish.

Let us remind ourselves of some fundamentals. A society dominated by liberal economics, preferable though it is to any totalitarianism, is one whose guiding principle is profit. This means that the flow of investment and the direction of economic change is primarily toward those things which bring the maximum money profit to their owners. This is why we have a housing boom for the upper third and none for the lower two-thirds of the population. This is why social security is so meagre, and why the capitalist press is actually trying to teach people that the welfare state is an evil – as if it were the duty of our governments to be indifferent to human suffering, and unwise to insure ourselves against it! This is why it is being suggested that we cannot afford better old age pensions while there is war in Korea – as though we could fight better against communism if we neglect our social responsibilities. Take the profit out of war, and we can pay for old age pensions. Even though liberal capitalism may have found some devices for ironing out the extremes of booms and depressions, it is still an undemocratic economy because it puts the interest of the minority of profit sharers ahead of the interest of the masses. It remains a society abounding in special privilege, and denying the principle of equality, of fair shares to all, which is fundamental to our way of thinking. It continues to support a capitalist class that now constitutes an irresponsible economic government, operating through one of the most undemocratic institutions in our society, the private corporation. It maintains several political parties whose inner structure and financing render them incapable of caring for the basic needs of the people. When Mr. Abbott raised rents 22%, or Mr. Martin announced there would be no health insurance for Canada, or Mr. Garson defended the suppression of the report on the flour-milling combine, or Mr. Gardiner opposed the creation of a world food pool under FAO, Canadian Liberalism was being quite true to its colours.[4] No protest has come from the Canadian Manufacturers' [Association] against any of these moves, nor will the money available to the Liberals at the next election be any the less.

The CCF proclaimed at Regina, and still proclaims, its belief in production for human need rather than in production for profit. By this we mean that the first claim upon our economic activity should be the satisfaction of basic human requirements for food, clothing, housing, education and leisure. Those come first. In war as in peace, these claims rank before private profit, though we all must submit to wartime restrictions. We do not oppose the making of profit in all its forms; on the contrary, the profit motive, under proper control, is now and will be for a long time a most valuable stimulus to production. Not a single democratic socialist party anywhere plans to nationalize all forms of production, and in the privately owned sector the profit motive must continue. But in a co-operative commonwealth this would not be the determining factor but a subordinate one. To secure the satisfaction of basic human needs economic planning is required, particularly of the amount and direction of investment, and of the broad channels of distribution. That such planning can be both practicable and democratic, and can result in a more equitable distribution of wealth as well as in increased production and high employment, the experience of Britain and the Scandinavian countries has conclusively shown. According to a report issued from London's International Chamber of Commerce, production in 1949 in western Europe surpassed pre-war levels by the following amounts: in Sweden, 45%; in Britain, 37%; in Denmark, 33%; in Norway, 31%; in Holland, 23%; in France, 22%; and in Belgium, 15%. It is significant that the top four countries are under socialist governments, and that the bottom two have indulged in the least planning. In Belgium, often cited in our press as a sane, free enterprise country ten percent of the workers are unemployed though the country receives more Marshall Aid per capita than England does.[5]

The fundamental differences between the CCF and the Liberals have not changed even though Liberal governments have introduced several reforms urged by the CCF and though their program (not their performance) overlaps in regard to some aspects of social security. They would let the capitalist profit-seekers shape our economic future for us; we would plan it consciously to serve human need. They would maintain the monopolistic practices that are now stifling initiative and slowing our rate of growth; we would replace them by social ownership and democratic controls for maximum production and lower prices. They would tolerate the inequalities of opportunity in the present system; we would remove them. They would hamper the growth of co-operatives and trade unions; we would promote it in every proper way. They would cling to their undemocratic type of political party, run from the top; we would make our democratic movement an even broader instrument for participation by the people in the processes of government. In clinging to private enterprise they would deny the creative power of mankind to mould its own destiny; we affirm it. They seek to arrest history; we march with it. They are Liberals; we are democratic socialists. Of the Progressive Conservative Party I need not speak; its sole function in Canada today is to make otherwise intelligent people feel they have to vote Liberal to save them from a fate worse than Liberal death.

This notion of the direction of the economy, consciously selected for humane purposes and brought about through planning, is so important that the question of social ownership now seems perhaps relatively less important. The aim of socialist planning has not changed, but the emphasis on nationalization has changed. In proportion as planning techniques have developed, and as the difficulties of too rapid a nationalization have been better appreciated, some reconsideration is taking place in the older view that immediate and widespread expropriation is fundamental. Opposition to certain forms of it has come from one wing of the socialist movement, the co-operatives. I would not presume to try to provide the proper formula for deciding how much and when to nationalize;this it seems to me is a matter of practical application rather than of principle. Nationalization is only one tool, and we must learn to use all the tools. Obviously a considerable degree of public ownership, such as was suggested in the Regina Manifesto, is required for Canada, for we suffer particularly from monopolistic ownership. But I suggest that for any socialist today to look upon every proposal for nationaliztion as the acid test of true socialism, an act of faith rather than of reason, is to be a little foolish. Within capitalism itself the control of industry has largely passed from owners to management and the 'sovereignty of economic property' has already been divided. The essential thing is to subject the decisions of management to social need. Social ownership is one way, a very important way, but not the only way of achieving this. Control of credit, of the allocation of raw materials, taxation, and competition from public and co-operative enterprises are other ways. While our fundamental purpose of production for use remains, we must keep an open and intelligent mind on the problem of the degree and timing of socialization.

Another element in socialist policy that has become more important in recent years is the whole matter of industrial relations. This goes deeper than ownership; trade unions may battle with governments as much as with private management. The studies and experiments on human relations in industry are vitally important for socialists to understand. Similarly the trade union movement has increasing responsibilities commensurate with its growing power, for the interests of labour are not exactly the same as those of society at large. The consumer is a very silent partner at the collective bargaining table. The rise of membership in trade unions has been one of the most encouraging signs of the past fifteen years; more perhaps than any other factor it has imposed some degree of social responsibility upon North American big business. The recent demands for industrial pensions have even convinced many industrialists that state pensions without a means test are a good thing, and many people who are not trade unionists are going to benefit from their struggles. But such special favours as the powerful unions can squeeze out of large corporations are no more secure than the corporations themselves, are dependent on continued prosperity in the economy, and may leave unprotected the mass of workers in smaller unions, besides the even larger group who are still unorganized. Trade unionism needs social democracy to fulfil its purposes; like the co-operative movement, it cannot do the whole job alone.

Another part of our program seems to have evolved considerably since Regina. When the CCF was born we were in a depression so extreme that no salvation seemed possible save on a national level. The provinces were nearly as bankrupt as the municipalities. Only Ottawa could have instituted the new policies of public investment, tax reduction and credit expansion which would have helped to reduce unemployment and to rescue the agricultural producer. But of course Ottawa did none of these things, being under first a Conservative and then a Liberal administration. The war, however, forced an abandonment of the old economic theories, and a poverty stricken nation with over a million people on relief miraculously found itself overnight with unlimited sources of money. If anyone ever doubts the importance of theory, let him reflect on that fact. After the war high prices strengthened the position of both provinces and municipalities, which are now capable of undertaking social services which previously they could not have contemplated. We are now more conscious than before of the important role a province may play in carrying out a socialist program. Saskatchewan has shown how successful this can be, though it has also shown the limitations. We are all federalists in the CCF to say the least; we have even heard the voice of the provincial autonomist in our midst. Let those who accuse us of an undue desire for centralization take note. In this sphere as in others we must strike a balance, separating out the functions appropriate to federal action from those appropriate to provinces and municipalities. Some matters, too, need regional administration, being neither federal nor provincial by nature, such as the use of water in interprovincial rivers. And of course we recognize more today the fundamental importance of world government. Since the proper division of functions can never be settled for all time, but changes with circumstances, the CCF must support a flexible method for amending the BNA Act, except for matters which may be considered fundamental human and minority rights.

These are some of the thoughts that come to me as I look over the period of Canadian socialism I have known. It seems to me we have grown in understanding. We have not altered our first principles, which stand as firm today as they ever did, and firmer. We know, however, more about the business of government, and we have seen social conditions change, and on the whole for the better, through the application of ideas we were the first to espouse. I like to think our doctrine has not altered, yet that we are less doctrinaire. No socialist is more dangerous than the one who knows it all, especially if he proves it by reference to some dead author. G.D.H. Cole, in his excellent little book called *Socialist Economics*, points out, for instance, that Marx said practically nothing about the problems which a constructive socialist society will have to solve. His great work was a critique of capitalism, not an analysis of socialist economic problems. He did not concern himself at all with a situation, such as western democracies face, where there is almost certain to be no violent overthrow of capitalism and no dictatorship of the proletariat. It is good for us to realize that our techniques for social change are under constant review and testing, while our sense of socialist values, our concept of the co-operative commonwealth in which human need is the first principle of action, stands firm and clear. The inner conviction that one's living principles are true is the mainspring of human action; with this it does not matter what changes and chances one meets in the outside world. Every member of the CCF should feel this inner conviction, feel it more today than ever before. The world in which human needs are best protected will be a world in which peace is most secure.

EDITOR'S NOTES

1 The Korean War had begun on 25 June 1950, and one month later was going badly for the South Koreans and their United Nations (American) allies. Although the

Canadian Parliament had voted to support the United Nations action in Korea, Canadian forces had not yet reached the theatre of war.

2 John Maynard Keynes was the eminent British economist who is credited with formulating, principally in his *General Theory of Employment, Interest and Money* (1936), the principles of countercyclical fiscal and monetary policy-making that were supposed to enable governments to prevent the recurrence of a 1930s-style depression.

3 Isaac Deutscher, *Stalin, A Political Biography* (London 1949)

4 Douglas Abbott, Paul Martin, Stuart Garson, and James Gardiner were members of the Cabinet led by Prime Minister Louis St Laurent. The FAO is the Food and Agriculture Organization of the United Nations.

5 The Marshall Plan, also known as the European Recovery Program, was a plan for American assistance of the European nations in economic recovery, first proposed by United States Secretary of State George C. Marshall in June 1947 and launched by President Harry Truman late that year.

XX

J.S. Woodsworth: Socialist and Canadian

In this review of Grace MacInnis's biography of her father, J.S. Woodsworth: A Man to Remember *(Macmillan 1953) Scott showed his appreciation of the spiritual qualities of the man and the ethical bases of his socialism. Scott first met Woodsworth in the late 1920s, but did not get to know him well until the following decade. He then worked with him until Woodsworth resigned the leadership of the CCF at the outbreak of the war in Europe, chiefly advising him on constitutional matters. Since the appearance of Grace MacInnis's book there has also been a fine scholarly biography by Kenneth McNaught,* A Prophet in Politics *(University of Toronto Press 1959).*

In noting that Woodsworth's socialism was not doctrinaire, Scott addressed a point that in the early and mid-1950s was hotly debated in the CCF. He was among those who had come to believe that the party's Regina Manifesto did not suit the party very well in the 1950s. Not until 1956, however, did the party's National Convention adopt a new program, the Winnipeg Declaration, which to a considerable extent modified – left-wing critics used the words 'watered down' – the earlier document.

From *Ontario CCF News,* February 1954

Here, at last, is the man we knew, seen from the doubly understanding viewpoint of a member of the family and a fellow worker in the socialist cause. J.S. Woodsworth is already something of a legend in Canada, because he met people from all ranks and classes and all who came in contact with him went away knowing they had been in the presence of someone simple and great. He is part of our national tradition, a man indeed who will be remembered; this book by Grace MacInnis will help those who never knew him to understand why.

THE SPIRIT OF THE MAN

For most people, perhaps the greatness of J.S. Woodsworth lay in his lifelong work for the needy, the downtrodden, the exploited, and in his leadership of the CCF Party during its first formative years. These are, of course, achievements which will go down in Canadian history. They will become even more significant as the struggle for the co-operative commonwealth continues, and as each one who is privileged to share in that struggle grows more conscious of the part that spiritual leadership plays in any democratic socialist movement.

In a deeper sense, however, it is the underlying spirit of the man, the indomitable courage, both moral and physical, and the largeness of vision, which are so truly the essence of his character and of which his work for humanity and for socialism is but the most natural outward expression.

HIS LIFE'S TURNING POINT

Two events in his life stand out for me as symbolizing this inner courage and vision. The first is that crisis of the spirit through which he seems to have passed on his solitary visit to the Holy Land, when the conflict between his conscience and the traditional Christian faith in which he had been reared was resolved, and he knew for certain that for him the truth must be followed no matter where it might take him. I could wish the book had spent more time on this turning point in his life, though for the chapter where it is briefly referred to, Grace MacInnis has chosen the appropriate title 'To Thine Own Self Be True.' It was because he had found his own true centre that he had the strength to leave the ministry of his church, and the courage to stand alone in Parliament in September 1939 against war and Canada's participation in it.

ON LEAVING THE CHURCH

It is clear from this account that J.S. Woodsworth went out from the church, not because he had grown less religious but because he wanted a truer outlet for the deepened convictions within him. He writes in a letter:

The more I think about such matters the more the distinction between sacred and secular diminishes. Theoretically, for me, there is no such distinction. It is artificial, false, the product of a narrow ecclesiasticism and a more wretched secularism. Practically the two are so interpenetrating each other that I am gradually attaining my theoretical position in actual life. A man is called to *live*. Life itself is the greatest responsibility and one which no one can escape. 'Called to the ministry,' yes, true; but no truer than 'called to the bar.' If we have the one spirit the difference of gifts is a minor consideration.

This is the faith the man had; he did not leave the church, he made the world his church. And for that faith he suffered persecution and hardship. It is a dangerous faith, even a revolutionary faith, for it is a constant challenge to all those who would institutionalize the spirit of man in order the better to stifle it.

AHEAD OF HIS TIME

Reading this history, one cannot but be struck by the remarkable insight Woodsworth had into the course of social evolution. He was ahead of his time, a lone voice speaking truths to deaf ears. He knew better than the so-called 'practical men' who sat before him in Parliament what was needed in Canada and what was coming. This insight came, not from a profound knowledge of economics, of business, of public administration – he did not have this – but from his sense of values and his feeling for human beings. His life is a further proof that wisdom comes from the heart rather than from the head, and that a heightened moral perception is one of the most practical qualities a man can possess.

Woodsworth had that profound sense of direction without which all practical plans are useless. He could not himself have set up a central bank or drawn a bill to nationalize the CPR, but he knew that finance should be the servant and, not the master of men, and that the purpose of an economic system is to provide useful things in fair abundance to everyone, and with these guides he came to better policies than did those more technically expert than he whose thinking was blocked by prejudice and self-interest at the very point where it should have begun.

PUTTING HUMANITY FIRST

For him socialism was right because it put humanity first and property second; but by the same line of approach he was not and could not have been a doctrinaire socialist. For socialism as a strict creed becomes another church out of which man will again have to escape.

If the CCF is to be true to the spirit of J.S. Woodsworth, it will not only maintain his moral attitude to social questions, but it will also have to maintain something of his distrust of too precisely formulated a program.

He saw socialism as an expression outwards of the inner belief in human beings and their equal right to the enjoyment of the good things of this earth. He did not see it as men conforming to an outside dogma imposed upon them.

Socialists, too, must 'follow the gleam,' as he did, even if it leads them to change their opinion. He himself did this when he sought to resign from the very party he had founded, on the issue of war. It is to the glory of the CCF that that difference of opinion was accepted without having to accept the resignation. Unity was maintained though disagreement existed. This too he left as a legacy.

'ALL EMBRACING LIFE'

The second event which stands out for me in this life is the very last in that life. It is the way he asked that his ashes should be cast upon the ocean. The Epilogue to the book tells in simple and moving words how the family took the funeral urn out into the Gulf of Georgia and returned J.S. Woodsworth to the elements from which he came. Why did he choose the sea and not the land? Partly because of what the sea symbolized to him, the 'all-embracing life of which we are but an infinitesimal part,' as he says in the letter which ends Grace MacInnis's story.

But I like to think, too, that he chose the sea because, unlike the land, it was not owned by any one state or people; it is our common wealth, outside the boundaries of the sovereignty which he had so long opposed as a source of hatred and war. For though he was a Canadian, and proud to be a Canadian, he was also a citizen of the world which he wanted so much to become *one*. It is the unity of mankind, and the mystery of the whole universe, to which he was attuned, and so he went out to sea.

XXI

Letter to the Editor, *The Gazette*, 1956

The letter that follows was a slightly flippant comment on a problem that bedevils all cultural agencies and public services: the tax monies needed to support them are seen as a drain; the profits of corporations, which also come out of the pockets of the same citizens, are seen as desirable.
From *The Gazette*, Montreal, 24 July 1956

Your cartoonist John Collins last Saturday depicted Mr. Davidson Dunton as a little boy 'Ambushed' and running away in disgrace because the CBC showed a small deficit in 1955. Would Mr. Collins like to pillory Mr. Alan Jarvis of the National Gallery in the same way? The National Gallery has had to be supported by the taxpayer ever since its foundation. And what about our schools? They are a sheer loss every year – a typical example of the State giving away something for nothing. Why not a cartoon pouring scorn on school principals and Ministers of Education?

There seems to be something wrong with the world. The more valuable something is, the less money it seems to bring in. Churches, Art Galleries, Symphony Orchestras, Public Libraries, the CBC – it is the same dismal story everywhere. They cannot make money, but have to sink to living off charity and the taxpayer. Only Coca Cola and other such fine examples of modern civilisation achieve financial independence. Can it be that God is not a businessman?

XXII

Letter to David Lewis, 11 October 1959

By the late 1950s Scott was helping to lay the groundwork for what would eventually be the New Democratic Party. In this letter to David Lewis he expresses his concerns about the foreign policy plank of the new party and his belief that an appropriate plank would attract more voter support than a policy of public ownership of industry. In 1950 Scott had accepted the leadership of the United States in a policy of defence against an apparently expansionist Soviet Union. Nine years later he exhibited greater scepticism concerning American foreign policy in the Cold War era, and recognized that provocative actions were no monopoly of the Soviets. Scott was clear-eyed concerning the implications of nuclear war, and the futility of defensive measures against it.

Thinking further about the program notes we are supposed to produce, I feel strongly that we should include some pretty bold ideas wherever we can, and I can see no better place than in foreign policy. We must still have a strong leaning toward public ownership in all appropriate fields, and not give way before the current attacks upon it; certainly Canada is in crying need of some major ventures in areas still privately controlled. Perhaps it would be unwise to make a frontal attack, as did the CCF, but things like gas and oil pipelines we should go after directly. This will give us a radical enough approach to satisfy most of the old-time CCFers, especially if we indicate a preference, or priority, for public enterprise. But this will not spark the imagination of masses of people; this can only be done, I feel sure, by a radical new look at Canada's defence relationships.

Surely the plain fact is that Canada is not adding to her own defence, but only to international tensions, by her present subservience to American policy. All the radar systems are worthless and should be dismantled.[1] They have merely succeeded in ruining the Eskimo and wasting money. With the dismantling goes the need for any American personnel in the North. Similarly the rationale for NORAD[2] disappears once we agree that we cannot stop missiles with planes, and that we refuse to take any part in retaliatory measures. To be able to retaliate you must keep yourself in a permanent position of menace to the enemy, and this we cannot and should not attempt to do. Only by letting ourselves become a base for American short-range missiles can we be menacing. Did you see the report on the new US nuclear base in Turkey in today's [New York] Times? Threatening to destroy all the good of Khrushchev's visit.[3]

The immense response we are getting to our Committee on Radiation Hazards shows the degree of latent public.support for the line of policy I am suggesting. For once you stop testing you must also stop all future use of atomic devices in war, and this means stopping war and the things that tend to war. This sounds idealistic but is, under today's conditions, imperative. We are no longer in the world that produced the Kellogg Pact outlawing war;[4] that was perhaps pure idealism, but we face stark realities. I think we should state those realities in clear terms, and not shy away from logical consequences. We must declare our policy to be that we take no part in preparedness for atomic war, *either by way of attack or defence*. Because there is no defence.

I don't think people vote primarily on domestic issues in our western countries today. The differences between right and left are less startling than they used to be, except perhaps with regard to labour legislation. This is important, and must not be overlooked, but the larger public considers this only a small part of any program. I am sure world ideas have a stronger appeal than ever before.

If we proclaim Canada's bold re-appraisal ... of her defence policy, then we are faced with what to do with the billions we can save on military expenditure. Here we are forced to be bold again, but surely in an exciting way. We can reduce federal taxes, pour more money into needed public works in Canada (including purchase of pipelines), and contribute generously to the International Development Authority (that Fleming wants to hamstring)[5] and economic aid. Reduced federal taxes leaves more for provincial taxation, thus helping provincial development plans or else leaving the individual with purchasing power to take up the slack left by cancellation of war contracts.

Along with all of this we must somehow formulate a theory of Canada's position in this world of giant powers. We must be bold a third time in asserting Canada has an individuality as a nation which is in danger of being lost and can and should be preserved. We must emphasise mass communications as an element in 'individuality defence.' [The] CBC must be restored to its first principles by generous public aid and an out-and-out attack upon commercialisation of the air waves. We should promise a Royal Commission on the press, following the English model, looking not so much to new legislation as to a public airing followed by some formulation of rules of guidance for journalists enforced through a permanent Commission of Journalism appointed by the industry, and before which complaints may be laid. We must develop positive restrictions on foreign ownership of certain key institutions (e.g. the banks, as the Gordon Commission suggested),[6] radio and TV stations (no non-US citizen can own the American ones), etc. And we should develop a policy of 'buying back Canada,' by nationalisation, outright purchase of shares, favouring of domestic investors, and other appropriate means. If this slows down foreign investment – it will never stop it – so much the better. For as Galbraith has said, we are bedevilled by a worship of mere production without having enough concern about what it is we are producing.[7]

A large emphasis in the new creed for Canada must be placed on education. A middle power like ourselves can make its best contribution in human minds. Minds freed from crass materialism, not trained to exercise dominion over other people's [minds], recognising the values in cultural diversity while conscious of the oneness of mankind. We must release the greatest undeveloped resource we have – the human spirit and the human brains of Canadians, the vast majority of whom never get near the top of their form. This means strengthening all schools and universities, fostering every form of artistic expression, lengthening the training period of all young people capable of further instruction, and infusing into everyone a feeling of excitement and adventure in this age of fantastic opportunities for human betterment. The 'new plateau' to be reached at this stage of our growth must be a spiritual and mental plateau.

I know I have not written a program. This is a preamble to a program. But unless we have a sense of direction I don't think we shall get far. We need a blueprint before we start nailing up the planks. So far we have not had one.

EDITOR'S NOTES

1 The reference is to the Distant Early Warning (DEW) Line
2 The North American Air Defence Command, the agreement for which was signed in May 1958
3 Nikita S. Khrushchev, Soviet leader from 1955 to 1964, visited President Dwight D. Eisenhower at Camp David in 1959. During that meeting each revealed to the other that he had serious difficulties with a military-industrial complex which demanded continued and heavy armaments expenditures.
4 The Kellogg Pact, or Kellogg-Briand Pact, renouncing war as an instrument of national policy, was signed in Paris in 1928 by representatives of the United States, Great

Britain, France, Germany, and eleven other countries. The prime movers were the American secretary of state, Frank Kellogg, and the French foreign minister, Aristide Briand.

5 Donald Fleming was minister of finance in the Cabinet led by John G. Diefenbaker.

6 The Royal Commission on Canada's Economic Prospects (*Final Report*, 1957), chaired by Walter Gordon

7 The reference is to *The Affluent Society* (Boston 1958) by the Canadian-born economist John Kenneth Galbraith.

XXIII

What Does Labour Need in a Bill of Rights?

In this address Scott linked the purposes of a Bill of Rights to the fundamental purposes of the labour union movement. The government led by John G. Diefenbaker had introduced a Bill of Rights to the House of Commons in September 1958. Nothing more was heard about the measure until twenty-two months later (it received second reading in early July 1960 and was passed into law in August). Nevertheless the government's action in 1958 quickened Scott's interest, for as early as 1934 he had proposed the inclusion of a Bill of Rights in the British North America Act.
Summary of a paper delivered at the Atlantic Provinces Labour Institute, a conference held at Dalhousie University, Halifax, 16–20 November 1959

Before dealing with the question of what Labour needs in a Bill of Rights, let us consider why there is a Labour movement. How did the Labour movement arise and what is its purpose? Trade guilds and similar organizations go far back in history: but when we speak today of the trades union movement, essentially we have in mind that organization of industrial workers which emerged with the Industrial Revolution.

The first clause, in what the International Labour Organization calls 'The Philadelphia Charter,'[1] points out that labour is not a commodity, and that labour is not to be treated merely as a factor in production and viewed as a ton of coal or so many board feet of lumber. One cannot produce commodities without labour, but labour is not a commodity.

Labour used to be called 'hands' because 'hands' designated the only part of the human being in which the employer was interested. The industrial system learned early how to divide the work of a man into pieces and to put a price on each piece. An employer could buy 'hours of labour' and thus measure the work of a man as he would measure a yard of cloth. The employer was committed to pay his men by the hour; between those hours labour could be discarded, for what happened then to Labour was not deemed to be any concern of the plant owner. The owner made allowance for depreciation of machinery, as part of the cost of the operation of the business, but the wearing out of the 'hands' was not recognized and was not taken into account. Society would look after the 'hands,' or the 'hands' would look after themselves.

In that system, where the maximizing of profits was the principal purpose of production, efficiency demanded that the cost of labour, and other production costs, be kept as low as possible. The whole nature of the system prevented it from regarding labour as essentially human, and the ownership interest in business predominated almost to the complete exclusion of the labour interest.

The trades union movement was founded and developed principally to change this limited concept of the relationship between man and his work, and between man and the tools with which he worked. Workers needed the right to confront the great aggregations of capital with something equivalent to the force that capital exerted. What a long time it has taken to establish at law the right to bargain collectively. The right is still opposed by many employers and the struggle continues. Whole areas of labour (most people who work for the state, for instance) are denied this right.

Labour has fought every inch of the way, over a century and a half, for what is decent and democratic. We think of the Chartist Movement in England, essentially a labour movement, and its bitter fights to achieve the secret ballot.[2] The Chartist Movement failed, in one sense, yet everything that it fought for is incorporated now in our law.

In the beginning, unions were illegal conspiracies operating in restraint of trade. People had to fight hard for the freedom of association and the right to strike. The collective withholding of labour was the only force that Labour could develop which could begin to compare with the power that went with ownership, the power to hire and fire without reason given or required to be given. In my opinion, the power of ownership is still many times greater than the power of Labour, even taking into account Labour's right to strike. To say that power has passed generally from the hands of ownership into the hands of Labour is but a smoke screen to camouflage the present real source of power.

One of the most serious problems facing Labour today rests in the fact that every major instrument of mass information is controlled and operated by the enemies of Labour.

In a recent television broadcast from Quebec, over the Canadian Broadcasting Corporation's French Language network, a forty-minute brief (which the Quebec Federation of Labour had presented to the Government of Quebec) was reduced for public consumption to six minutes, while the thirty-five minute reply of the Premier of Quebec was given in full.[3] The public heard what the Premier of Quebec had to say about Labour, but little of what Labour was saying about itself.

A program in the current CBC-TV series called *Background* was presented recently for the ostensible purpose of giving to the Canadian people background information about the proposed new Canadian political party.[4] More than two-thirds of this program was devoted to speakers who opposed the new party in no uncertain terms. If the program had been called *Viewpoint*, the offering of different points of view would have been justified. The program was called *Background*, however, with the implication that Canadians were being given objective background information by which they could make up their own minds on an important matter. This type of thing, I am sorry to say, seems to be even more prevalent now on the CBC, under the Conservative Government, than it was under the former Liberal Government. It is my opinion, however, that CBC news coverage and opportunities for the expression of different viewpoints have been so far ahead of the press of Canada as to show that, for the fairest distribution of news, we require publicly owned and operated institutions like the CBC, rather than privately owned and operated institutions like newspapers.

Illustrations like the foregoing serve the emphasize the struggles of Labour and the needs of Labour, and lead to the question 'What will a Bill of Rights do for Labour in relation to the kind of struggle that is going on now?' Labour in the United States has been evolving under a Bill of Rights ever since there was a trades union movement in the United States. Canadian Labour has evolved in a country without a Bill of Rights. I see very little difference between the nature of the struggle in Canada and that in the United States.

Labour, as part of the citizen body, has a genuine interest in, and need for, a Bill of Rights. Everyone needs civil liberties and to have security protected by law. In so far as a Bill of Rights will aid in the protection of civil liberties, a Bill of Rights is good for Labour, as it is good for farmers, teachers, business men and everyone else. There is a general need for the basic freedoms: freedom of speech, freedom of the press, freedom of religion, and so forth.

Among the basic freedoms, freedom of association is one particularly important to Labour. Undoubtedly, a Bill of Rights will contain a declaration of the right of association. If it is the right kind of Bill of Rights, a bill which will restrict legislatures from passing laws against rights (as state governments are restricted by the American Bill of Rights), it will help Labour by making more secure the right of association. If we had such a Bill of Rights in Canada, there would be, for instance, a new ground for setting aside anti-Labour legislation in Newfoundland.

If a Bill of Rights merely mentions the traditional freedoms, I do not think that it will do much to ease the path of Labour. A society in which people are educated to understand rights and to become more conscious of civil liberties is of course a good society for Labour. Everything that strengthens democratic sentiment is good surely for the Labour movement and it is good for everybody else. A society in which there will be more opportunities for both sides of a case to be heard, in which people will be more alert to the needs of their fellow-citizens, will be a healthy society.

I suggest that it is possible to put into a Bill of Rights something more than political freedoms. The Universal Declaration of Human Rights of the United Nations (which is not the law of any land, but rather a declaration of good ideas and good principles) proclaims basic freedoms and a great deal more. The Declaration reads,

Everyone has the right to freedom of peaceful assembly and Association.
No-one can be compelled to belong to an association.

This clause involves the tricky quesiton of the closed shop. My view is that trade unionists should have the same right as lawyers or doctors to organize a professional type of association. Certainly, lawyers have to belong to a professional association or they cannot practise law. The concept of a citizenship in industry, where there is free bargaining between employers and employees, so that in a given industry there may be a closed-shop arrangement to make this bargaining possible, does not impress me as a violation of a right.

The Declaration continues:

Everyone, as a member of society, has the right to social security and is entitled to realization, through national effort and international cooperation and in accordance with the organizational resources of each State, of the economic, social and cultural rights indispensable for his dignity and the free development of his personality.

Everyone has the right to work, to free choice of employment, to just and favourable conditions of work and to protection against unemployment.

Everyone, without any discrimination, has the right to equal pay for equal work.

Everyone who works has the right to just and favourable remuneration, insuring for himself and his family an existence worthy of human dignity, and supplemented, if necessary, by other means of social protection.

Everyone has the right to form and to join trade unions for the protection of his interests.

The Declaration deals with the right to leisure, to adequate standards of health and housing, and to the right to an education.

... Education shall be free, at least in the elementary and fundamental stages. Elementary education shall be compulsory ...

provinces by judicial interpretation, (3) insufficient control over corporations and insurance companies, and (4) lack of clarity in federal-provincial financial arrangements. At that time, a federal power to implement international treaties was thought to exist; Mr. Bennett had just ratified three conventions of the International Labour Organization and had enacted legislation which was only later referred to the courts by Mr. King and held *ultra vires*. The constitutional aspects of national planning were already reduced to what seemed like manageable proportions, implying change but no drastic overhauling of the Canadian system of government.

It will be interesting now to contrast what *Social Planning* proposed with what has actually happened in the growth of the Canadian constitution since 1935. Many changes have taken place, both in the law and custom of the constitution. With a few notable exceptions, they have tended to be along the lines suggested in so far as the distribution of legislative power is concerned. In 1934 the central bank, demanded in the Regina Manifesto, was created, and by 1938 was made a wholly owned state bank. A national currency emerged, signed by public officials rather than by bank presidents. The Rowell-Sirois Report surveyed the experiences of the depression years and recommended a variety of changes in government responsibility; the provinces were to keep the lesser social services, but the Dominion was to assume unemployment insurance, contributory old age pensions, jurisdiction over minimum wages, maximum hours and minimum age of employment, and the power to implement ILO conventions; it was, in addition, to deal with marketing even when intraprovincial trade was affected, and to supervise all insurance companies except those confined to one province. These recommendations were thus specifically designed to overcome the Privy Council's disastrous decisions of 1937 on Mr. Bennett's 'New Deal' legislation, which had struck down the first unemployment insurance and federal marketing laws as well as the statutes implementing the three ILO conventions.[1] In its financial recommendations the Rowell-Sirois Report was even bolder; all provincial debts were to be assumed by Ottawa, and provincial subsidies based on population were to be replaced by national adjustment grants calculated to meet the proved fiscal needs of the provinces. Future provincial debts were to be in Canadian currency only, unless approval was obtained from the Finance Commission. The provinces were also to withdraw from personal and corporation income taxes, and succession duties. The Report has passed into history, but it left behind, beside a reflection of the left-of-centre trend of opinion in the 1930's, the unemployment insurance amendments to the constitution of 1940 and a distribution of tax fields that was accepted in subsequent federal-provincial taxation agreements.

The war years changed Canada's constitutional position in international affairs, notably by establishing her independent right to declare war and make peace, but

A Bill of Rights, guaranteeing rights like those proclaimed in the United Nations Declaration of Human Rights, is needed by Labour. Certain basic freedoms, like the freedom of speech, press, association and religion, can be guaranteed absolutely by prohibiting people from interfering. Where social and economic rights are involved, however, somebody has to pay for them. This is a reason for leaving such rights out of a Bill of Rights. There is no use writing into a constitution, 'Everyone shall have a decent standard of living.'

It is not enough merely to include these rights in a bill. Further action is required by the state through social insurance laws and other measures. There is good reason for leaving such rights out of a Bill of Rights.

It is my view that the Prime Minister's proposed Bill of Rights would be greatly improved if it consisted of two parts: (1) a part guaranteeing those rights which *can* be guaranteed in a Bill of Rights, and (2) a part containing what might be called a declaration of social goals of aims. This is how the matter is dealt with in some of the newer Asian constitutions which embrace the rights proclaimed in the United Nations Declaration. The Constitution of Pakistan, for instance, says that the state of Pakistan *will seek to achieve* certain specified goals. To have the state committed to a permanent national policy of aiming at raising standards and improving conditions is surely a good thing.

If social and economic goals were stated in a Canadian Bill of Rights, we would be provided with a positive guide for all governments. We would strengthen thereby an important concept. As we improve the techniques of production, the general standard of living should rise. In Canada, every year the amount of productivity per head increases (except when there is an economic recession), and provides a growing fund out of which more wages can be paid. (I recognize that this is an average situation and that it does not apply to all industries.) In our society, constantly improving with reference to production, every year there is more to divide up.

It is evident that Labour has a least the same interest in a Bill of Rights as has everybody else in our society. A Bill of Rights declares principles of good government which are a continuing educational force in society. The more democratic the society, the better off is labour. However, if a Bill of Rights is confined to the political rights of free speech, press, association, religion, and so forth, I do not see that a bill will make a significant difference in Labour's fight for better wages or in Labour's defence of the right to strike or to picket. Such a Bill of Rights would be valuable in general, but I do not think that it would have direct application to Labour's principal concerns. It would not increase educational opportunities in Canada, nor would it strengthen the right to collective bargaining.

If a Bill of Rights is made a fundamental part of the law or of the constitution, binding on all governments (and not passed, as has been proposed, merely as a statute without effect on provinces), it will strengthen the freedom of association which itself is under attack at this very moment.

In my view, Labour has a general reason, and (in part) a special reason for wanting to see a Bill of Rights adopted in this country.

EDITOR'S NOTES

1 The Philadelphia Charter was adopted by the International Labor Organization (ILO) at a meeting in Philadelphia in 1944 and later annexed to the ILO Constitution. It reaffirms the principles to which the ILO is dedicated. Taken from the charter is the ILO's motto: 'Poverty anywhere constitutes a danger to prosperity everywhere.'
2 Chartism was a British working-class movement which took its name from the 'People's Charter,' first published in 1838. Its six points were annual parliaments, universal male suffrage, the secret ballot, equal electoral districts, the removal of the property qualification for membership of Parliament, and payment of members. Three mammoth petitions were presented to the House of Commons before the movement collapsed in 1849.
3 In September 1959 Jean-Paul Sauvé of the Union Nationale succeeded Maurice Duplessis as premier of Quebec after the latter died.
4 The reference is to what in due time became the New Democratic Party.

XXIV

Social Planning and Canadian Federalism

In 1961 the NDP was formally launched, with T.C. Douglas as its leader. Michael Oliver, professor of political science at McGill, was the national chairman of the party. Social Purpose for Canada *was intended to do for the new party something of what* Social Planning for Canada *had done for the CCF. Scott's contribution constituted the most obvious link between the two books, concentrating as it did on the legal and constitutional questions raised by the NDP program. Among the contributors to the new volume was a Quebec lawyer, Pierre Elliott Trudeau, who also wrote about constitutional matters.*

In this paper Scott paid more attention than previously to the necessity that provincial planning be established alongside federal planning.
From *Social Purpose for Canada*, ed. Michael Oliver (Toronto: University of Toronto Press 1961), pp. 394–407

From the day of its founding the CCF party anticipated that the building of a

socialist society would require constitutional change in Canada. A Britis[h] America Act drafted for a predominantly agricultural community in 18[6] hardly be expected to fit an industrialized economy operated on princ[iples] economic planning. Yet the degree of change required was not at all cl[ear.] Regina Manifesto in 1933 did not propose any specific shift in the distrib[ution] legislative powers as between Ottawa and the provinces; it contented itsel[f] statement that 'What is chiefly needed today is the placing in the hand[s] national government of more power to control national economic devel[opment]. All were agreed that there must be more central authority, for reasons ob[vious] anyone faced with the conditions in Canada at the time. But this was centr[alization] for planning's sake, not for centralization's sake. Indeed, the Manif[esto] speaks of 'the increasing industrialization of the country and the co[nsequent] centralization of economic and financial power which has taken place i[n] two generations.' Private centralization had obviously already taken pla[ce] hands of big business – a centralization before which the provinc[es were] powerless. What was needed was a countervailing public power to re[present] national interest. Only the Parliament of Canada was seen as big enoug[h for this] task. In CCF thinking, strengthening federal authority for this purpose [merely] took away jurisdiction, not from provincial governments, but from [an] irresponsible minority of financiers and industrialists.' That the CCF opp[osed] extreme centralization is evident from its reference, in the Manifest[o, to the] historic distinction between 'matters of common interest' and 'local [matters] adopted by the Fathers of Confederation at the Quebec Conference of 1[864,] from its description of public ownership as being 'Dominion, Prov[incial or] Municipal.' The party, despite its socialist objectives, always acce[pted the] principles of Canadian federalism.

By 1935, when *Social Planning for Canada* was published, the fiel[ds where] federal powers needed reinforcement were being clarified. In that boo[k it was] argued that a great deal of the supposed weakness in federal authority was [due not] to the BNA Act, but to 'long years of planned inactivity on the part of Li[beral and] Conservative governments' (p. 504). The non-use of existing pow[ers was] more striking than the absence of powers. Unquestioned authority e[xisted to] deal with international trade, interprovincial trade and commun[ications;] banking, currency and interest; there was the declaratory power over loc[al works] which could bring them within federal jurisdiction; federal taxing pow[er was] virtually unrestricted. The desire in the old parties for reform was o[bviously] less than the constitutional authority for reform. Yet certain areas [were] beyond federal reach and, in the opinion of the authors, required federa[l control.] These were said to be related to (1) social legislation, particularly in re[spect of] labour matters, where it was felt concurrent powers might be adequat[e for the] Dominion, (2) aspects of intraprovincial trade and commerce give[n]

they did not compel a change in the distribution of legislative powers. They did, however, enormously increase the knowledge of what might be accomplished within the existing distribution. Perhaps most of the wartime economic planning could have been justified under the 'emergency' doctrine which, as enunciated by the courts, permits extensive federal legislation based on the 'peace, order and good government' clause of the constitution of a kind not permissible when there is no emergency. Indeed, given a sufficiently dangerous situation, Canada becomes virtually a unitary state; we possess a theory of the *état de siège* in our law, though no mention of it appears in the BNA Act. Apart from emergency powers, however, there were other sources of federal authority in the ordinary law capable of extensive use for economic planning during the war; classes of subjects such as defence, interest, banking, taxation and the spending power fully justified federal control of military production and monetary and fiscal policy at that time.

The emergence of monetary and fiscal planning was one of the major developments of the war experience of 1939–45. Maynard Keynes put more substance back into federal powers than Lord Haldane had ever taken out, and the techniques he suggested are now widely accepted if not always consistently applied. The federal Government after the war followed Keynesian policies with varying degrees of eagerness and success, and no changes in the law of the constitution were found necessary. Existing federal powers, supplemented by agreements with most of the provinces, sufficed. Parliament, having jurisdiction over 'The Public Debt and Property,' was competent to dispose of federal Crown money by gift or conditional grant, so long as the law providing for the expenditure did not purport to change any existing law in the provinces. This enabled federal spending to be directed to the achievement of a wide variety of social and economic goals. Hence, for example, were established family allowances,[2] pensions for the blind, a national housing programme, grants to universities, allowances for disabled persons and floor prices for agricultural products. Some of the federal grants are made direct to recipients without provincial intervention, as are family allowances; others form the basis of federal-provincial agreements, as does hospital insurance; both are instruments of social planning involving no constitutional change. A co-operative federalism can achieve much with this approach. The 1951 amendment defining federal jurisdiction over old age pensions was useful, but probably only clarified a power that previously existed. It introduced a new principle into the constitution, however, by specifically subjecting federal old age pension law to existing or future provincial laws.[3] In all other instances of concurrent powers in the BNA Act, a valid federal law prevails over any provincial law in conflict with it.

Besides constitutional amendment, judicial interpretation has been clarifying important aspects of federal jurisdiction. On four matters of serious national concern the courts have rendered decisions which denied federal powers and which have left us with unresolved governmental problems. these are judgments in the Snider case (to refer back to 1925),[4] which reduced federal jurisdiction in labour matters to federal undertakings; the Labour Conventions case (1937)[5] which reduced the power to implement treaties to matters otherwise within federal jurisdiction; the Marketing Act case (1937)[6] which overthrew a nation-wide marketing scheme supported by every provincial legislature; and the Delegation case (1951)[7] which held that a delegation of powers from Parliament to legislature or vice versa was unconstitutional. The first three of these decisions upset existing federal statutes; the last imposed a new limitation on all legislatures in Canada. The seeming victory for the provinces was a hollow one, except in so far as it fixed the status quo; the marketing situation is today very confused, and what positive use can provinces make of the power to implement treaties when they can have no diplomatic representatives abroad, or of the power to make laws on labour relations when more and more industries in each province are controlled by a single national board of directors which deals with a single trade union? The futile attempts of provincial governments to settle the Packinghouse Workers' strike in1947, while the federal Government sat helplessly on the side lines, is a standing example of the danger of confiding large issues to small jurisdictions in a federal state.[8]

More recent judicial interpretation has suggested that some of these decisions may be modified and their more extreme effects overcome. When the Empire Treaty of 1919 which supported federal jurisdiction over aeronautics was replaced by a purely Canadian treaty, the courts found that the subject was one which fell within the 'peace, order and good government' clause of the constitution, though there was no national emergency at the time.[9] If this clause, which was intended by the Fathers of Confederation to serve as the residuary clause of the constitution, and which Lord Haldane reduced to a war emergency power, could be restored to its original place in the law, a number of difficulties in national planning could be overcome. Matters which have 'grown up' through social change to become truly national could then be legislated on in their national aspects. It would be rash, however, to imply that this point has been reached. In regard to delegation, some of the effects of the 1951 reference case have been overcome by a subsequent holding that delegation, not from legislature to legislature, but from legislature to subordinate administrative bodies, is permissible.[10] The logic of this is unconvincing, but an example of its working may be seen in the federal delegation to provincial transportation commissions of the power, granted Ottawa in the Winner case,[11] to regulate trucking and bus services crossing provincial boundaries.[12] Delegation here produced decentralization; it could be used in the reverse direction. As pointed out above, the constitutional position of marketing legislation is very unsatisfactory, owing to the 1937 decision, but even here there are signs that the courts may begin to take a more realistic view of the trade and commerce clause. The notion of 'interprovincial trade' is becoming clearer, and is more frequently found in federal statutes; of even greater significance is the acceptance of the notion that trade within a province may enter into a 'current' or 'flow' or trade, a 'stream of commerce' which may take it out of provincial jurisdiction and bring it under the federal power. Germinal ideas of this nature are to be found in the Ontario Farm Products Marketing Act reference of 1957[13] and the Murphy case of 1958,[14] more especially in the masterly judgments of Judge Rand. What Professor Bora Laskin calls the 'thaw' in the frozen trade and commerce clause[15] seems to have set in, and Canada may be beginning to follow the trend of American decisions some fifty years later.

In another large field of constitutional law recent developments are of particular interest to socialists. This is the area of human rights. Unless these expand as society grows, the socialist goal is unattained, for no amount of economic security can make up for their loss. Freedom, like full employment, can be made a goal of planning; it is not accidental that the book of essays on planning published by the CCF in 1944 was called *Planning for Freedom*, or that it contained a special chapter on freedom. In a series of judgments during the 1950's the Supreme Court of Canada had occasion to take its stand on several issues involving fundamental liberties, and it made constitutional history by its elucidation of the basic concepts of freedom to be found in the BNA Act. The definition of sedition was narrowed in the Boucher case,[16] freedom of religion emerged triumphant over provincial limitation in the Saumur[17] and Birks[18] cases, freedom of speech and of the press were preserved in the Padlock Act case,[19] and the responsibility of public officials, even the highest, to the citizen whom they have illegally injured was sustained in the Chaput,[20] Roncarelli[21] and Lamb[22] cases. Improvements in the statute law, for the better protection of basic freedoms, are seen in the growing adoption of Fair Employment Practices Acts and Fair Accommodation Practices Acts. In 1960 came the Canadian Bill of Rights which, though making much less change in the law than many have supposed, set out in one document enacted by Parliament a number of the traditional civil liberties.[23] There was only one counter-trend observable in the decade, but it was a frightening one – the attack on freedom of association which was launched by several provinces in their anti-trade union legislation; this forms part of the provincial picture which is dealt with below.

Other chapters in this book make clear the importance of the control of investment in any form of economic planning. Is this control possible within the present distribution of powers? To some extent, obviously so. Monetary policy affects investment, at least quantitatively. Fiscal policy provides different forms of direct public investment. Tax incentives can be given to induce capital to flow into selected areas. All these devices are being used by federal authorities today. Can more drastic controls be exercised, for example to prohibit investment in undesirable enterprises or over-expanded industries? Could Ottawa, instead of subsidizing the development of Elliot Lake, have forbidden the mining development of that area? The answer in this instance might well be affirmative, because the export of the ore can be controlled, and in addition all mines for the production of uranium and other prescribed substances are 'works for the general advantage of Canada' under the Atomic Energy Control Act. The unregulated development of uranium production in Canada, with private capital being allowed to make its own decisions as to investment, is a good example of bad planning; the Canadian taxpayer pays the cost of all the services the private investors require, and allows them such quick profit that the risk of a collapsed market is assumed by workers' families much more than by capital. The workers do not receive equivalently quick wages.

If we ask ourselves about federal control of investment in a private industry that is not producing a commodity specifically within federal jurisdiction, we meet grave constitutional difficulties. For the Privy Council long ago laid down the ridiculous rule that federal authority to regulate trade and commerce did not include regulation of any particular trades (for example insurance or margarine) in which Canadians would otherwise be free to engage in the provinces. It would appear that the only particular forms of trade and commerce which Ottawa may directly control, regardless of their magnitude, are ones that can be brought within specific federal powers, such as banks and interprovincial communications. Any other kind of enterprise desiring to expand its plant by investing its own reserves or funds raised in Canada would seem to be free from federal interference, regardless of the social utility of the investment; such control as might exist would seem to be a provincial matter. While the flow of foreign capital can probably be federally regulated, a prohibition of its entry for a particular trade purpose might be considered as colourable legislation, designed to evade the constitutional prohibition, and hence *ultra vires*. The same danger would exist if export licences were used to control particular schemes. Companies with federal charters might be subject to special forms of investment regulation, but, according to another Privy Council decision,[24] a provincial company can do business across the country provided other provinces give it permission, so some large businesses might escape by this door. The 'works and undertakings' of a company can be declared to be for the general advantage; here is a power seemingly available for investment control. But it bites off more than is needed, and is a clumsy device for the purpose. Short of constitutional amendment, or some form of delegation, the most useful legal basis for a national investment policy would be a further 'thaw' in the trade and commerce power so that federal legislation could embrace regulation of a trade as a whole where it was carried on throughout the country by transactions that ignored provincial boundaries. But even if this occurs, a considerable area of investment remains within provincial jurisdiction, and provincial co-operation is therefore required.

Apart from federal regulation of investment in areas directly within federal jurisdiction, there is another method that can improve the possibilities of co-ordination and synchronization of national investment policies. This is the offer of financial inducements to provinces and municipalities to accept federal leadership and timing in the management of public investment.[25] The offer by Mr. Diefenbaker to share the cost of municipal public works timed to relieve winter unemployment is an example. While it has its merits, this device has so far been little developed and only occasionally applied. A province may have plans of its own which it prefers, or may be actively opposing federal plans because of pressures from private investors: indications of this have been evident in the development of the Columbia River project in British Columbia. Canadian federalism is more difficult to operate than that of the United States where, because of the larger number of states, no single state can exert any special influence on the central government.

This brings us to the role of the provinces as agencies of planning. During the 1930's their helpless financial situation made them drowning victims needing rescue rather than lifeboats bringing safety and security: hence the CCF emphasis at that time on federal action. Another depression could reduce them to the same state. Alberta's bold attempt to fight the economic battle alone fell foul of the BNA Act in 1937–8; as Professor J.R. Mallory says, 'the Aberhart programme provided the *reductio ad absurdum* which was required to demonstrate the unsuitability of the provinces as agencies of major fiscal and economic policy.'[26] The emphasis there must be on the word 'major.' When war expenditures and wartime planning ended the economic depression, and as the capture of power in both Ontario and Saskatchewan seemed possible, the CCF began to pay greater attention to provincial responsibilites and opportunities. As early as 1943, E.B. Jolliffe reminds us, CCF members of several provincial legislatures met to discuss mutual problems; he was then the leader of thirty-four CCF members of the Ontario legislature as against only thirty-eight Conservative supporters of the Drew Government. Writing in *Planning for Freedom* (pp. 74, 75), he says: 'it is generally recognised now in the CCF that there is an important job to be done by a provincial administration. Part of that job under our present constitution, can only be done by the provinces; it cannot be done by the Dominion.' Also in 1943, the CCF book *Make This Your Canada* (p. 151) declared that 'central planning over the whole economy must fit in with, take account of and give opportunity for regional, provincial and municipal planning. The last thing desired is complete centralisation.' Several further conferences of provincial representatives were held in the following years, the Saskatchewan Government giving first-hand information and advice. The CCF party was the first party in Canada to initiate the 'interprovincial caucus.' While economic planning for Canada will certainly mean more action by the federal government, it does not mean less action by provincial governments; on the contrary, their role increases proportionately. Economic planning will be 'even more essential and important than it is today,' as *Make This Your Canada* put it (p. 151). The charge of 'centralization' against the CCF, if used so as to imply a disregard of legitimate provincial autonomy, is largely a fear-raising slogan put across by reactionaries in order to keep capitalists in power, with the result that the economic domination of our society by the power élite is further protected.

The most obvious example of the need for provincial planning is in regard to natural resources. These all started (except in the Northwest Territories) as provincial Crown property, that is, in public ownership. Even today most of them remain in public hands. Under the BNA Act it is the provinces who must make the concessions, leases and sales that transfer them to private corporations. The terms of these grants largely determine the manner in which economic development will take place and the amount of return the public treasury will receive for the province's permission. Under a provincial Premier like Duplessis, heading a political machine universally recognized as susceptible to corruption and bribery, and confronted with vast sums of American capital seeking profitable outlet, the nature of a province's economic planning is easily imagined. In his case, not content with giving away huge resources for a minimum of return to the public, he even sold to a private corporation dominated by American capital the publicly owned distribution system for gas in Montreal which a previous Liberal administration had itself taken away from the old Montreal Light, Heat and Power Company. And all this was under the guise of preserving Quebec's autonomy. No wonder that a present Liberal cabinet minister has written that what Quebec needed was a Mossadegh.[27] All but one of the Canadian provinces rejected the CCF proposals for provincial socialization and planning; the resultant degree of Americanization and big-industry control is only now beginning to be appreciated. In Saskatchewan, the gas distribution system is a provincially owned public utility.

It is in the development of provincial resources that very large amounts of investment take place, and as has just been pointed out, provincial governments can exercise control, if they wish, over many of these enterprises. It is thus possible for the separate provincial investment policies to run counter to federal policy. Provincial administrations may be counted on to want to maximize investment at all times in their own province, even when national planning may require a slowing down. Quebec has special cultural reasons for wanting to control her economy. provinces may borrow at will, either in Canada or abroad, and, as in the 1930's, may find themselves overloaded with a debt that must be repaid in a depreciated currency. All these forms of provincial autonomy will make over-all control of investment very difficult without co-ordinating machinery and a spirit of co-operation. In Australia, dangers of this kind led to the imaginative step of creating a Loan Council to control the borrowing of both the state and

Commonwealth governments; each state is represented on the Council, but the Commonwealth has two votes and a casting vote. The rejection of the Rowell-Sirois Report in 1940 left Canada without any plan for co-ordinating federal-provincial financing, and since then we have proceeded by a series of *ad hoc* arrangements which have become so subject to individual exceptions and special deals as to make of Ottawa a kind of United Nations seeking agreement among ten sovereign states. In October 1960, and again in February 1961, the federal Government actually proposed as a 'new plan' that the provinces should revert to levying their own taxes to meet their own needs. Thus the pre-1940 anarchy would be restored, the rich provinces would become richer and the poor poorer. Even Quebec was not prepared to accept this degree of autonomy; Premier Lesage is reported as describing Mr. Diefenbaker's proposals as a backward move that would 'endanger the satisfactory functioning of our federal system' and as liable to 'increase regional inequalities.'[28] The equalization formula which formed part of the revised proposals presented by Ottawa in February was still, according to Lesage, 'unthinkable, unbelievable, utter and complete deception.'[29] The failure of post-war governments, whether Liberal or Conservative, to grapple seriously with the financial problems of Canadian federalism, or even to set up a permanent federal-provincial secretariat as recommended by the Rowell-Sirois Report, is a reflection of their lack of national purpose and their dominance by outmoded notions of free enterprise.

Obviously federal co-operation is needed even in the development of provincial resources. The federal government built the railway into Labrador down which Quebec's iron ore is carried. The Central Mortgage and Housing Corporation assists in the building of new towns without which the workers at remote provincial mines could not be housed. Everywhere provincial development dovetails into some federal undertaking. The vaster the provincial resources, the more likely they are to be beyond complete provincial control. If they require a market outside the province, they cease in that aspect to be provincial. The planning of new power dams on rivers is perhaps wholly a provincial matter if the rivers are wholly within a province and the province happens to be large enough to finance the projects. In poorer provinces this may be impossible, and federal or other aid must be sought. The rivers may be interprovincial or international, limiting the authority of one provincial government, and requiring interprovincial agreements or federal-provincial-American co-operation. In a federal state, whether planning be by governments or private corporations, intergovernmental co-operation is essential. In Canada we have made some but far from enough progress in working it out.[30] There is a place also for purely interprovincial co-operation, and for that reason the initiative of Premier Lesage of Quebec in calling the provincial governments together in December 1960 is to be welcomed, though it is not yet clear what form of co-operation will emerge.[31]

A good example of a successful form of federal-provincial co-operation in Canada is to be found in the work of the advisory committees under the Prairie Farm Rehabilitation Act (1935) and the Maritime Marshland Rehabilitation Act (1948). The drifting soils of the prairies and the unreclaimed marshlands of the maritimes were wasting agricultural assets beyond the means of those provinces to restore. Federal initiative and provincial co-operation have resulted here in a truly impressive programme of agricultural planning. Agriculture is of course a concurrent power under the constitution, so Ottawa may legislate within the field; the trouble is that the field has been extremely narrowly defined by the courts. The form of co-operation now adopted, in which plans are mutually agreed on and cost is shared, avoids legal pitfalls. To March 31, 1958, PFRA provided the necessary assistance to construct 421 community projects for water conservation; it undertook major irrigation projects in southern Alberta and minor ones in British Columbia; it has promoted major reclamation projects in all four western provinces, notably on the South Saskatchewan River; and MMRA works constructed or in progress affect hundreds of thousands of acres in Nova Scotia, New Brunswick and Prince Edward Island.[32] Another example of a similar approach is the Eastern Rockies Forest Conservation Board (1947) which provides for co-operation between Ottawa and Alberta for the conservation of the forests on the eastern slope of the Rockies which is part of the watershed of the Saskatchewan River. As the value of these forms of co-operation becomes more evident, the willingness to embark upon them may be expected to grow.

Economic planning is only a small part of a province's responsibility for planning. Fields such as education, welfare and community planning provide even larger opportunities for provincial experimentation. These matters are more exclusively within provincial jurisdiction, though in each the federal government has an important role to play. Despite Quebec's change of mind, which finally led her to reject what she had first accepted, federal grants to universities are likely to continue in other provinces which feel that university autonomy in educational matters is great enough to permit them to decide for themselves whether or not to accept a gift. So too the federal government's responsibility for large areas of social welfare needs no emphasis; here federal authority rests on a combination of specific powers (unemployment insurance, pensions, etc.) plus the spending power (family allowances, contributions to hospitals, etc.). Community planning remains wholly within provincial jurisdiction, but the federal government is not prevented from participation in specific schemes such as the development of new town-sites (Elliot Lake) or slum clearance (Regent's Park). Ottawa alone can decide where airports and railway stations are to be located. In all these three fields, however, the provinces are primarily responsible, and are likely to remain so. The constitutional problem here is financial rather than legal: it is more difficult to find the money than find the legal authority. Socialist planning that envisages enlarged functions of provincial government in activities that are inevitably costly must make provision for the necessary funds. One place where provinces must learn to look, besides any arrangement they may have with Ottawa, is in their own treasure house of natural resources, at present exploited primarily in the interest of shareholders. Only under an unplanned capitalism would one find Canadian children receiving a scanty education in overcrowded schools while Texan shareholders reap huge profits from Canadian oil and natural gas. A proper system of redistribution, based on need rather than population, will also be needed to enable poorer provinces to keep pace with those more fortunately endowed.

There is another function of provincial governments, already mentioned, which concerns deeply all Canadians. This is their responsibility for many aspects of civil liberties. While the fundamental freedoms of religion, speech, association and the press are predominantly in federal care, there is a division of authority in the broad field of human rights which makes the provinces important agencies for the preservation of certain liberties. Although the criminal law is federal, it is administered by the provinces, and the way a law is enforced, particularly if police are involved, can expand or narrow the freedoms it guarantees. Municipal governments also play a large part in the creation of a free society, though their authority is derived from and can be no wider than that of the province. What a province may do to harass and confine the trade union movement is becoming evident from anti-union legislation in Quebec, Newfoundland, British Columbia and Alberta.[33] There are styles in freedoms as in clothes; it is fashionable today to oppose racial discrimination, so we have made considerable advances in the enactment of provincial Fair Employment Practices Acts, for example; but although the black man may work with the white, neither may be free to exercise to the full his trade union rights. Capitalism does not worry about the colour of its workers so much as about their power.

When we have discussed the role of the federal government on the one hand, and of provincial and municipal governments on the other, and of the great necessity of continued co-operation among them we have still left out a whole area of social and economic planning – the area which is supranational. For no nation state can live unto itself alone in the contemporary world, least of all a country with the peculiar geographical situation and political relationships of Canada. Neither the federal government, nor the provincial governments, nor both combined, can make foreign markets secure, or guarantee the bases of stable economic progress. Canada cannot isolate herself, even if she would, from world conditions, though by better planning she can cushion the shock of external influences and redistribute their burdens more equitably. It is sterile now to confine discussion to the old conflict of jurisdiction between Ottawa and the provinces; too many problems have grown outward beyond our frontiers. The principle that the size of government must be as large as the size of the problems with which government must deal not only leaves the provinces far behind as adequate agencies of planning but increasingly leaves the federal government behind also. Defence becomes North American defence and defence of the Western world; trade likewise takes on its global aspects. Even the subjects seemingly confined more easily within national boundaries, such as health, education and welfare, have their international relations. The old two-way federalism blends into world federalism the beginnings of which are evident in a multitude of specialized agencies of the United Nations and in the United Nations itself. To be a good Canadian citizen one must be a good world citizen; to be a good socialist one must be an international socialist. National constitutions are the bricks and stones in a world structure, and one contribution to world peace and stability which nation-states can make is to see that their constitutions render it possible for them to fulfil their international duties. That is why it is imperative that Canada's power to implement Canadian treaties should be defined as clearly as was her original power to implement Empire treaties.

AUTHOR'S NOTES

1 The unemployment insurance reference will be found in [1937] Appeal Cases 355; the marketing reference, *ibid.*, 377; the ILO reference, *ibid.*, 326. Comments on the cases will be found in 15 *Canadian Bar Review* (1937).

2 The Family Allowance Act was upheld in *Angers* v. *Min. of National Revenue*, [1957] Ex. CR 83

3 BNA Act, s. 94A

4 *Toronto Electric Commissioners* v. *Snider*, [1925] Appeal Cases 396. See F.R. Scott, 'Federal Jurisdiction over Labour Relations – A New Look,' *McGill Law Journal* (1960), at p. 153. [Writing the judgment was Lord R.B. Haldane, whom Scott refers to more than once in this article. – Ed.]

5 See n. 1 above.

6 *Ibid.*

7 *A.G. of Nova Scotia* v. *A.G. of Canada*, [1951] SCR 31

8 The story of this attempt is told in Scott, 'Federal Jurisdiction over Labour Relations.' The strike in the Dominion Bridge Co. in 1960 was caused by the Company's refusal to accept nation-wide bargaining for certain items.

9 *Johannesson* v. *Mun. of West St. Paul*, [1952] 1 SCR 292, and note by Bora Laskin in 35 *Canadian Bar Review* (1957), at p. 101

10 See the *Willis* case, [1952] 2 SCR 392 and note by John Ballem in 30 *Canadian Bar Review* (1952), at p. 1050.

11 [1954] Appeal Cases 541; [1954] 4 DLR 657; note in 32 *Canadian Bar Review* (1954), at p. 788

12 Statutes of Canada, 1953–4, c. 59

13 1957 SCR 198

14 1958 SCR 626

15 *Canadian Constitutional Law* (2nd ed., Toronto 1960), p. 318

16 [1951] SCR 255

17 [1953] 2 SCR 299

18 [1955] SCR 799

19 [1957] SCR 285; and see note by Andrew Brewin in 35 *Canadian Bar Review* (1957), at p. 544.

20 [1955] SCR 834

21 [1959] SCR 121

22 [1959] SCR 321. See also F.R. Scott, *Civil Liberties and Canadian Federalism* (Toronto, 1959), pp. 37 ff.

23 The legal nature of the Bill of Rights is analysed in 37 *Canadian Bar Review* (1959), at pp. 1 ff.

24 The *Bonanza Creek* case, [1916] 1 Appeal Cases 566

25 See on this, W.A. Mackintosh, 'Federal Finance (Canada),' in Geoffrey Sawer, ed., *Federalism: An Australian Study* (Melbourne, 1952), pp. 100–5.

26 *Social Credit and the Federal Power in Canada* (Toronto, 1954), p. 189. [William Aberhart was the Social Credit premier of Alberta, 1935–43. – Ed.]

27 René Lévesque (now the Hon. René Lévesque, Minister of Natural Resources), 'Pas plus bêtes que les Arabes,' *Cité libre*, mai 1960, p. 17. [Mohammed Mossadegh was the Iranian prime minister whose government nationalized the Anglo-Iranian Oil Company in 1951. Two years later he was replaced in a CIA-sponsored coup which returned the Shah to the throne. – Ed.]

28 *Montreal Gazette*, Oct. 27, 1960

29 *Ibid.*, Feb. 24, 1961

30 On the idea of 'co-operative federalism' see J.A. Corry, 'Constitutional Trends and Federalism' in A.R.M. Lower *et al.*, *Evolving Canadian Federalism* (Durham, NC, 1958), chap. III; see also A.W. Macmahon, ed., *Federalism, Mature and Emergent* (New York, 1953), *passim*.

31 See reports of the meeting in *Montreal Gazette*, Dec. 3, 1960. The idea was proposed in the Tremblay Report on Constitutional Problems, 1956. For comment on this Report, see: F.R. Scott, 'French-Canada and Canadian Federalism' in Lower *et al.*, *Evolving Canadian Federalism*, chap. II; and A. Brady, 'Quebec and Canadian Federalism,' 25 *Canadian Journal of Economics and Political Science* (1959), at p. 259.

32 For a brief description of these projects, see *Canada Year Book*, 1959, pp. 408–11.

33 For criticism of this legislation see 4 *Canadian Labour* (1959), nos. 4–5. The most outright attack on freedom of association is found in the Newfoundland legislation (Statutes of Newfoundland, 1959, cc. 1–2), commented on by Stanley Knowles, 'The Facts about Newfoundland,' 4 *Canadian Labour* (1959), nos. 4–5.

XXV

Confederation Is a True Alliance

Scott's continuing close contact with the French Canadian community brought him an invitation in 1963 to address the Société Saint-Jean-Baptiste of Quebec City. Here he discussed the nature of the Confederation pact between French and English Canadians. Later in the year Prime Minister Lester B. Pearson appointed the Royal Commission on Bilingualism and Biculturalism, co-chaired by Davidson Dunton and André Laurendeau, and made Scott one of its members. He served on the commission for seven years.
Translation of an address to the Saint-Jean-Baptiste Society, Quebec City, May 1963[1]

... The question put to me is somewhat abstract. You ask me if a true alliance is possible between French and English Canadians. But the question implies a total absence of an alliance between the two communities, whereas an alliance does in fact exist, even if it is strongly criticized. Personally, I think that it is more a matter of making modifications, however far-reaching, to Confederation than of a completely new alliance. But as you know I am not a separatist.

What are the governing principles of the present alliance? Do not forget that this alliance has lasted for nearly a century, a period during which there were many wars and significant political and social changes, which we have weathered in spite of all the strains and disagreements.

Also keep in mind that during this same period Quebec has made tremendous progress. This progress has made French Canadians so strong and proud that you are now asking yourselves whether you should put an end to the former state of affairs and start a new life as an independent nation. One of the governing principles of the alliance was the preservation of your culture in Quebec, and in this respect it has certainly been successful.

But what were the other goals of Confederation? At this point, I would like to cite several examples which are not specifically mentioned in the subject proposed for discussion. One of the objectives of Confederation was to give Quebec a democratic and parliamentary system through which the French and Catholic majority would be its own master, and note that this is a result of its majority status and not of its race since – let us be quite clear on this point – democracy and racism are incompatible. The minority in Quebec, be it of British or any other origin, also has its place and its rights. In addition, Confederation guaranteed the provincial legislature vast room for legislative action, where the French Canadian majority could do as it pleased. The best illustration of this important fact is the provincial budget, which has grown to a billion dollars per year.

Some people speak of colonialism, but in fact it is a rather unusual colony that can freely spend a billion of its dollars. This amount is three times greater than the federal budget of thirty years ago!

I know that there are two principal obstacles to freedom of action in the provincial domain at the present time, the question of finance or taxation and the question of economic control. Let us begin with the first problem. The allocation of public revenues is a much-debated issue in all federations: identical financial problems arise in the United States, Australia and India. How much should remain with the central government? How much should go to the member states? These are not questions of law but of policy. The allocation of revenues can easily be changed without changing the constitution. Since 1867, furthermore, the taxation system has undergone continual change. There is never enough money to satisfy all the demands of all the governments; if one gets more another must receive less – even Social Crediters are subject to this law.[2] Everything ultimately depends on arriving at reasonable agreements. Bear in mind, however, that under our present system of government it is the federal representatives who have the duty to decide on the measures necessary for Canada's defence as well as the other needs of the central government. This is why ultimatums from the provinces do not help very much in resolving the problem.

The second question which raises significant difficulties and limits freedom of action in the provincial domain is that of economic control. Let me simply say here that it is not the English presence but rather the capitalist system that is French Canada's enemy. If we believe in free enterprise we must accept its implications and its consequences. This is exactly the same issue which confronts the other provinces in face of the American economy.

Having been a socialist, in the English sense of the word, for a number of years I am not one of those who believes in free enterprise. I have often preached that Quebec should exercise its political power to control the economic system. In the past, the response has often been that one cannot be a Catholic and a socialist. This was before the time of Pope John XXIII and his masterful encyclical, *Mater et Magistra*, which should be circulated in all the schools of Canada, whether Catholic or not.[3]

The idea of planning is accepted today. However, it is clear that a province cannot plan in isolation; there must be co-ordinated planning.

I venture to say that Confederation is a true alliance which has to a certain degree served the domestic needs of Quebec. But outside Quebec it is another matter. I believe that it is the duty of the other provinces and the federal government to make changes and institute new arrangements that better recognize the French fact. I have always fought for a greater recognition of minority rights in the rest of the country, the two important issues in this case being bilingualism and separate schools. We can state that there is not a single province which is not bilingual to some degree since all federal laws are official in both languages throughout Canada. But this is not enough!

Five provinces out of ten have separate schools, but again this is not enough!

Here, then, is an opportunity for a new alliance. Why should we try? So that we are not obliged to destroy a federal system that has given us much in the past and that can still give us a great deal in the future. We should keep in mind that successful heterogeneous federations exist throughout the world.

EDITOR'S NOTES

1 The following students in the Department of Translation, Glendon College, York University, collaborated in translating this address: Sharon Anderson, Carole Blanchard, Pat Dimitroff, Dora Faber, Margaret Hopper, Miria Ioannou, Madeleine Magnus, Karen Muir, Linda Poulson, Valerie Smith, and Sally Tremain. Their professor was Jane Couchman.
2 Social Credit, to almost everyone's surprise, gained twenty-six seats in Quebec in the federal election of June 1962. In the federal election of April 1963 the Créditistes sustained some losses but still took twenty seats.
3 Issued in 1961, *Mater et Magistra* was the most important statement in thirty years of the church's views on the social responsibilities of Roman Catholics.

XXVI

Global Attack on Our Institutions

This article and the following are comments on the invocation of the War Measures Act in October 1970, by the federal government led by Pierre Elliott Trudeau. The first was published during the crisis; the second appeared the following year in a special publication of the Canadian Association of University Teachers, a 'Symposium on the War Measures Act.' Besides Scott, the contributors to this symposium were James Matkin, Abbé Louis O'Neill, Claude Ryan, Marcel Rioux, Gerard McNeill, and Terry Copp.

Scott saw a fundamental issue in the crisis as the necessary refusal of a duly elected government to accede to the illegal demands of terrorists, the Front de libération du Québec (FLQ) who had kidnapped the British trade commissioner in Montreal, James Cross, and the Quebec minister of labour, Pierre Laporte. (The latter was eventually murdered by his abductors.) Along with a good many

other people Scott had come to the view that drastic action was called for if
violence, which had been escalating gradually over seven years, were during the
October crisis not to result in large-scale bloodshed. He believed that this in
turn might make the settlement of the differences between Quebec nationalism
and Canadian federalism impossible by peaceful means. He opposed some of
the excesses that accompanied the use of the War Measures Act, but he neverthe-
less approved the use of the act as the lesser of evils. In retrospect he came to
*see the position taken by Gérard Pelletier (*La Crise d'octobre, *1971) as one that*
very closely approximated his own views.

Although he deplored the use of terrorist tactics, and opposed the goals of the
FLQ, Scott recognized that the FLQ phenomenon, and the support it attracted,
pointed to abuses in Quebec and Canadian society that needed to be addressed.
Not surprisingly, he associated these abuses with capitalism.
From *The Gazette*, Montreal, 24 October 1970. Reproduced with permission of
The Gazette

Quebec is in grave trouble. Therefore Canada also is in trouble. Therefore all
Canadians who are concerned about the future of our common country must try to
understand what is happening and be willing to help.

In many parts of the world there are revolutionary movements attempting to
overthrow existing societies. Some of them deserve to be overthrown. Others, of
which Quebec is one, do not need a violent upheaval because not only are they in
full evolution but other more humane means of changing their institutions are
available. For example, the legitimate activities of the Parti Québécois, which
aims to prove by democratic means that the majority in Quebec is in favor of
independence, are not in question now. This party has existed for some years, it is
distinct from the FLQ, and its activities are not rendered illegal by the proclamation
of the War Measures Act.

It is not separatism in Quebec that is outlawed, it is a determined and
well-organized revolutionary movement applying new techniques of terror aimed
at the polarization of our society and the fracturing of those elements which
enable Canadian federalism to exist at the moment and give assurance that it
can exist in the future. It is a global attack upon all institutions in our present
system.

CHE GUEVARA FAILED

If an organization like the FLQ were to enter Ontario or British Columbia, aiming to
overthrow the social system by force, we all know it would have no chance
whatever of success. Che Guevara tried this in Bolivia,[1] a country where the native
population was infinitely more oppressed than it is in Quebec, and no one would

support him. But in Quebec the same kind of revolutionary movement has more success. We must ask ourselves why this is?

Obviously one reason is that an FLQ type of movement, whose philosophy and tactics are not specifically French Canadian but are merely showing now in French Canada, has more support in Quebec because it feeds on nationalism and the general notion of Quebec independence. This term also needs understanding, because sincere people in Quebec who say they are indépendantistes or séparatistes are not necessarily aiming at a new independent state totally unrelated to its surrounding communities.

The intelligent separatist knows that Quebec would not be a viable country without a great many of the economic and political contacts it now has with English Canada and with North America. René Lévesque[2] himself has said he favors independence in order that Quebec might by herself think out her proper role in North America, and then, as it were, re-enter into a Canadian federalism adjusted to meet this new situation.

OPTIONS OFFERED

There is at the moment in Quebec a government newly elected which clearly offered the Quebec people an option on staying within Confederation and working out the necessary adjustments without a break in the fundamental relationship. This government represents the great majority of the Quebec electorate, and must be considered as the only authoritative voice of Quebec. It was this government, with the full support of the city government of Montreal, which requested Mr. Trudeau to give him emergency aid.

In the light of this double request, how could a federal prime minister have possibly refused to respond? It may well be debated and should be debated, whether the War Measures Act is the right kind of emergency legislation for this kind of emergency or whether the particular measures were not too severe. Mr. Trudeau himself knows this, and has suggested the necessity of a new substitute statutory power to deal with something less than the War Measures Act was intended to deal with. But at that moment when this request came Ottawa could scarcely have refused to acquiesce without laying itself open to a charge of gross irresponsibility towards the most important centre of French Canadian culture in Canada.

All this surely is clear. It is equally clear that the present emergency provides no ultimate solution for the problems out of which the emergency arose. The FLQ could not have developed from mere extremist propaganda to emotional appeal, with considerable support at least among the youth in the universities and schools, if it did not play upon basic aspirations in the people. This youth, as represented by the organization of its teachers, 70,000 strong, is by no means in support of the methods of the FLQ, but is in support of its fundamental aim of an independent Quebec though not necessarily of its brand of socialism.

FUNDAMENTAL CHOICE

Quebec is therefore facing and will continue to face its fundamental choice: does it believe that the future of its language and culture in North America is better secured by steady growth within Canadian federalism?

Or does it really believe that its future is better secured by creating a small independent fortress state which is not likely to begin its life without social and economic upheavals possibly forcing its government towards totalitarianism and cut off from the expanding centres of French culture outside Quebec?

It is a tragedy, in Pierre Trudeau's otherwise remarkable handling of the problems of a prime minister in Canada in these difficult days, that he has been led into economic policies which have imposed particular hardships upon Quebec and the youth of Quebec. If there was any province in which unemployment should have been carefully avoided, so as not to make it worse than in other parts of Canada, it is Quebec. Yet it is precisely in Quebec that unemployment is worst and is likely to grow more serious. This is no time to ask whether Quebec is receiving more favorable treatment than other provinces in monetary terms. It must receive better treatment if its problems are worse than those of other provinces.

The purpose of economic planning is to equalize economic benefits as far as possible across the country. They are extremely unequal now in Quebec. There must be economic measures taken to open opportunities for employment and for youthful careers in Quebec, and in the French language, if we are to have any hope of reducing the frustration and alienation which feed the FLQ. Some imaginative action on the part of Ottawa fully supported by all provinces of Canada is more necessary because it is obvious that the FLQ by its subversive activities, deliberately designed for this purpose, has probably frightened investors who might otherwise have put private money into Quebec resources.

REALISM NEEDED

What is needed in this situation above all is a sense of realism, and much good will. The realist who knows his facts will understand that nothing, not even the FLQ terrorism, will prevent the more creative and imaginative minds in Quebec from continuing their struggle to improve their cultural position and to enlarge their individual opportunities as members of the French-speaking comnunity.

This is the essential issue. Either Quebec is going to produce some kind of French culture in North America, of which every person in Quebec can be proud, and all persons outside also appreciative and respectful, or it is not worth trying.

Surely all English Canada must believe they ought to succeed in this effort. They must not be deflected from this purpose by the activities of terrorists whose primary aim is not so much the expansion of a culture as the achievement of political power for Maoist or Communist ends.

More and more people are coming to believe that the capitalist system, with its structures and values, is an obstacle in the way of developing a truly humane French culture, as it is to the development of a humane English culture in Canada. This problem both communities in Canada are tackling, though in my opinion with not sufficient vigor. We are accustomed to accept great injustices, partly because we did not really see them, and partly because we did not think there was any way of overcoming them easily. This time has passed. The productivity of modern technology could rehouse the population that needs better housing, could feed the people who have insufficient food, and could give employment to all who honestly sought it, in useful and inspiring activities, if we put the resources at our command to this great social purpose. But the present profit-seeking organization of the economy renders this extremely difficult. An increasing appreciation of this fact is the source of the revolutionary activities of so many people.

We have witnessed, in several parts of Canada resulting from the crisis in Quebec, young people expressing support for the FLQ. This does not necessarily mean that they like violence, nor that they support the tactics of kidnapping and murder. What it does mean, in my opinion, is that they support the global attack of the FLQ upon the false values, the corporate structure, the brainwashing by advertising, that everyone can see is a characteristic of our present economic system. In whatever means we take to deal with the present crisis in Quebec, and whatever new measure we adopt to prevent its recurrence, we must never forget this profound new widespread outlook, formerly held only by avowed socialists.

I still believe that we can hold off the violent revolutionaries while we apply ourselves to the solution of the problems which they rightly emphasize. I think to imagine that there are quick solutions to these problems is juvenile, and to label our society as nothing but oppressive and aggressive and violent is oversimplifying and greatly exaggerating. By comparison with almost any previous condition of the human race in any part of the world, our present society contains as many humanitarian and democratic activities as have ever been seen before. It is therefore a question of the speed of change and the degree to which one trust the processes, cumbersome though they may, in our present democratic institutions ...

EDITOR'S NOTES

1 Ernesto 'Che' Guevara was an Argentinian-born revolutionary leader who was instrumental in Fidel Castro's victory in Cuba in 1959. He was killed in Bolivia in 1967 while trying to organize a peasant revolt.

2 At the time René Lévesque, a former provincial Liberal cabinet minister, was leader of the Parti Québécois; later (1976–85) he was premier of Quebec.

XXVII

The War Measures Act in Retrospect

From CAUT/ACPU, vol. 2, no. 4, May 1971. Reprinted by permission of the Canadian Association of University Teachers

On October 23, 1970, I wrote in my diary eight reasons why I had supported the application of the War Measures Act to the critical situation in Quebec. They were all examples of an outbreak of civil disorder in the past. The first dates from 1918, when I heard the machine guns on the streets of Quebec City during the conscription riots, and saw for the first time a crisis leading to bloodshed which left deep and lasting wounds in the body politic. My second experience was in 1936 when I was chairman of a reception committee for the three delegates of the Spanish Republican Government who were in Canada seeking aid against Franco's invading forces;[1] that night Montreal was given over to marching bands of students and demonstrators who, with the virtual connivance of the police, roamed about breaking windows and preventing public meetings for the delegates from being held. The civic and religious authorities were then on the side of the demonstrators; had such a situation developed last October, and we were on the brink of it with Chartrand, Vallières and Gagnon[2] addressing large student gatherings, bloodshed in the streets could scarcely have been avoided even if sections of the police force were disaffected, for the army was there. The doctors, be it remembered, were on strike, so the hospitals were wholly unprepared for such an emergency. Montreal had just witnessed two riots with violence during the previous year: one that left St. Catherine Street a shambles after the police strike, and the other when marchers went into St. Léonard to protest against the local Italian demand to have instruction in English in the public schools. 'No English Wops' was one of the placards being carried, and a certain Paul Rose was one of the leaders.[3] This particular riot resulted in heavy damage to Italian property, and the eventual reading of the riot act. The march had been advertised on the French TV an hour before it started with a request for mass support. All this after seven years of increasing bombings, increasing bank hold-ups (they were averaging two to three per day by early October, many claimed by the FLQ) and thefts of rifles and dynamite. On top of this came the two kidnappings and the fantastic spectacle of duly elected governments talking to the secret conspiratorial FLQ which had seized a temporary political power and was maintaining it by threats of assassination.

Something had to break, and for a few dreadful days it seemed as though civil government might break. We have Claude Ryan's admission that he thought so too;[4] he even toyed with the idea that if Bourassa was incapable of continuing, 'Lévesque is a logical possibility' (see *Rumours of War*, p. 181).[5] René Lévesque was not even a member of the legislature. What a near victory for the FLQ! Panic spread everywhere, even though the army was already present. We had the army, a police force which had been able to round up and secure conviction of a number of bomb-setters, and a Criminal Code which many think was 'adequate.' Why was such escalation of terror possible if the Criminal Code was adequate to meet the situation? Ordinary processes of law enforcement had obviously and frighteningly failed. Perhaps in some other society they might have worked, but in Quebec at the time, for a variety of reasons, they did not.

Canada was lacking in legislation to deal with any emergency short of apprehended war, invasion or insurrection, other than the calling in of troops to help the civil authorities. Apart from these political crises, a power blackout in wintertime or a strike in essential services could place the lives of millions in jeopardy. Calling in the military can maintain order against riotous street demonstrations, but troops cannot ration food. Nor can they ferret out a well-trained secret conspiracy. One lesson – among many – we can learn from October is the need to take a new look at emergency powers, including the War Measures Act. No modern industrial society, where a natural disaster or a determined few can imperil millions, can risk drifting along without forethought and foresight. But the Quebec and federal governments had only the War Measures Act to deal quickly with a deteriorating situation. All the evidence pointed, not to a popular insurrection, but to a further erosion of civil government, and to what Gérard Pelletier has called 'uncontrollable civil disorders.'[6] This is how it looked to me.

A shock treatment was needed to restore the balance. It was given, and it worked. There was only one death, and it was not caused by the forces of law and order. Six million Quebecers had their right to self-government restored. They can make René Lévesque Prime Minister by votes, but not by bombs. He would not want it otherwise.

The invocation of the Act, however, and the way it was carried out, must be sharply distinguished. I sympathize with the dilemma facing the NDP in having to vote for both together. It was not necessary, in my opinion, and that of the Civil Liberties Union of which I am a member, to have had such drastic Regulations accompanying the Act. The lesser powers of the Turner Act would have been more than adequate at the start.[7] There must have been hundreds of unnecessary arrests. Our whole society is partly to blame for these. Emergency powers require emergency police training, and this we have never provided. Too many people think of police as 'pigs,' so they tend to create that kind of force; this is polarisation at its worst. In the past 30 years I have noticed a great improvement in the general behaviour of the Montreal police toward parades, demonstrations and sit-ins, but the blanket powers of search and detention under the first Regulations were just too much for the whole body of police accustomed to the simple old ways. Reparation is surely owed for unjustified treatment and detention, just as it is owed for false arrest under the ordinary law.

In this respect, the Report of the Committee to Aid Persons Detained under the Emergency Powers Legislation, presented to the Quebec Government by the Civil Liberties Union and a special committee appointed for the purpose, is of prime importance, though it is not even mentioned in *Rumours of War*. It represents something quite new, and potentially useful in other situations. Fourteen representative citizens of Montreal met as early as October 25th to ask the Minister of Justice, Mr. Jérôme Choquette, to select three of their members to form part of a committee of investigation of the detainees, with complete freedom to visit all prisons in the province. Permission was granted, and with one representative of the Department no less than 162 persons were visited. Financial help was given where necessary, families were informed of the situation, consultation with lawyers arranged, and charges of police brutalities received and passed on. The whole Report, too long to summarise here, was published in *La Presse* and *The Montreal Star*. It was handed to the Quebec Ombudsman and is under consideration by the government. This does not excuse the abuses, but it makes any comparison between Canada and Brazil or Greece – which some who should have known better have made – wholly misleading.[8]

What French Canada as a whole thought of the War Measures Act was dramatically shown by the Gallup Poll of December 5th: 86% approved. English-speaking Canada approved 89%. I have never known such unanimity between French and English on any matter so easily capable of dividing them – especially when there are so many politicos and journalists desperately trying to divide them. A certain 'Montreal writer' Ann Charney, to whom the *Canadian Forum* devoted five pages in its somewhat hysterical January issue, stated: 'If there had been some illusion of unity between the English and French in Montreal, on Friday the protective screen crumbled and the gulf was there for all to see.' What percipience! There are plenty of differences between English and French in Canada, but not a difference as to whether violence or votes are to be the means by which we reach for solutions. I would have thought this result at least would hearten our civil libertarians, but it seems to make some of them even more afraid of the future. I do not see that poll as an approval of police methods: it was rather a relief at being freed from fear.[9]

That the future is fraught with dangers to civil liberties is abundantly clear. The future always is, more so today than perhaps ever before in Canada. Partly this is due to movements of world opinion over which we have little or no control. But it is also partly – though only partly – due to our apparent indifference to social and economic injustices which people believe could be greatly reduced by more vigorous democratic planning aimed at full employment, the elimination of regional disparities, and above all at changing competitive money-making into various forms of human co-operation. We need a new view of man's place in a technological society which puts him first and mere growth second. We must put a more 'human face' on our uses of power. It is tragic that the Bourassa government has been so hampered in its first attempts at reform by the FLQ crisis that the solutions are now harder to come by, and that Ottawa's economic policies have allowed a degree of unemployment that people cannot be expected to tolerate for long. In my opinion this is exactly what the FLQ wanted. They want guerrilla warfare in the streets, and guerrilla tactics in the law courts. They want to prove that violence is the only way out. They want to show that liberal democracy cannot evolve into a more social democracy. Maybe it won't, but the great majority of Quebecers have not given up a belief that it can ...

EDITOR'S NOTES

1 General Francisco Franco was the leader of the insurgent forces in Spain during the civil war in that country (1936–39). Assisted by armed forces from Nazi Germany and fascist Italy, the insurgents were victorious, and Franco became the leader of the new Spanish state, remaining its dictator until his death in 1975.
2 Michel Chartrand was a Montreal trade unionist and supporter of the FLQ; Pierre Vallières and Charles Gagnon were leaders of the FLQ. Vallières, author of *Nègres blancs d'Amérique: Autobiographie précoce d'un 'terroriste' québécois* (translated as *White Niggers of America* [Toronto 1971]) was the chief theorist of the FLQ.
3 Paul Rose was a member of the FLQ and one of the kidnappers of the Quebec minister of labour, Pierre Laporte. Rose was later convicted of Laporte's murder.
4 Claude Ryan was editor of the Montreal newspaper *Le Devoir*. He later served as leader of the Quebec Liberal party, and is currently (1986) provincial minister of Education.
5 Robert Bourassa was Liberal premier of Quebec from 1970 to 1976 and regained this position in late 1985. The book referred to is *Rumours of War* (Toronto 1971), by the Toronto journalist Ron Haggart and the Toronto lawyer Aubrey E. Golden.
6 Gérard Pelletier was in 1970 secretary of state in the Trudeau cabinet. In 1971 he published *La Crise d'octobre*, soon afterwards translated into English, his personal statement on the events in Quebec.
7 The Public Order Temporary Measures Act was introduced into the House of Commons by John Turner, then minister of justice, in November 1970, and passed into law the following month.

8 Both Brazil and Greece at the time had authoritarian governments in which a military junta played a central role. `

9 Scott later wanted to add: 'I was on the side of the majority of Quebec on that question.' Often, of course, he had found himself in the minority!

XXVIII

FHU and the Manifestos

The historian Frank Hawkins Underhill died in September 1971. In The Canadian Forum, *which both men, Underhill in particular, had worked so hard to keep alive, Scott reminisced about aspects of their early friendship and collaboration. Underhill played a crucial part in the early development of the LSR, and provided the first draft for what became the CCF's Regina Manifesto in 1933.*

Unlike Scott, Underhill did not stay with the CCF. In the later 1940s, while Scott served as national chairman of the party, Underhill became increasingly disillusioned with it, and around 1950 left it altogether. To some extent he made his peace with the Liberalism he had abandoned in the 1920s. Scott, however, preferred to believed that his reconversion was not total.

From *The Canadian Forum*, vol. 51, November 1971, pp. 8–9. Reprinted by permission of *The Canadian Forum*

My first memory of Frank Underhill is in August 1931. Percy Corbett, then Dean of Law at McGill, was invited to attend the Institute of Politics which Williams [College] held every summer at Williamstown, Mass., and he took me along as his secretary. He also invited FHU to come as speaker at several sessions. The great depression was well along, the British Empire was turning itself into a Commonwealth, everyone was wondering whether England's war debts to the United States would be paid, and in the middle of our conference the British government abandoned the gold standard. We did not lack topics of conversation, even if no one seemed to know really what was happening.

FHU was sure of one thing, however, and that was that Canadian politics had to change. He foresaw a realignment of movements and parties in Canada. This was not the topic of the Williamstown conference, but it became the principal, almost the sole matter for discussion one Sunday when Corbett, FHU and myself took the day off to climb Greylock, a mountain in the nearby Berkshires. On the way up, while eating our picnic lunch and on the way down FHU expounded and expanded his thesis: the old parties were bankrupt, a new party must be and obviously would be formed, it must be saved from the fate of the Progressives who fell into the all-embracing arms of Mackenzie King,[1] and the only way to make sure of this was to found some kind of Canadian Fabian Society which would provide a solid intellectual base for a new party programme. Research would underpin reform, and provide an analysis of Canadian society which would expose the nature of capitalism and the function of the Liberals and Conservatives as defenders of a system crying out for radical change. Whatever new party came along must be given an ideological foundation which would make a fusion with these parties forever impossible.

Thus was conceived the League for Social Reconstruction. We had no name then, but we had the plan out of the fertile political mind of FHU. He and I discussed the next steps. He said he knew enough people in Toronto University to form a group who could start work immediately, and I said I knew of a few around McGill whom I might rely on. So when we left Williamstown shortly after, it was agreed we should organize meetings in Montreal and Toronto, should decide on a future conference of our two groups, and above all should try to formulate a policy statement, a Manifesto in fact, which should clearly define our political position. The League was to have two classes of members, like the Fabian Society: those who accepted the Manifesto and were full members, and those who subscribed to the general aims of the League, received its publications, but were not committed to the whole of its democratic socialist philosophy. Thus it would avoid sectarianism.

In the course of that autumn of 1931 the plan evolved. We studied the work and organization of the League for Industrial Democracy under Harry Laidler in the United States; we first toyed with the name League for Economic Democracy, but eventually decided on League for Social Reconstruction as being wider in its implications. The initials LSR formed a new word that was constantly on my tongue and in my thoughts, and in those of my closest friends, for the next ten years.

The founding meeting of the LSR took place in Toronto in January 1932. This was seven months before the CCF was launched in Calgary, and a year and a half before the Regina Manifesto was adopted by the Party, which had sprung into being through the social forces at work in Canada exactly as FHU had predicted on the top of Greylock. The temperature the day we met fell to 17 below [Fahrenheit], which gave us a true-north-strong-and-free feeling. The principal work of the meeting was the final amending and approval of the Manifesto. Drafts of this document had been circulating among the members of our two groups the previous autumn but my memory is unclear as to the manner in which it was first prepared. I suspect FHU was a dominant influence, though by then we had many other good minds with us, whose names are well known today. It was group thinking – of which I have had a long experience – at its best. I stress the importance of the LSR Manifesto because since then most of the talk has been about the Regina

Manifesto, undoubtedly a more important document because of its political acceptance but second in line nevertheless. One has only to compare the two to recognize the fundamental similarity, even to words and phrases. FHU did the first draft for Regina, but he started from the LSR base. It was a broad base, and many individuals helped to form it. None of them, except our Honorary President J.S. Woodsworth, was present when the CCF party was born in August 1932. The intellectuals came in later, before they had time to do much of the research they were beginning. This only came out in any quantity in what P.C. Armstrong, then 'economist' for the CPR,[2] called in his diatribe against it THE BOOK, namely *Social Planning for Canada*. And a great deal of that research came out of the Royal Commission on Price Spreads.[3] Let us be careful about damning Royal Commissions.

So the CCF was saved from the fate worse than death. It escaped Mackenzie King – all save a few dropouts. The NDP is also safely standing on its own feet. FHU's plan worked. How ironic that he should have wavered for a time! Yet by then Mackenzie King was dead. And his [FHU's] was never a total change of heart. Did he not hold his nose while voting [Liberal] those few times? And did he not say he hoped to see the day when Ed Schreyer would become Prime Minister of Canada?[4]

EDITOR'S NOTES

1 The Progressives, a collection of agrarian-based political groups, polled 22.9 per cent of the popular vote in the federal election of 1921, principally in the three Prairie provinces and Ontario. With sixty-four seats they had more than the Conservatives, but their political philosophy and lack of cohesion kept them from forming the official Opposition. In the years that followed Prime Minister King courted them assiduously. The Progressives also fell victim to internal divisions and to the lure of old political affiliations. After the election of 1926 they continued to be a strong force only in Alberta.
2 See above, 'A Decade of the League for Social Reconstruction,' note 6.
3 This royal commission, which reported in 1935, is also known by the name of its chief instigator and first chairman, Harry H. Stevens, from 1930 until October 1934 R.B. Bennett's minister of trade and commerce.
4 Edward Schreyer, first NDP premier of Manitoba (1969–77), became governor general of Canada in 1978. When his term ended in 1984 he was named high commissioner to Australia.

XXIX

The Rebirth of Democracy

*Scott became national chairman of the CCF in the summer of 1942. By this time
the party was gaining in strength, and Scott agreed with David Lewis, the
national secretary, that there was a need for a book stating the party's program
and ideas in a popular form. Published in 1943,* Make This YOUR Canada *was
the result of their joint effort to meet this need.*

*At the Frank Scott conference held in Vancouver in February 1981 David
Lewis said that the final chapter of the book, reproduced here, was 'composed
mainly by Scott. It contains his concept of an important aspect of the philosophy
democratic socialism ... and of the bond which makes democracy and socialism
one.' Lewis held it to be 'an eloquent and valid statement of the democratic
socialist's thesis.'*

*Although the chapter was prompted in part by the particular circumstances of
the Second World War, it is used to conclude this selection of Scott's political
writings not only because it was to some extent a collaborative piece but also,
and more important, because Scott continued to see it as a summing up of his
views about the relationship between democracy and socialism.*
From *Make This YOUR Canada*, by David Lewis and Frank Scott (Toronto:
Central Canada Publishing 1943), pp. 187–97. Reprinted with the permission of
Sophie Lewis and Stephen Lewis[1]

We are living today in a period of revolutionary change. The world wars and a
world economic depression have occurred within the space of one generation.
Many empires and nations have been overthrown; economic systems have
collapsed and been transformed. Social experiments of new and startling kinds are
everywhere being tried. Science, in its constant search for more terrible weapons
of destruction, is producing every day more reasons why men should be united.
The pace of social change has been accelerated beyond all experience, and we can
be sure of only one thing – that we can never go back to our old ways of living or
our old habits of thought.

Because we all wish to come through these catastrophes into a better and happier
world, we are deeply conscious of the need for a social faith which we can express
in our personal conduct and in our national policies. We realize that without vision
we perish. It is the nations with a sense of purpose that have the power. We have
seen Germany turn her tremendous energies to the one goal of world domination,
and in ten years come close – very close – to succeeding. We have seen Japan set
out to be master of Asia, and come equally near to victory. We have seen the

Russian people embark upon a colossal plan of organized social revolution, and emerge with a powerful new system capable of withstanding the onslaught of the world's mightiest armies. And on the other hand we saw the democratic countries, though possessing enormous potential strength, being placed on the defensive because they lacked any dynamic aim or objective. Their democracy, frustrated by economic crisis and social injustice, had become static, and had lost its capacity to evoke men's belief and action.

At the last moment, when their defences were nearly down and their foes were close upon them, the democracies found in sheer self-defence the will to survive. This was scarcely a creative faith, but it had the force of primitive instinct. It united a great company of nations determined to retain or to regain their freedom. Out of this simple yet powerful idea the United Nations were born. But since the cause of their union was a resistance to attack rather than agreement to achieve a positive goal, it gave their war effort at first a purely defensive quality. Hence it has been said that we knew what we were fighting against, but not what we were fighting for. We were still less positive than our enemies in this respect; they knew what they would do if they won. We were content for long to say 'First we must win the war,' or 'Nothing matters now save victory.' What we would do with victory we did not seem to know.

This early or defensive stage of the struggle is passing. It need hardly be pointed out how inadequate it was. We can see all too clearly how rapidly the United Nations can fall apart if the immediate threat to survival is removed and there is no unifying international objective to give positive direction to future policies. Similarly within our own country we can see how easily our plans for post-war reconstruction will collapse if Canada falls back into the antagonisms and selfishness of the pre-war years. Whether we look at the national or the international scene we are confronted with the same urgent need for a clear understanding of the positive purposes for which we fight and the fundamental principles on which we can build a long term programme of domestic and world reconstruction.

All this we now understand. And in looking for this purpose in the struggle, in searching for the vital, forward-looking faith which can make victory certain and at the same time make it lasting, we are finding it where we should have looked in the first place. We are finding it in a renewed understanding of the meaning of democracy. The present world fight against the anti-democratic forces has revived our democratic faith. The bitter trial has helped to sharpen our understanding. Everywhere democracy has begun to possess again something of the dynamic content that made it a revolutionary watchword in the 18th and 19th centuries. Democracy was once a fighting creed. It made men stand up against overwhelming odds, made them overthrow foreign invaders and domestic tyranny, and gave them a vision of a new society they were determined to create. In the revolutionary democratic tradition, enlarged by the wider horizons of today, lies sufficient incentive to evoke in people of all races the will to change the world.

This war is becoming a people's war because we are grasping this great truth. The people, roused by the burdens and the sacrifice, are finding their own strength, sensing their own potentialities, and seeing their role of leadership in the revolutionary process. The essence of the discovery lies in the recognition that democracy had not failed us, but that we had failed democracy. We had let it wither and come near to dying. We rested satisfied with a portion only of its full possibilities. We tolerated its corruption and obstruction by enemies in our midst, often just as deadly as the avowed fascists outside our borders. This blindness is falling from our eyes. We no longer use the term democracy merely to describe our existing societies, where a limited political freedom struggles in the midst of economic dictatorship. We no longer use it as a name for a social order which is obviously breaking down all around us. We use it to mean the kind of society we intend to build out of the chaos – freer, stronger, richer, and much more concerned with human welfare than any we have known.

Democracy is a living principle holding this promise of the future. It is something we want badly and have not got. To get it, we must expand our present freedom to include economic and social democracy. The social planning long proposed by socialists must be added to our political democracy. The analysis of our economic development shows that freedom can no longer live by the mere negative absence of restraint. It can live and flourish only under conditions which provide opportunities for full enjoyment by all of the riches of modern society, and for full participation by all in the collective processes which create those riches.

This is the faith mankind needs. It is the dynamic basis for a new association of the peoples of the world, capable of leading to victory and of lasting beyond victory. This is what is now freeing men's hearts and minds for a forward march, and is giving them a direction and a goal. With this belief the global war and its social disruption cease to be an appalling disaster only, and become both a challenge and a great opportunity. The defeat of fascism becomes the first step to new achievement. The changing world is a world we intend to dominate by democratic means for democratic ends. We can create, as well as survive. We can unite in common action the friends of the awakening democracy in all countries on the surface of the globe. In this sense we fight a people's war, and are determined to win a people's peace.

What are the tested principles on which this conception of democracy rests? The first and perhaps the most central is the belief in human personality. Democracy believes in people. It proclaims afresh, as it has always proclaimed, the essential value of every man, woman and child on this rich earth. All truly democratic action seeks to establish a social order in which the welfare of the individual will be the first concern of the community. This idea of the sacredness of personality, of the 'dignity of man,' democracy shares with all the great religions. It cuts at the root of all false teaching about superior and inferior races, and leads directly to the notion of the brotherhood of man.

In its earlier days, as we have seen, and particularly during the laissez-faire period of modern capitalism, the welfare of the individual was expected to result automatically from the free pursuit of his own interest by every citizen. The idea that collective action could produce common good was strongly opposed. Democratic theory then was individualistic to the core. When industrial enterprise was small in scope, when the economy was expanding and opportunity for independent self-advancement was more frequent – as on the North American frontier – this concept of democracy was perhaps adequate. It no longer suffices. The whole structure of the world has changed. Today we have learned through our bitter experience that happiness and freedom are a collective result. No man can be really free without the aid of a well-ordered society to provide him with the health, education, and opportunities for useful work and self-expression that he needs. This was the main lesson of the world depression. No separate nation can be secure and free, without a world community on whose economic resources it can draw, with which it can have fruitful intercourse, and from which it can have protection against aggression and violence. This is the main lesson of the world wars.

Hence, though democracy is still primarily concerned with the welfare of the individual and the dignity of man, it recognizes that collective action, democratic planning and international co-operation are fundamental to attaining these objectives. Democracy therefore no longer makes a sharp antithesis between the individual and the state. It recognizes that a true democracy is a community, not simply an aggregation of units. It sees the interdependence of peoples, and how the fate of milions everywhere may hang on the decision of a few in some distant part of the world. This sense of community, and of reliance one upon the other, is something that had not developed in our old democracy, either within the nation or between nations. Canada, by her neglect of her unemployed, her depressed areas and her youth during the 1930's, provides a striking example of a state that was not a national community. The toleration, if not assistance, in the decline of the League of Nations by the states that might have maintained it showed the power of the forces opposed to the idea of world community. We would not unite voluntarily in the constructive arts of peace, so we are now united involuntarily in the destructive processes of war. We are being forced to keep political pace with our scientific expansion and global interdependence. Therefore we are lost if we still believe that every communal act, every growth of central planning and supra-national organization, is a destruction of liberty. Communal action is the condition of liberty.

If the new democratic community is to be built, it must put into practice certain principles and give effect to certain values. It must uphold, as we have said, the sacredness of human personality, without which no democracy can exist. Democracy seeks not to build a powerful state or a dominant race, but to create a national and world order which will provide the right environment for the fullest development of personality. Because men are of different races, and express themselves through their traditional cultures, the democratic community is one which welcomes and safeguards the varieties of cultural groups. And because personality cannot be enriched and enlarged without education, health, useful work, and the enjoyment of personal property, democracy must develop the necessary economic processes by which these are provided.

No mere belief in personality is of much value, however, unless democracy first makes certain that all men are free. For personality cannot attain full development unless the individual is able to make his contribution ot the world, able to speak his mind and to participate in the processes of his government, and able to worship God in his own fashion with others of his faith. The tragic spectacle of the enslaved populations in occupied areas of Europe and Asia provides a new reminder of this simple truth. There can be no peace and security, no respect for personality, where the individual or the race is in subjection. But in the pursuit of freedom we come again upon the need for collective action to attain and to maintain that freedom. Democracy means freedom for all, not just for some; the liberty of individuals must conform to the community rules which are established in the interests of all. Individual rights are not absolute, but are qualified by their communal purpose. There can be no freedom to dominate others; no right of private enterprise which exploits others. Freedom can exist only in an organized society, and law is the 'social engineering' which designs that society.

The old Anglo-Saxon word 'freo' which is the root of our word 'free,' brings out the communal basis of liberty very clearly: it means 'to be loved.' The free man was the loved man, the respected member of a group, someone within the family circle. Christianity and other religions have always taught this principle of love of one's neighbour. No man is really free in a society which does not care whether he lives or dies, is underpaid or unemployed, ill-housed or poorly nourished. In such a society he becomes a slave to poverty, disease, ignorance and fear – even if it has given him the right to vote, to strike, and the theoretical right to look for a new job. Freedom is found by common action within society and through society.

We now see that this principle is just as true of international as of domestic affairs. Nothing could be more 'free,' in the individualist sense, than the sovereign state. Yet how free is it? If small, it is free to be conquered; if large, it is free to wage periodic warfare for purposes of aggression or of survival. It is not free to dwell in peace, or free from fear. It is a slave to the results of the anarchy it produces. International anarchy condemns men to militarism; only international order can free them from militarism. And in both the national and international spheres our community welfare depends so largely on a right ordering of our economic life that today we cannot be free as individuals or as states unless the economic resources of the world are planned and organized to provide welfare and opportunity for all people everywhere.

Then democracy in our time must translate into reality the forgotten principle of equality. A truly democratic spirit lives in the vivid phrase used by one of Cromwell's soldiers: 'I think the poorest he that is in England hath a life to live as the richest he.'[2] Every man is the equal of every other in that he has a life to live. The inequalities of men are superficial or physical; the equalities are profound and spiritual. Democratic equality rests on the basic right and value of every personality. The little Kaffir boy, the northern Eskimo, the Chinese peasant and the Indian villager have as much right to good education, good food and housing, to health, peace and the opportunity of self-development, as anyone else. Therefore racial equality, equality of the sexes, equality of opportunity and equality before the law are all vital conditions of true democracy. Hence all class or racial privileges, all hereditary titles and offices, and the unfair distribution of wealth that creates inequality are anti-democratic and evil. So too we must condemn any form of economic or political imperialism in the international sphere. Perhaps in no respect do our modern democracies violate their principles more than with regard to the practice of equality. Nazi propaganda aimed at the 'pluto-democracies' and at our racial prejudices touches us at our weakest spot. It has been well said that 'fascism finds democracy vulnerable precisely where democracy ceases.'

Finally, democracy must be international in its outlook. Its principles demand the recognition of rights for all people, regardless of race, religion or colour. Hence it is a force that breaks down the barriers that divide men today. But it goes farther than that. The individual democrat who feels the truth of human brotherhood and who sees the crying need for world order knows that he shares a world-wide responsibility and duty. Wherever men live and die for freedom, there will his heart and hand be. He must concern himself with world affairs. He knows that the universal quality in democracy makes it the only possible basis for the future international institutions which must be set up if we are to rid ourselves of the anarchy of a world of so-called 'independent' states. Men will not tolerate a world society based on racial supremacy or imperialism. Therefore, no matter what the difficulties of building a world organization may be, its creation is an essential part of the programme of every political party that is truly democratic. The new democratic faith is a world faith or it is nothing. It cannot sit behind a Maginot Line or a hemisphere boundary.[3]

It is these basic principles and objections that form the hope and belief of hundreds of millions of people throughout the world today. They give us a standard by which to measure our policies, and a goal toward which we should bend our energies. They alone are worth the labor and sacrifice, worth the 'blood, sweat and tears.'[4]

THE CHALLENGE

Merely believing in a set of values is not enough to create those values, though it is an essential first step. Democracy will not come by just describing its nature in glowing terms. It will only come by hard work and personal dedication to its service. It imposes duties, and does not merely confer rights. It takes the combined effort of millions working together to make a democracy – men and women who are practical as well as idealistic, tough-fibred as well as intelligent. And in both the national and international spheres it must find expression through political action.

This is the challenge we are meeting during this war. This is the challenge we shall face when the war is won. Democracy must expand and become again creative. It must move forward, unafraid, to the next logical and progressive stage in the evolution of human organization. The democratic socialist society must replace the rapacious system of monopoly capitalism. Unless we advance to the co-operative commonwealth, we may be forced back into fascist darkness. We have our chance now in Canada. Let us arise and take it.

1 Scott wrote in 1982: 'My thanks are due to Sophie and Stephen Lewis for their permission to include here a chapter from *Make This YOUR Canada* which, though drafted by me, was published under joint authorship with David Lewis.'
2 The statement was made by the Leveller, Colonel Thomas Rainborough, at the Putney Debates in 1647.
3 The Maginot Line was a defensive line built by France between the two wars along her border with Germany. By attacking through Belgium in 1940, the Germans simply bypassed it, and ultimately took its forts from behind.
4 The reference is to Winston Churchill's repeated use of these words during the war, most dramatically in his first speech to the British House of Commons as prime minister, on 13 May 1940: 'I have nothing to offer but blood, toil, tears and sweat.'

A Bill of Rights, guaranteeing rights like those proclaimed in the United Nations Declaration of Human Rights, is needed by Labour. Certain basic freedoms, like the freedom of speech, press, association and religion, can be guaranteed absolutely by prohibiting people from interfering. Where social and economic rights are involved, however, somebody has to pay for them. This is a reason for leaving such rights out of a Bill of Rights. There is no use writing into a constitution, 'Everyone shall have a decent standard of living.'

It is not enough merely to include these rights in a bill. Further action is required by the state through social insurance laws and other measures. There is good reason for leaving such rights out of a Bill of Rights.

It is my view that the Prime Minister's proposed Bill of Rights would be greatly improved if it consisted of two parts: (1) a part guaranteeing those rights which *can* be guaranteed in a Bill of Rights, and (2) a part containing what might be called a declaration of social goals of aims. This is how the matter is dealt with in some of the newer Asian constitutions which embrace the rights proclaimed in the United Nations Declaration. The Constitution of Pakistan, for instance, says that the state of Pakistan *will seek to achieve* certain specified goals. To have the state committed to a permanent national policy of aiming at raising standards and improving conditions is surely a good thing.

If social and economic goals were stated in a Canadian Bill of Rights, we would be provided with a positive guide for all governments. We would strengthen thereby an important concept. As we improve the techniques of production, the general standard of living should rise. In Canada, every year the amount of productivity per head increases (except when there is an economic recession), and provides a growing fund out of which more wages can be paid. (I recognize that this is an average situation and that it does not apply to all industries.) In our society, constantly improving with reference to production, every year there is more to divide up.

It is evident that Labour has a least the same interest in a Bill of Rights as has everybody else in our society. A Bill of Rights declares principles of good government which are a continuing educational force in society. The more democratic the society, the better off is labour. However, if a Bill of Rights is confined to the political rights of free speech, press, association, religion, and so forth, I do not see that a bill will make a significant difference in Labour's fight for better wages or in Labour's defence of the right to strike or to picket. Such a Bill of Rights would be valuable in general, but I do not think that it would have direct application to Labour's principal concerns. It would not increase educational opportunities in Canada, nor would it strengthen the right to collective bargaining.

If a Bill of Rights is made a fundamental part of the law or of the constitution, binding on all governments (and not passed, as has been proposed, merely as a statute without effect on provinces), it will strengthen the freedom of association which itself is under attack at this very moment.

In my view, Labour has a general reason, and (in part) a special reason for wanting to see a Bill of Rights adopted in this country.

EDITOR'S NOTES

1 The Philadelphia Charter was adopted by the International Labor Organization (ILO) at a meeting in Philadelphia in 1944 and later annexed to the ILO Constitution. It reaffirms the principles to which the ILO is dedicated. Taken from the charter is the ILO's motto: 'Poverty anywhere constitutes a danger to prosperity everywhere.'

2 Chartism was a British working-class movement which took its name from the 'People's Charter,' first published in 1838. Its six points were annual parliaments, universal male suffrage, the secret ballot, equal electoral districts, the removal of the property qualification for membership of Parliament, and payment of members. Three mammoth petitions were presented to the House of Commons before the movement collapsed in 1849.

3 In September 1959 Jean-Paul Sauvé of the Union Nationale succeeded Maurice Duplessis as premier of Quebec after the latter died.

4 The reference is to what in due time became the New Democratic Party.

XXIV

Social Planning and Canadian Federalism

In 1961 the NDP *was formally launched, with T.C. Douglas as its leader. Michael Oliver, professor of political science at McGill, was the national chairman of the party.* Social Purpose for Canada *was intended to do for the new party something of what* Social Planning for Canada *had done for the* CCF. *Scott's contribution constituted the most obvious link between the two books, concentrating as it did on the legal and constitutional questions raised by the* NDP *program. Among the contributors to the new volume was a Quebec lawyer, Pierre Elliott Trudeau, who also wrote about constitutional matters.*

In this paper Scott paid more attention than previously to the necessity that provincial planning be established alongside federal planning.
From *Social Purpose for Canada*, ed. Michael Oliver (Toronto: University of Toronto Press 1961), pp. 394–407

From the day of its founding the CCF party anticipated that the building of a socialist society would require constitutional change in Canada. A British North America Act drafted for a predominantly agricultural community in 1867 could hardly be expected to fit an industrialized economy operated on principles of economic planning. Yet the degree of change required was not at all clear. The Regina Manifesto in 1933 did not propose any specific shift in the distribution of legislative powers as between Ottawa and the provinces; it contented itself with the statement that 'What is chiefly needed today is the placing in the hands of the national government of more power to control national economic development.' All were agreed that there must be more central authority, for reasons obvious to anyone faced with the conditions in Canada at the time. But this was centralization for planning's sake, not for centralization's sake. Indeed, the Manifesto also speaks of 'the increasing industrialization of the country and the consequent centralization of economic and financial power which has taken place in the last two generations.' Private centralization had obviously already taken place in the hands of big business – a centralization before which the provinces were powerless. What was needed was a countervailing public power to restore the national interest. Only the Parliament of Canada was seen as big enough for this task. In CCF thinking, strengthening federal authority for this purpose therefore took away jurisdiction, not from provincial governments, but from a 'small irresponsible minority of financiers and industrialists.' That the CCF opposed any extreme centralization is evident from its reference, in the Manifesto, to the historic distinction between 'matters of common interest' and 'local matters,' adopted by the Fathers of Confederation at the Quebec Conference of 1864, and from its description of public ownership as being 'Dominion, Provincial or Municipal.' The party, despite its socialist objectives, always accepted the principles of Canadian federalism.

By 1935, when *Social Planning for Canada* was published, the fields where federal powers needed reinforcement were being clarified. In that book it was argued that a great deal of the supposed weakness in federal authority was due, not to the BNA Act, but to 'long years of planned inactivity on the part of Liberal and Conservative governments' (p. 504). The non-use of existing powers was more striking than the absence of powers. Unquestioned authority existed to deal with international trade, interprovincial trade and communications, banking, currency and interest; there was the declaratory power over local works which could bring them within federal jurisdiction; federal taxing powers were virtually unrestricted. The desire in the old parties for reform was obviously less than the constitutional authority for reform. Yet certain areas remained beyond federal reach and, in the opinion of the authors, required federal action. These were said to be related to (1) social legislation, particularly in respect of labour matters, where it was felt concurrent powers might be adequate for the Dominion, (2) aspects of intraprovincial trade and commerce given to the provinces by judicial interpretation, (3) insufficient control over corporations and insurance companies, and (4) lack of clarity in federal-provincial financial arrangements. At that time, a federal power to implement international treaties was thought to exist; Mr. Bennett had just ratified three conventions of the International Labour Organization and had enacted legislation which was only later referred to the courts by Mr. King and held *ultra vires*. The constitutional aspects of national planning were already reduced to what seemed like manageable proportions, implying change but no drastic overhauling of the Canadian system of government.

It will be interesting now to contrast what *Social Planning* proposed with what has actually happened in the growth of the Canadian constitution since 1935. Many changes have taken place, both in the law and custom of the constitution. With a few notable exceptions, they have tended to be along the lines suggested in so far as the distribution of legislative power is concerned. In 1934 the central bank, demanded in the Regina Manifesto, was created, and by 1938 was made a wholly owned state bank. A national currency emerged, signed by public officials rather than by bank presidents. The Rowell-Sirois Report surveyed the experiences of the depression years and recommended a variety of changes in government responsibility; the provinces were to keep the lesser social services, but the Dominion was to assume unemployment insurance, contributory old age pensions, jurisdiction over minimum wages, maximum hours and minimum age of employment, and the power to implement ILO conventions; it was, in addition, to deal with marketing even when intraprovincial trade was affected, and to supervise all insurance companies except those confined to one province. These recommendations were thus specifically designed to overcome the Privy Council's disastrous decisions of 1937 on Mr. Bennett's 'New Deal' legislation, which had struck down the first unemployment insurance and federal marketing laws as well as the statutes implementing the three ILO conventions.[1] In its financial recommendations the Rowell-Sirois Report was even bolder; all provincial debts were to be assumed by Ottawa, and provincial subsidies based on population were to be replaced by national adjustment grants calculated to meet the proved fiscal needs of the provinces. Future provincial debts were to be in Canadian currency only, unless approval was obtained from the Finance Commission. The provinces were also to withdraw from personal and corporation income taxes, and succession duties. The Report has passed into history, but it left behind, beside a reflection of the left-of-centre trend of opinion in the 1930's, the unemployment insurance amendments to the constitution of 1940 and a distribution of tax fields that was accepted in subsequent federal-provincial taxation agreements.

The war years changed Canada's constitutional position in international affairs, notably by establishing her independent right to declare war and make peace, but